movement education

This is a volume in the

SAUNDERS SERIES IN PHYSICAL EDUCATION.

DAVID L. GALLAHUE, *Consulting Editor*
Indiana University

movement

Saunders College Publishing
Philadelphia

education

JOHN S. FOWLER, *Ph.D.*
University of Colorado at Boulder

Address Orders to: 383 Madison Ave.,
New York, NY 10017
Address Editorial correspondence to:
West Washington Square
Philadelphia, PA 19105

This book was set in Caledonia by Centennial Graphics.
The editors were John Butler, Carol Field, and Mary Agre.
The art director was Nancy E.J. Grossman.
The text and cover designer was Adrianne Onderdonk Dudden.
The production manager was Tom O'Connor.
The cover printer was Lehigh Press, Inc.
Fairfield Graphics was printer and binder.

LIBRARY OF CONGRESS
CATALOG CARD NO.: 80-53928
Fowler, John S.
Movement education.
Philadelphia, Pa.: Saunders College
480 p.
8101 801010

MOVEMENT EDUCATION ISBN 0–03–057881–7

1234 56-1 987654321

CBS COLLEGE PUBLISHING
Saunders College Publishing
Holt, Rinehart and Winston
The Dryden Press

Preface

A PRACTICAL GUIDE TO TEACHING MOVEMENT EDUCATION TO CHILDREN AGES THREE TO TWELVE

The use of the term "movement education" seems to be in a state of continuous evolution. This text represents the views of the author in presenting a particular philosophy of movement education. Because there is also some confusion concerning the interpretation and meaning of the term, depending upon which text or other source is considered, movement education for the purpose of this book is defined as an approach to teaching motor skills, including basic movement skills, games, dance, and other activities, that utilizes a process of discovery learning and incorporates the movement factors proposed by Rudolf Laban (described later). Hence, movement education implies a method of teaching as well as the content of what is to be taught.

This book is designed to help the reader understand the teaching of movement education to children ages 3 through 12 as well as gain an appreciation of its underlying theory and rationale. Many teachers and students already will be familiar with some of the ideas presented in the following chapters and will have some background in the traditional program of elementary school physical education, which comprises such activities as calisthenics, relays, games and team sports, stunts and tumbling, and rhythms. Therefore, much of the material contained in this book is discussed not so much with a view to stating positions dogmatically, but rather with the purpose of assisting readers to understand what has been presented, enabling them to relate the information to their own experience and situation. For the reader who feels the need for further study and information, a study guide and discussion questions are included at the end of each chapter.

It is difficult to determine precisely how much detailed material teachers need from a textbook. The author believes that with a good background in child growth and development, an understanding of some of the ways in which children learn, an appreciation of subject matter, and a desire to try different ideas, the teacher can use this book to implement and support a program that grows out of the work of children. This is in contrast to a style of teaching that uses ready-made lesson plans taken from a book or is based on the idea that "If it's Tuesday, shouldn't I be playing Red Rover?" The philosophy of teaching presented in this book is based upon carefully observing or monitoring children as they respond to tasks or instructions given by a teacher, who then decides what to do next based upon these observations. The program should be related to the individual needs, interests, and abilities of children in a particular school.

The text provides practical material for teaching, not only for the early stages of teaching movement education, but also for later stages when teachers begin to feel comfortable and secure with the approach. The book affords the necessary resource materials and ideas to enable teachers to go ahead and plan more independently. The hope is that teachers will be able to develop different and unique ways of utilizing the suggestions in the text as they observe the varied and often original responses of the children. All of the practical material in the text has been used with children by the author and found to be successful in a variety of educational settings.

Undertaking a change in teaching style or examining different teaching methods can be an interesting and challenging experience for a teacher. Plans to initiate or facilitate a change in teaching style should be carefully considered and scheduled over a sufficiently long period to enable the results to be evaluated. New approaches can be tried out in more controlled circumstances for varying amounts of time. It is easy to become discouraged if things do not work out perfectly immediately; however, persistence will be rewarded as both the teacher and the child begin to achieve success with the new material.

On the other hand, teachers also may feel that new or different ideas concerning the curriculum are the best ideas, and these sometimes can be too readily accepted without any real understanding of their implications. A good teacher should be willing to try out new ideas only after careful study that leads to a belief that the methods possess some merit. Ultimately, each teacher has to formulate his or her individual philosophy of teaching based upon a sincere belief that what is being done is worthwhile and of benefit to the children.

Through a program of movement education, children are encouraged to:

1. Develop an understanding and awareness of the wide range of movements of which the body is capable as they learn basic movement skills
2. Discover their own movement capabilities, limitations, and potential as basic skills are used in games, gymnastics, dance, and other activities
3. Develop qualities of self-discipline, self-confidence, and self-direction, and acquire a good self-concept
4. Learn how to learn
5. Learn how to cooperate with others in socially useful ways.

The time is long overdue for academic and physical education to become more compatible. Movement education can help physical education to become a viable part of the school curriculum. As a subject area, movement education should not have to justify its importance or be regarded as a frill in the program that is only paid token attention. School principals, curriculum planners, administrators, and parents need to become aware of the vital role that a good movement program can contribute to the total educational process. Movement plays a vital and critical part in a child's early development and education. The materials and ideas presented in this text can assist teachers toward providing an education in movement.

Finally, the author wishes to acknowledge the help of all those who reviewed the manuscript and assisted with the clarification of material by offering constructive criticism and positive support. These include Bob Pangrazi of Arizona State University, James B. Robertson of Springfield College, Betty Roberts of Marshall University, Margaret M. Thompson of the University of Illinois at Urbana-Champaign, Barbara A. Passmore of Indiana State University, Patricia Tanner of the University of South Florida, and Margaret Toohey of California State University at Long Beach. In addition, thanks are due to the editorial staff at Saunders College Publishing, especially John Butler and Carol Field.

JSF

Contents

1 signs of change: the movement movement

Changes can be seen taking place in elementary schools throughout the United States, not only in the way physical education is being taught, but also in its content. Programs at conventions and conferences, college courses, and workshops have been implemented to promote movement education. Whole textbooks devoted to movement education have been published for elementary school teachers and physical education specialists. It is worth examining the origins of these changes and the concepts and ideas behind movement education.

The main impetus to change originated in England over 30 years ago and included a move toward more informal teaching methods and the use of discovery learning; increasing use of different kinds of apparatus on which children could climb, hang, swing, and balance; and adoption of a system for analyzing and teaching basic movement that was developed by Rudolf Laban.

Probably the most important change which took place in elementary schools was the result of Laban's work. Laban left Germany in the late 1930s, when Hitler began his rise to power, and settled in England. He had spent many years in the study of movement in various settings, including drama and dance. Once in England, Laban developed a following of people who were interested in his work and ideas. His theories and methods were not totally unknown in England or in the United States since people had visited Laban in Europe tc study his methods of teaching. Laban and his associates conducted courses in modern dance, and gradually physical education and dance teachers, particularly women, began to work with his movement elements and themes. Many men were skeptical of these new ideas, partly because of the association of Laban's work with dance and partly because of the way in which they had been trained to teach physical education.

What Laban in fact had developed was a system for analyzing movement based upon certain movement factors which he labeled time, weight, space, and flow. Quite simply, the time factor referred to the ability of the body or parts of the body to move at different *speeds* (with speed as a function of time), that ranged from fast to slow. Movements also could accelerate or slow down, or have a rhythmic quality. Weight referred to the amount of muscular tension in the movements of the body. Movements could be described as being *heavy* or *light*, or possibly somewhere in between. The space factor suggested descriptions of the body's use of space. The body or body parts, could move in different *directions* (forward, backward, and sideways), in different *pathways* (direct or indirect), and on different *levels*. Finally, flow referred to the ongoing character of a movement, which could be *bound*, or easily

Fig. 1-1 *"Bound" movements.*

Fig. 1-2 *"Free" movement.*

stopped, or *free,* which suggested a more continuous kind of movement. The *relationship* of body parts to each other or of the body to other bodies or objects could also be described. Laban used the term *effort* to describe the qualitative aspects of a person's movement. Effort was a combination of the way in which a person used the different elements or factors of time, weight, space, and flow.

Laban's work also suggested that experimentation or exploration of movement ideas or themes should be used as the approach to teaching. In movement education, a theme is, in essence, a movement idea that emphasizes or highlights certain aspects of movement. Laban developed 16 basic movement themes by using the factors described above. Themes were categorized under such headings as body awareness, space awareness, the shape of movements, elevation (jumping and landing), and partner and group work. Laban originally applied themes to drama, mime, and dance as people learned how to use the effort factors. Since then, other students have applied the themes to gymnastics and games. (See the study guide for references.)

The total scheme or framework for study of basic movements, and which later evolved into movement education, was developed by considering what, where and how the body moves and in what relationships. A simple development of each category would show:

1. *What the body is doing.*
   a. The whole body can move.
   b. Different parts of the body can move (*i.e.*, the head, arms, legs, feet, and so on).
   c. The body can support itself on different parts.
   d. The body can make different shapes.

Generally, as it moves through space the body is, in a functional sense, performing a *locomotor* skill, such as walking, running, and hopping. Moving the body from one place to another usually can be accomplished by some kind of transfer of body weight that uses different body supports. For example, walking is accomplished by means of a foot-to-foot transfer, rolling uses adjacent body surfaces, and jumping is usually a foot-to-foot transfer with part of the movement being in the air (flight). Many gymnastic movements include different kinds of weight transference.

If most of the movement takes place in one spot, the movement is generally described as *non-locomotor.* Examples of non-locomotor movements include balancing, curling and stretching, twisting, and rocking. Finally, the body can *manipulate* an external object, such as a ball or bat.

2. *Where the body is moving (using space).*

The body or body parts can move in the following ways:
   a. In different directions—forward, backward, sideways, up and down.
   b. At different levels—low, medium, high.
   c. In relationship—to each other, to other people, to objects.
   For example, near to, far away from, behind, over, etc.

3. *How the body is moving (using effort).*

The body or body parts can move using the following factors:
   a. Different amounts of time (speed)—fast or slow, accelerating, decelerating, rhythmically.
   b. Different amounts of weight (force or muscular tension)—heavy, light.
   c. A certain pathway through space—direct, indirect.
   d. Different kinds of flow—free or continuous, bound or controlled.

This framework will be used later in Chapter 6 through 9 when practical ideas for teaching movement education are developed.

At the time Laban began work in England, elementary classroom teachers usually were conducting their own physical education classes. Lessons were based on the programs suggested in the *1933 Syllabus of Physical Training for Schools,* a government publication which contained recommendations for teaching elementary school physical education. The teacher was encouraged to

Fig. 1-3 Exercise in unison.

follow the daily table of exercises or lessons, which were ready-made prescriptions that took little account of children's individual differences, needs, interests, or abilities. The exercises usually were performed in unison, following teacher demonstration and command. Many of the exercises involved isolated movement of different body parts, with the class arranged in team lines or files. The program also included games, rhythms, relays, and other activities. Programs similar to these were also conducted in the United States.

Open Education

Changes were beginning to take place in elementary education, however, particularly in England. In some classrooms, teachers began to experiment with different seating arrangements, with the desks or chairs and tables arranged in clusters so that small groups of children could work together. Certain areas of the classroom were devoted to different activities, such as math, reading, science, pets, and so on. New schools were designed in a variety of ways to allow different types of interaction between teachers and children, between children, and between teachers. This meant different and novel utilization of space. Larger spaces were constructed so that two or more classes could work together under the

Fig. 1-4 *Relay races.*

guidance of two or more teachers. In older buildings walls were knocked down or altered to create more space. As the individual differences in children were increasingly recognized, a move was made away from teaching the entire class the same thing at the same time. Instruction became more individualized, that is, children were allowed or encouraged to progress at their own rate and at the level of their ability. Some children might be seen to be finishing off a writing assignment, while others were doing math, painting, reading, or feeding the gerbils! Bells did not ring every 30 minutes and the school day became more integrated. If children were absorbed in a project or in other types of work, they were encouraged to complete it. Team teaching often was utilized, with teachers offering their special interests and strengths to more children. One teacher would be responsible for planning and recording the progress of a group of children. This kind of educational setting was a demanding one for the teacher, who had to serve as facilitator, guide, adviser, and resource person.

This approach to teaching and learning came to be known as "open" education, in contrast to the older, more traditional and formal methods of teaching. Blackie (1967) and Silberman (1970) have described the scene in British elementary schools. Some of these ideas also were implemented in the teaching of physical education.

DEVELOPMENT IN NORTH AMERICA

In North America, teachers in the public schools and at the college level were becoming aware of what was happening in England. Anglo-American workshops in physical education that were held in England provided a useful interchange of ideas and experiences. Movement education was frequently included as a topic at these workshops. Many foreign educators also visited and worked in England to study physical education and movement programs conducted in different parts of the country, while their English counterparts visited the United States and Canada to give demonstrations and lectures about movement. Thus, programs began to develop in America as people learned about Laban and the theories of movement. Many people involved in physical education and in dance were already familiar with the work of Laban and had been working within his framework; however, the areas of gymnastics and games provided new ground for application of movement factors.

The changes occurring in British elementary schools also created considerable interest in the United States and in other parts of the world. The British Infant School (kindergarten through second grade) was much written about and discussed by teachers and other educators, with some elementary schools in North America implementing the theories of open education. These developments are well documented by Silberman (1970, 1973), Weber (1971), Rogers (1971), and Featherstone (1967).

ATTEMPTS TO CHANGE

Some confusion initially arose when teachers in other countries believed that the key to initiating change was to incorporate large open spaces in schools. Many new schools which were built utilized the concept of open space, while others enlarged existing areas or added open space facilities. Difficulties arose, however, when teachers had to function in these large open spaces without having had sufficient preparation or understanding of how to proceed. Many teachers even tried to build walls around their group of children by using bookcases and room dividers, with instruction then proceeding in the traditional way. Actually, the size of the space had little to do with whether a teacher utilized an open or closed approach to instruction. Some schools had self-contained classrooms and some open space areas, and it was in this situation that teachers and parents were able to determine the environment in which children would learn best. Eventually, good programs were developed in which teachers received a thorough introduction and careful instruction to prepare them to utilize the whole concept.

It should be pointed out that the growth of open education in England took place over a number of years, but teachers in other places who adopted this concept expected success almost immediately. If things tended to develop more slowly they returned to the methods of teaching with which they felt most comfortable. It must also be noted that by no means were all schools in Britain modeled on open education patterns. School principals were free to develop their own curricula and methods of organization. Implementation and adoption of open education methods in the United States have not been particularly widespread.

The changes in elementary education that occurred in America had, until comparatively recently, little effect on physical education. Physical education teachers have not always been aware of developments in other areas of education. College professional preparation programs in physical education now are beginning to consider alternative teaching strategies for individualizing instruction and teachers are being exposed to new ideas through conferences and convention programs.

TEACHING METHODS

Several things happened as teachers began to implement or experiment with the new concepts. When Laban's theories were first utilized, teachers employed them rather mechanically. Children were asked, sometimes even commanded, to move in different directions at various speeds and levels, and using varying amounts of force. Movement factors were applied to a particular skill such as running, and then simply permuted, taking one or more factors at a time. For example, the teacher might say, "Let me see you run. Who can run backwards? Now try sideways." This pattern would continue, with the teacher merely suggesting other factors to vary the skill which was being performed. This kind of teaching did not produce or encourage any kind of thinking on the part of the child. It was essentially the old "command" style of teaching and teachers soon ran out of ideas after they had utilized all the factors. A lot of movement was produced in terms of quantity, but little developed in the way of quality of movement as it was not repeated and refined. Usually this approach was something that teachers tried only for a short time as they did not understand how to develop the program.

A more sophisticated approach which encouraged children to explore movement and discover their own limitations and abilities developed as teachers began to utilize a method based on questions instead of commands. The teacher usually prefaced activities with "Who can find another way to cross the balance beam?" or "Can you find a different way to do that?" This approach often was referred to as the "find another way" method. Children were encouraged to make original responses and were challenged by the form of the question or task. Movement factors were used and children could develop ideas on their own without too much prodding from the teacher. If ideas were not forthcoming from the children, the teacher had to suggest ideas to get a variety of responses. As children explored the tasks it often seemed that they produced responses simply for the sake of variety. The success of the method was measured by the variety or number of different ideas produced.

Gradually teachers gained insight into how to develop movement responses of children. Through courses, conferences, and relevant literature the intent of Laban's theories became a little clearer. The sequence of events was, in actuality, for the children to be encouraged to explore and discover movements as a response to a task or problem proposed by the teacher. The teacher then carefully observed the responses and decided what the child should do next based on those observations. Children then repeated and refined certain selected movements. The activity that was learned depended upon whether the teacher had decided to systematically follow Laban's basic movement themes, was simply applying the movement factors to basic movement skills, or had developed some other way to structure the learning process. Movement quality was achieved by repetition and refinement, and by focusing the child's attention on certain aspects of the movement. Questions might be asked about how the movement started or finished, or on how a particular movement could be improved. The teacher might ask "Did you mean to put your hands on the floor so quickly?" or "Why did you choose that direction?" Usually the children's work was developed around the framework described earlier, that is, by looking at what, where, and how the body was moving. If the teacher's objective was to guide the development of a child's movement responses toward a specific goal, the method was essentially that of "guided discovery." If the responses were more open-ended and the children were free to develop things in their own way, then the method was designated as "problem solving."

Laban intended that application of his principles be based on an understanding and internalization of those principles. The person who had received a thorough education in movement would then almost intuitively know the qualities of effort needed for a particular skill or movement. The individual's application of the required qualities was described as "body awareness." In addition, the individual's use of effort qualities and gesture reflected aspects of personality and inner attitudes. This latter aspect was derived from the work Laban had done with people in dramatic movement on the stage, in mime, and in dance.

Teachers and other interested individuals have tried to understand the total implications of Laban's work. Generally teachers have used what appealed to them and seemed applicable to their teaching in an eclectic manner. They developed programs in their own way and combined the older, more traditional activities with some of the newer concepts of movement education. If teachers used movement education it usually was only with the primary grades and then mainly involved only locomotor skills. Application of Laban's principles to other areas of the physical education curriculum has been underway for a number of years as teachers have explored the possibilities of using movement factors and themes in games, gymnastics, and dance. Utilizing Laban's ideas and approach through discovery learning has led to adoption of the terms "education gymnastics," "educational dance," and "educational games."

Movement education as a complete approach to physical education in the elementary school has been increasingly accepted among teachers and in college professional preparation programs. This acceptance has been facilitated by a better understanding on the part of teachers of the underlying structure of movement education and of the needs of children and the goals of education and learning. Bruner (1966, 1975) stresses the importance of understanding the underlying structure of any subject that is to be taught. Teaching the basic principles of the subject first and then using and reviewing them at progressively more advanced levels as children mature forms the foundation of a curriculum. Bruner supports the notion of spontaneous learning based on the child's curiosity and the desire to attain competence—a key factor in the movement education philosophy.

Later Developments in England

About 20 years after the publication of the *1933 Syllabus of Physical Training* in England, the Ministry of Education published two books dealing with the physical education of the young child. The first one, *Moving and Growing* (1952), examined the movement capabilities of young children. It discussed the wide variation in individual growth, described how to plan a movement period or lesson, and stressed exploration, repetition, and creativity as factors that aided learning. The second book, *Planning the Programme* (1953), complemented *Moving and Growing*. Various lesson frameworks were described, including one which suggested that a lesson might be built around the qualities of strength, space, and time. No mention was made of Rudolf Laban, in fact, neither book offered any other references. A few examples described how students might use movement factors which obviously were Laban's, although not credited to him, but it was categorically stated that a lesson framework was not included "because its use depends upon the ability of the teacher to evolve movements freely," and one could not do this by reading a book (Her Majesty's Stationery Office, 1953).

After studying these books, teachers had to rely on courses and conferences to learn more about these new ideas. Individual teachers had been experimenting on their own, while college teachers had developed some theories of movement, and gradually these ideas were shared. Demonstrations also were given with children in various parts of Britain and a center, the Art of Movement Studio, was opened in 1946. Lisa Ullman, a former pupil and co-worker of Laban, was principal and carried on with Laban's work after his death in 1958. At the studio teachers could attend courses and conferences to further their knowledge and gain experience in Laban's methods.

In 1972, after another 20-year interval the British Government published a new book on physical education in elementary schools. The book, *Movement: Physical Education in the Primary Years*, examined the influence of Rudolf Laban. It was suggested in the book that children, under the skillful guidance of a teacher, can develop activities on their own that are meaningful to them. Topics studied in the book included gymnastics, games, dance, swimming, track and field, and outdoor education. As in the two books published earlier, it was suggested that teachers develop their own programs based on the previous experiences of the children they were teaching. A catalog of specific activities and lessons was not provided. Essentially, teachers were encouraged to think for themselves and develop their own curricula based on very clear ideas of purpose and direction.

Thus, the "movement movement" was born over 40 years ago and has been continually developing and evolving ever since in England, the United States, and in other countries. Naturally, teachers are free to adopt those teaching strategies and curriculum elements which they find most suitable and which accommodate the guidelines established by their school or school district. Movement education is just one alternative among many other approaches to effective teaching and learning.

It is the intent of this book to provide the reader with some feeling and appreciation for the goals of a movement program, and a look at children in terms of their growth, development, and learning. The book will offer a large number of practical suggestions and ideas to assist the teacher in becoming a movement educator. Hopefully, each person using this text will take from it what he or she needs, discover possibilities for further development, and become independent enough to see the text as a resource and not simply as the final source of all knowledge on movement education.

Summary

This chapter has discussed briefly some of the changes that have taken place in the content and method of teaching elementary school physical education over approximately the last 40 years. The "movement movement" began in England under the influence of Rudolf Laban and those broader changes which were taking place in elementary education.

Laban, who settled in England in the late 1930s, proposed a different way of analyzing movement based on factors which he labeled time, weight, space, and flow. Laban developed a systematic way for people to explore various movement themes by using those movement factors which would develop "body awareness." Although much of Laban's work had been in the areas of dance, drama, and mime, teachers in England and other countries began to experiment by applying Laban's ideas to gymnastics and games.

Teachers, particularly in the British Infant's School, were developing different ways to work with children. They began to individualize instruction and explore approaches to permit different types of interactions between teacher and child, child and child, and teacher and teacher. The concept of team teaching evolved as well as various plans for unique classroom organization allowing creative use of space. The "open" education approach to learning was developed; it stressed that self discovery was perhaps more effective than formal instruction and utilized an informal rather than a direct approach to teaching and learning.

Both the influence of Laban's work and the changes taking place in elementary education affected physical education teaching in England. Physical education instruction became more informal as teachers used discovery methods and began applying the theories of Laban within a framework of what, where, and how the body moves. The use of different kinds of climbing and balancing equipment in elementary schools also had a stimulating effect on the physical education program.

Through teacher exchanges, conferences, relevant literature, and other methods, the concepts of movement and open education which originated in England spread overseas. In America, people were not unaware of the work of Laban, especially in the area of dance, although teachers on both sides of the Atlantic were not always aware of how to develop quality in movement. Children were encouraged to find different ways to respond to the tasks established by the teacher, producing a large quantity of movement; however, to achieve quality of movement, the responses of the children had to be repeated and refined under the skillful guidance of the teacher. One important aspect of the work in England was the lack of detailed curricula; it was the task of individual teachers to develop their own programs.

Movement education has been in a state of continuous evolution since the late 1930s. Some teachers have utilized these concepts only with primary grade children and for short periods of time, while others see movement education as a complete approach for all grade levels.

The purpose of this text is to help teachers understand movement education through an examination of its underlying ideas and principles, together with practical suggestions for teaching the subject.

Bibliography

Board of Education. *Syllabus of Physical Training for Schools, 1933.* London: His Majesty's Stationery Office, 1933.

Board of Education. *Syllabus of Physical Training for Schools, 1919.* London: His Majesty's Stationery Office, 1919.

Blackie, John. *Inside the Primary School.* London: Her Majesty's Stationery Office, 1967.

Bruner, Jerome S. *Toward a Theory of Instruction.* Cambridge, Mass: Harvard University Press, 1966.

Bruner, Jerome S. *The Process of Education.* Cambridge, Mass: Harvard University Press, 1977.

Featherstone, Joseph. *An Introduction: Informal Schools in Britain Today.* New York: Citation Press, 1971.

Gilliom, Bonnie Cherp. *Basic Movement Education for Children: Rationale and Teaching Units.* Reading, Mass: Addison-Wesley Publishing Co., 1970.

Laban, Rudolf and Lawrence, F. C. *Effort.* London: Macdonald and Evans, 1947

Laban, Rudolf. *Mastery of Movement,* 3rd ed. Revised by Lisa Ullman. London: Macdonald and Evans, Ltd., 1971.

Laban, Rudolf. *Modern Educational Dance,* 2nd ed. Revised by Lisa Ullman. New York: Frederick A. Praeger, 1963.

Logsdon, Bette J. *et al. Physical Education for Children: A Focus on the Teaching Process.* Philadelphia: Lea and Febiger, 1977.

Ministry of Education. *Physical Education in the Primary School. Part One. Moving and Growing.* London: Her Majesty's Stationery Office, 1952.

Ministry of Education. *Physical Education in the Primary School. Part Two. Planning the Programme.* London: Her Majesty's Stationery Office, 1953.

Rizzitiello, Theresa, ed. *Annotated Bibliography on Movement Education.* Washington, D.C.: AAHPER, 1977.

Silberman, Charles E. *Crisis in the Classroom.* New York: Random House, 1970.

Silberman, Charles E. *The Open Classroom Reader.* New York: Vintage Books, 1973.

Stanley, Sheila. *Physical Education: A Movement Orientation.* Toronto: McGraw-Hill, 1969.

Thornton, S. *A Movement Perspective of Rudolf Laban.* London: Macdonald and Evans, 1971.

Weber, Lillian. *The English Infant School and Informal Education.* Englewood Cliffs, N.J.: Prentice-Hall Inc., 1971.

References to Other British Sources

The following list of references published in England will give the reader some idea of the number of publications that appeared in the 1960s and early 1970s. They are presented chronologically rather than alphabetically.

Randall, M. W. *Modern Ideas on Physical Education.* London: G. Bell and Sons, Ltd., 1952.

Morison, Ruth. *Educational Gymnastics for Secondary Schools.* Liverpool: I.M. Marsh College of Physical Education, 1960.

London County Council. *Educational Gymnastics.* London: London County Council, 1962.

Inner London Education Authority. *Movement Education for Infants.* London: ILEA. 1963.

Cameron, W. McD., and Pleasance, P. *Education in Movement: School Gymnastics.* Oxford: Basil Blackwell, 1963.

Johnson, F. J. M. "Leicestershire Education Committee Suggested Indoor P.E. Scheme for Juniors." In *Bulletin of Physical Education.* British Association of Organisers and Lecturers in P.E. Vol. VI, No. 4, August 1964.

Clegg, Sir Alexander. "Physical Education in its Relation to Examinations and General Subjects in the Curriculum." In Carnegie Old Student's Association *Conference Papers,* Vol. 1, Nos. 1 and 2. November 1964.

Mauldon, E., and Layson, J. *Teaching Gymnastics.* London: Macdonald and Evans, 1965.

Jordan, Diana. *Childhood and Movement.* Oxford: Basil Blackwell, 1966.

Scott, H. "Physical Education Through Movement Experiences." In Carnegie Old Student's Association, *Conference Papers,* Vol. 1, No. 3, November 1966.

Bilbrough, A., and Jones, P. *Physical Education in the Primary School.* London: University of London Press, 1968.

McIntosh, P. C. *Physical Education in England Since 1800.* London: G. Bell and Sons, Ltd., 1968.

Cameron, W. McD., and Cameron, M. *Education in Movement in the Infant School.* Oxford: Basil Blackwell, 1969.

Morison, Ruth. *A Movement Approach to Educational Gymnastics.* London: J. M. Dent and Sons, Ltd., 1969.

Department of Education and Science. *Movement: Physical Education in the Primary Years.* London: Her Majesty's Stationery Office, 1972.

Briggs, Megan M. *Movement Education.* London: Macdonald and Evans, 1974.

Selected References Published in the United States

As with the British sources, this is a chronological listing.

Barrett, Kate Ross. *Exploration: A Method for Teaching Movement.* Madison, Wis. College Printing and Typing Co., Inc., 1965.

Hackett, L., and Jensen R. *A Guide to Movement Exploration.* Palo Alto, Calif.: Peek Publications, 1966.

Hanson, Margie R. "The New Look in Elementary School Physical Education." In *Physical Education for Children's Healthful Living.* Washington, D.C.: Association for Childhood Education International, 1968.

Porter, L. *Movement Education for Children.* Washington, D.C.: American Association of Elementary, Kindergarten and Nursery Educators, 1969.

Rekstad, M., *et al. Promising Practices in Elementary School Physical Education.* Washington, D.C.: AAHPER, 1969.

AAHPER. *Trends in Elementary School Physical Education.* Washington, D.C.: AAHPER, 1970.

Gilliom, Bonnie Cherp. *Basic Movement Education for Children: Rationale and Teaching Units.* Reading, Mass: Addison-Wesley, 1970.

Kirchner, G., *et al. Introduction to Movement Education.* Dubuque, Iowa: Wm. C. Brown, 1970, and 2nd ed. 1978.

Sweeney, Robert T. *Selected Readings in Movement Education.* Reading, Mass.: Addison-Wesley, 1970.

Tillotson, Joan S. "The Future of Elementary School Physical Education." In *The Next Fifty Years: Health, Physical Education, Recreation, Dance.* Ed. L. Neal. University of Oregon, School of Health, Physical Education and Recreation, March 1971.

Rekstad, M., *et al. Preparing the Elementary Specialist.* Washington, D.C.: AAHPER, 1973.

Kruger, H., and Kruger, J. M. *Movement Education in Physical Education.* Dubuque, Iowa: Wm. C. Brown, 1977.

Logsdon, Bette J., *et al. Physical Education for Children: A Focus on the Teaching Process.* Philadelphia: Lea and Febiger, 1977.

Rasmus, Carolyn J., and Fowler, John. *Movement Activities for Places and Spaces.* Washington, D.C. AAHPER, 1977.

Study Guide British Sources

If the reader is interested in British sources, the book by Thornton (1971) provides some excellent background on Rudolf Laban, so this probably should be read first. Laban's books then can be studied to complete or complement this information.

Peter McIntosh describes the history of movement education very well and discusses its early development in his book (1968). The book by Bilbrough and Jones is a landmark text that has encouraged many people to try a different way to teach. Interestingly, the book does not mention Laban or give any other references since it is largely based on the author's own experiences.

The government publications of 1933, 1952, 1953, and 1972 provide a picture of developments taking place over almost 40 years. Evolving from a book of daily lesson tables, they show the transition to a situation in which teachers are encouraged to develop their own material.

A section of Silberman's *Crisis in the Classroom* (pp. 253–256), describes movement education in primary schools, and a section of *The Open Classroom Reader* by Bullough (pp. 781–789), discusses movement, drama, and dance.

Special references for developments in games and dance will be found in the study guides following chapters eight and nine, respectively.

The work of Morrison has had an impact on teaching gymnastics in school and should be examined. The books published by the authorities in London also have been influential and widely used.

The British Journal of Physical Education often carries articles and editorials pertaining to movement education. For details, write to The Physical Education Association of Great Britain and Northern Ireland, Ling House, 10 Nottingham Place, London, W1M 4AX, England.

American Sources

Selected Readings, edited by Robert Sweeney (1970), would be a good book to browse through, since it contains a wide variety of articles which provide indepth background material. The ACEI publication, *Physical Education for Children's Healthful Living*, offers a number of articles describing current developments and suggesting possible changes.

Muska Mosston published *Teaching Physical Education: From Command to Discovery (1966)*, a book which examines styles of teaching and describes and differentiates between guided discovery and problem-solving methods. This text has become a classic in the field and should be required reading.

In 1969, Sheila Stanley, working in Canada, developed a book about movement education that discusses discovery learning and Laban's theories of movement, applying these theories to gymnastics, games, and dance. This book was followed in 1970 by two others, *Basic Movement Education for Children*, by Gilliom, and *Introduction to Movement Education*, by Kirchner, Cunningham, and Worrell. Both books contain abundant material for teachers to use. Gilliom's book employs a thematic approach, with movement problems arranged according to three different levels. Gilliom does not utilize lesson plans but rather suggests that the teacher work through problems according to the individual child's rate of progress. This is an excellent book for the teacher who would like some ideas on how to start teaching movement education. The activities cited are mainly of the gymnastic type, with a little material on ball skills and rhythms. Kirchner *et al.*, on the other hand, suggests planning lessons based on themes and divides the material into separate categories for the primary and intermediate grades. This book also deals mainly with gymnastics.

Many other textbooks in elementary school physical education include chapters on "movement exploration" or movement education, but suggest the approach as something to try as a 3-week unit. Other authors have tried to integrate both traditional and problem-solving methods but have often left teachers wondering how to put such a program together.

Writing in 1971, Tillotson, in a publication dealing with the future, strongly supported "open" education and movement education, with teachers employed in learning centers rather than in schools and being managers or facilitators instead of instructors.

As changes occurred in teaching physical education, the focus began to center on the problems of "What is teaching?" and "What does the teacher do to facilitate learning?" Answers were sought as to how teaching and learning could be personalized, humanized, and individualized. Articles describing the state of the art appeared in the Journal of Physical Education and Recreation (JOPER). The September 1977 issue of JOPER carried a special feature, "Games Teaching," edited by Marie Riley. This article was followed a year later by others on "Educational Gymnastics" (September 1978), and on "Dance and the Child" in (September 1979). These articles provide the reader with more information on current ideas and developments.

In 1977, two books appeared that offered a review of developments in movement education in the United States. The text by Logsdon *et al.* discusses the elementary school, a philosophy of physical education, and movements of the child, and mechanical principles before examining the work of Laban and the application of his work and ideas to educational dance, games, and gymnastics. The book also contains a chapter on instructional methods in terms of helping teachers to become better observers of children, and therefore better teachers, and considering why teachers take particular actions or make particular responses. The final chapter evaluates the movement education program. This is a book that demands careful reading and study but it does clarify many questions and problems concerning the teaching of movement education. The second book published that year is by Kruger and Kruger and approaches movement education in a slightly different way. This book examines a curriculum with dual tracks: a learning track for developmental movement education, or the acquisition of tool skills; and a learning track for basic movement education, which involves development of an awareness of body, space, effort, and relationships.

Another book that originally was published in Germany in 1955, by Liselott Diem, was translated into English and published in America in 1957 with the title of *Who Can.* This delightful little book, with its marvelous illustrations, was reprinted by AAHPER in 1977 and may be obtained from AAHPER. The book presents a series of 20 tasks for exercise and activitiy on the floor and on apparatus, with each task prefaced by the question, "Who can. . .?"

Miscellaneous Readings

EDUCATION—THE CHANGING SCENE

Holt, John. *How Children Fail.* New York: Dell Publishing Co., 1965.

Holt, John. *How Children Learn.* New York: Pitman Publishing Co., 1967.

These are two delightful books about children and what goes on in the interactions between children and adults, both in and out of the classroom.

Leonard, George B. *Education and Ecstasy.* New York: Dell Publishing Co., 1968.

The book by Leonard provides some fascinating insights into what goes on in schools and looks at some possibilities for the future.

Postman, Neil, and Weingartner, Charles. *Teaching as a Subversive Activity.* New York: Delacorte Press, 1969.

The authors criticize current educational methods and suggest alternatives. The book has an especially good chapter on the method of inquiry.

Brown, Mary, and Precious, Norman. *The Integrated Day in the Primary School.* New York: Ballantine Books, 1968.

Two practicing teachers in England discuss their development of an "open" school.

Goodell, Carol, ed. *The Changing Classroom.* New York: Ballantine Books, 1973.

A collection of readings dealing with many of the new ideas that began to emerge in education in the late sixties and early seventies. Discusses theories and practices.

Rogers, Carl R. *Freedom to Learn.* Columbus, Ohio: Charles E. Merrill Publishing Co., 1969.

Rogers discusses the way that learning can be facilitated in an atmosphere affording freedom to learn.

Movement Education—Critiques

Lawrence F. Locke has written a critique of movement education which is in the *Selected Readings in Movement Education* edited by R. Sweeney (1970). It can also be found in Brown and Cratty's *New Perspectives of Man in Action,* published by Prentice-Hall, Inc., Englewood Cliffs, New Jersey, in 1969. Locke also wrote "The Movement Movement," which appeared in JOHPER in January 1966. These articles were written some years ago but present a challenging and perceptive view of the subject.

Siedentop examines movement education in his book, *Physical Education: Introductory Analysis*, (2nd ed. Dubuque, Iowa: Wm. C. Brown, 1976) and discusses the Locke critique, and adds other discussion. A useful chapter which challenges the movement educators to tighten their theoretical structures.

Seminar Questions and Activities

1. Visit a local elementary school and talk to the physical education teacher about the kind of program in operation. See if you can observe some classes. Describe what you see in terms of program orientation. Is the problem traditional, or inclined toward movement education? See Bilbrough, A., and Jones, P. *Developing Patterns in Physical Education*. London: University of London Press, 1973, p. 18.
2. Develop a chart which illustrates Laban's framework of movement. How could you use the chart to help you in developing a child's movement?
3. Try to visit a school which is utilizing an open education philosophy. What impressed you about the school or left you puzzled? Discuss your concerns or thoughts with a teacher or your instructor.

2 movement: its place and purpose in the curriculum

Introduction

This chapter examines the knowledge, skills, and attitudes related to movement that children work toward achieving by the time they reach the end of their elementary school education. The purpose here is to present the reader with some goals which will be discussed so that he or she can gradually develop an individual philosophy of teaching. A key question to be considered in developing this philosophy is how movement education contributes to the total education of the child.

It must be remembered that the movement education program is not the only curriculum area in which children are involved in school. They usually will spend a great deal more time in the classroom than in the gymnasium or on the playground. A daily period specifically designated for movement is essential, yet many children may receive only 20 minutes of such activity two or three times a week. Despite this fact, a well-taught and well-planned movement program can have a tremendous influence upon the growing child who is learning to use his or her body, developing attitudes about exercise and activity, and acquiring knowledge related to the body and movement. In addition, the child's participation in a movement program can influence peer-group acceptance, assist with the development of a good self-concept, increase self-confidence, and affect many other aspects of development.

The movement education program may be taught by a specialist teacher or by the child's regular classroom teacher. Whoever is responsible for teaching movement in a school should realize the importance of providing adequate time for children to allow them to participate successfully. Other curriculum pressures, or the limitations of inadequate space and other resources, often have dictated how much time is available for teaching movement. We have seen the way children can be short changed in such areas as music, art, and movement because of the emphasis on or pressure of getting children back to learning "basic" subjects. The most basic subject, however, is movement and through participation in a movement program children can learn to think and feel and use their senses and imagination as well as learn to express feelings and communicate.

It is the right of every child to enjoy movement in its broadest sense. This would include such activities as games, gymnastics, dance, outdoor activities, and swimming. Skills in these areas, as well as the associated knowledge and attitudes concerned with socioemotional and intellectual development, need to be fostered. Healthful and beneficial lifetime habits of exercise and activity can start in pre-school and be developed throughout the school years. Needless to say, such experiences, to be effective, must provide some measure of success and enjoyment or children will be discouraged and lose interest at an early age. It also is important to identify as early as possible those children who may have motor problems, as these children may also have some kind of learning disability. Thus, total development of the child depends upon both academic and motor learning.

Developing a Philosophy

The teacher of movement education, whether a specialist or a classroom teacher, will need to develop an overall personal philosophy about teaching which is based on sound principles and beliefs. This philosophy should be capable of justification and, if necessary, defense.

A personal philosophy of movement education for children will grow from a person's beliefs about children, his or her training in education, and the nature of the subject matter taught. These beliefs, or values, often are based on the kinds of experiences a person has had concerning school, the particular subject involved, and his or her degree of success as a participant. Unpleasant associations often linger on and the teacher may consciously or unconsciously place less emphasis on particular subjects in the curriculum because of these associations. In the movement area, this lack of emphasis may be rationalized by the notion that children's exercise and play needs are provided for at recess or during the noon hour.

The specialist who has a background in teaching motor skills should have a very clear idea of the direction to be taken and the goals to be developed as a result of professional preparation and experience. The classroom teacher, on the other hand, may not be too certain of the elements comprising a movement program. Emphasis on the program may vary according to the teacher's own particular opinions and values. Therefore, before starting to teach, it is essential to put down on paper the bases for goal statements. These should include the pertinent areas of child growth and development; the nature of and conditions for learning; and the implications of these goal statements for the child's movement education. Program development then can follow, based on the goal statements developed.

One of the dangers in using a textbook is that concepts such as goals and objectives often tend to be memorized rather than understood. Goals, and a rationale for each, are discussed later in this chapter. The reader should carefully examine these statements and, rather than blindly accepting them, review them with consideration given to current position papers on physical education and movement in the elementary school (see chapter study guide). The goal statements should also be measured against personal beliefs, experiences, and values. Ideally, teachers should develop their own program goals, with the goals that follow serving as guidelines.

Stating Goals

In general, goals are broad statements that detail the overall purposes for a particular program, with the focus resting primarily on what it is hoped the students will achieve through the program. Objectives, as distinct goals, are more detailed statements or the steps by which the goals may be achieved.

Goals and objectives in education and physical education often are stated in very idealistic terms. The actual connections between the goals and the achievements of students are not always made or are even apparent. Goals must be more than statements about learning to play basketball or dancing the Virginia Reel. The focus must be on the children's achievements rather than on specific subject matter.

If goals are stated in a purposeful and meaningful way and related clearly to the goals of the overall school curriculum, then school principals and other concerned individuals will be able to recognize the place, purpose, and value of a movement program.

Physical education teachers have often failed in the past to convince others of the vital role physical education plays in the total development of children. Because of this, when budgets become tight physical education often is regarded as a "frill" and one of the first subjects to be eliminated. With clearly defined goals and teachers who are accountable for their programs and student achievement, movement education will gain acceptance and equality within the total curriculum.

GOAL STATEMENTS

Broad, interrelated goals are developed below for a movement education program based on the physical, socioemotional, and intellectual areas of child development. The goals are not stated in any hierarchical scheme and are similar to the goals of a traditional physical education program; however, the methods and materials used to achieve the goals will be different. A discussion of each goal is provided.

Physical Aspects

To provide the opportunity for the student to:

1. Become physically fit through a program which includes vigorous exercise and makes progressively increasing demands on the body systems.
2. Acquire an understanding and appreciation of the nature and maintenance of total fitness and health.
3. Become aware of his or her own movement capabilities, limitations, and abilities as the student learns how to manage his or her body competently in a variety of different movement experiences.

   These goals would include the development of muscular strength and endurance, flexibility, agility, coordination, speed, and balance as well as benefiting the cardiorespiratory system.

   Movement experiences are built around locomotor, non-locomotor, and manipulative movements, and their application in gymnastics, games, and dance. Levels of development will be related to the individual child's own needs and abilities.

Socioemotional Aspects

To provide opportunity for the student to:

1. Learn to cooperate and collaborate in socially acceptable ways through participation in individual and group activities.
2. Develop positive attitudes, feelings, and values about sportsmanship, competition, and other people, and the role of exercise and activity in life.
3. Enjoy participation in different kinds of physical activity through satisfying, successful movement experiences.
4. Learn to share and care for equipment.

Fig. 2-1 *Enjoying activity.*

5. Develop a good self-concept and self-esteem with regard to the body and physical activity while promoting the qualities of self-discipline, self-confidence, and self-direction.

Intellectual Aspects

To provide the opportunity for the student to:

1. Develop the knowledge and understanding associated with movement concepts and the physical laws of movement. Learn the "why" as well as the "how" of exercise and activity.
2. Develop creative and original responses to problems or tasks involving basic movement, gymnastics, game skills, rhythms, and dance.
3. Choose movement activities from a range of possible alternatives and learning styles.
4. Experience the joy of discovery in learning to move.
5. Learn how to learn.

DISCUSSION OF GOALS

Teachers need to think about the implementation of goals before, during, and after teaching. Some goals afford short-term or immediate attainment, while others, such as attitudes and values, essentially require long-term development. The discussion that follows should help teachers and students to begin clarifying their own values and attitudes concerning what they believe their program should be attempting to achieve with children.

1. Physical Aspects—Vigorous Exercises

Children need some vigorous exercise everyday to stimulate growth, strengthen bone and muscle, and develop the heart and lungs. Present day society, especially in the inner city and in urban areas, tends to create limitations on the opportunities for young children to exercise. In many places children are driven or bussed to school instead of walking. Apartment living, especially in high-rise apartments, may place restrictions on the amount and kind of exercise and activity available to children. Parents often are unwilling to let children play in a neighborhood park, even if it is nearby, unless they can be closely supervised.

It is doubtful that the movement program in school can satisfy the child's total need for exercise in the short amount of time usually allowed. However, through participation in a movement program children can be encouraged to take part in activities at other times. Recess, the periods before and after school, and the lunch break are times when children can exercise and satisfy part of this need. Equipment such as balls and bats could be made available to children for use at these times. A program of movement education also can provide children with some idea and knowledge about activities that can be practiced or played outside of the classroom. In other words, the movement program should afford some carryover activities for children to pursue in other situations.

Play will not always be vigorous, but generally children love to run and chase, to roll and tumble, to climb and swing. More and more parks and playgrounds are moving away from swings, slides, and merry-go-rounds toward equipment that encourages climbing and hanging rather than just sitting. In addition, the newer equipment is designed to foster more imaginative and challenging use by children. The spaceship can become a rocket, a castle, or a submarine as play develops.

Children have different capacities for exercise, so teachers should realize that to make everyone do the same number of repetitions of an exercise, particularly where strength and endurance are involved, or run three laps of the field may be convenient for the teacher but certainly may not be the best way to enhance development or encourage a positive attitude about exercise in children. As children are encouraged to respond to the increasing demands, or overload, placed on the heart, circulation, and muscles during exercise, teachers should be aware of individual differences and capabilities. A child's level of performance in certain

Fig. 2-2 *Climbing is a challenge.*

activities can be determined, with subsequent activities adjusted to suit that child's particular needs.

PHYSICAL FITNESS TESTING

The use of physical fitness tests and their place in a program of movement education also needs to be examined. Many schools use the physical fitness tests developed by the American Alliance for Health, Physical Education, and Recreation (AAHPER, 1976). In general, the test battery is designed for use in grades 4 and above and includes a 50-yard dash, sit-ups, pull-ups, standing long jump, shuttle run, and a 600-yard run/walk or an 8-minute distance event. Children who scored at the 85th percentile or above for their age in all events qualified for the President's Physical Fitness Award. The test is currently under review (1980) and probably will have a different format when revised.

Some school districts require physical education teachers to administer the tests to their classes, while in other schools it is left to the individual teacher to determine whether the tests are given. If the tests are used as a screening device for children who are identified as having low scores, with these children receiving special help, they can be worthwhile. Too often, however, the re-

Fig. 2-3 *The space ship.*

sults are not used in any meaningful way, thus posing the question of why the test was given. In other situations children have spent a great deal of class time specifically working on the test items for the sole purpose of improving test scores! To work toward attaining the President's Physical Fitness Award can be a rewarding experience for children, providing that a balance of activities is maintained in the program and that other equally important aspects of the total movement program are not sacrificed because of the time needed by some children to obtain a satisfactory standard in the tests. Testing procedures can be lengthy unless the teacher is well organized and has developed efficient testing techniques. A positive benefit of testing is that the results do give the teacher and student some idea of individual levels of performance. The tests can motivate some children, affording them a goal worth achieving. Test results generally should not be used as part of a grade.

PHYSICAL FITNESS AND MOVEMENT EDUCATION

In some quarters there has been and still is a tendency to equate physical fitness with physical education. The criticism has been made that movement education does not really encourage the development of physical fitness in children. Some discussion, therefore, is necessary to clarify the relationship of fitness and movement education.

Physical education lessons often begin with a few minutes of calisthenics. Such exercises as "Jumping Jacks," toe touching, and push-ups are performed, with the class led by the teacher or a student. These exercises usually do not continue long enough or are performed strenuously enough to have any real effect in terms of developing strength, flexibility, or endurance. There is little overload to increase strength and children usually do not even get out of breath. Improvement in flexibility is doubtful because so little effort is exerted in stretch positions, although the habit of stretching certain muscle groups before beginning any vigorous exercise is a useful one to acquire. Children should be taught and encouraged to develop a simple stretching routine. Vigorous, sudden stretches should be avoided; stretches should be done slowly, with the main effort falling in the final position. Until recently, when more specialized apparatus has become available for children to use for climbing, hanging, and swinging, the main physical weakness among children has been in the strength of the arm and shoulder girdle muscles. With the appearance of such equipment as cargo nets, geodomes, and different kinds of climbing frames for use both indoors and outside, children will have more opportunity for improving their arm and shoulder strength.

A movement education program does not contain a specific segment that can be designated as being solely the "physical fitness" portion of the program. Muscular, cardiovascular, and organic fitness improve as children learn basic skills, develop games, and participate in other kinds of activity. The concept of physical development and fitness underlies the total program. Children will be frequently involved in activities that involve flexibility, strength, agility, balance, coordination, endurance, and speed as they respond to tasks and challenges set by the teacher.

Teachers involved with a more traditional approach can try the ideas suggested in later chapters to discover how physical fitness becomes an integral part of movement education.

BODY MANAGEMENT GOALS

As children learn to move they gradually become more aware of their own capabilities and limitations. The experiences provided in a program of movement education help children to understand and appreciate the consequences of moving at different speeds, using different amounts of force, and employing direct or indirect movement. The child also learns about the body's use of the different aspects of space, that is, direction, pathway, and level, and the various body supports and shapes. The development of body

Fig. 2-4 Body management.

awareness will lead toward competent body management as children master locomotor, non-locomotor, and manipulative skills and are able to apply them in play, gymnastics, games, and dance.

By kindergarten, children have already acquired and mastered a great many movement skills. These skills will need further refinement and development as the children move through the elementary school. New skills will be learned and added to the increasingly broad repertoire of movement possibilities. Children will need plenty of time to adequately explore their own movement capabilities, therefore, the problem of time for practice and refinement needs to be considered. When physical education is only allocated three 20-minute periods a week, children do not have enough time to really practice and master gross motor skills. Very young children at the pre-school and primary grade levels may need, for example, to throw and catch a ball a large number of times before they attain competence. Programs that primarily consist of allowing children to play games do not always provide the opportunity for them to master basic skills because more time is spent playing than practicing. Many adults today are unable to throw a ball properly because they never had the chance to acquire the correct pattern in the elementary years.

Fig. 2-5
An individual activity.

Not every child will become, or will even want to become, a varsity athlete or indulge in serious competitive activities. Many will find outlets for exercise and recreation through such activities as bicycling, dancing, swimming, and sailing, others will play tennis or volleyball, ski, or climb mountains, while others may have little opportunity for any of these adventures. Thus, one might ask the question, "What body management skills is it necessary for a child to learn?" Is there some kind of structure underlying movement education that can provide a person with the necessary basis for acquiring the skills needed for sports, recreational activities, games, gymnastics, and dance? If we were to list some of these basic skills the following would be included.

LOCOMOTOR SKILLS

The ability to walk, run, jump, and land with the correct pattern and with good form or quality of movement. Other locomotor skills include hopping, galloping, skipping, rolling, and sliding. The body can, of course, move as the body weight is transferred onto a variety of different supports on the floor and on apparatus. These skills can be explored singly or in combination.

NON-LOCOMOTOR SKILLS

This category includes many of the different ways the trunk or individual body parts can bend, stretch, twist, and rock. The body also can balance on different supports on the floor and on apparatus. Balance can be explored in terms of losing balance or overbalance. The body can also support itself by hanging on different body parts.

Fig. 2-6 *Learning to push.*

MANIPULATIVE SKILLS

The functional skills of lifting and carrying, pulling and pushing need to be explored in terms of correct body management. Manipulative skills in which a ball or bat is used will be important as the child learns to throw and catch, or kick and hit a ball, which leads to participation in simple game activities.

Efficient movement is based upon an awareness of the mechanical principles of movement, the laws of motion, economy of effort, and an understanding and application of Laban's movement factors.

If children are provided with a good background in body awareness and management and are able to develop skill in a variety of activities in which they enjoy participating, it ought to be possible for each child to find success and a sense of achievement in movement.

2. Socioemotional Aspects

Learning how to get on with other people is an important aspect of education. Personal relationships between teacher and child as well as between child and child need to be developed. The physical education or movement teacher works with children in a somewhat different environment than that of the classroom teacher. Children are generally freer to move about and need more careful management than if they were in a more confined space. Essentially, of course, the teacher is trying to encourage children to learn. If children are absorbed and involved in what they are doing, then management usually will not be a major concern of

Fig. 2-7 *Learning to kick.*

the teacher in terms of maintaining discipline and control. Because children are in close proximity to each other for most of the school day, they do need to learn to cooperate and work together. In movement education there are some unique opportunities for developing social interactions.

MOTIVATION

In managing the learning or behavior of children, teachers use a variety of methods and devices. Competition is frequently used to get children to cooperate. Teachers ask: "Let's see which is the first team to line up," or "The quietest team can go first today," or possibly "The best team today gets a gold star." Encouraging children to be "first" or "best" is a questionable motivational tool. The motivation necessary for a child to perform a task, sit down quietly, or stand in line at the door can come from within the child or simply can spring from a desire to please the teacher. This internal desire and possible self-reward is described as "intrinsic motivation." Working or performing a task for external reward is "extrinsic motivation." In a way, we are talking here about behavior modification, that is, how can we encourage or persuade children to do what we want them to do or learn?

Normally in movement education there are few occasions when children do not want to participate; however, it may be necessary

Fig. 2-8 *The smile of success.*

with a particular class or an individual child to use some form of external reward. Praise and positive reinforcement for good behavior or a good performance certainly help to encourage learning and desirable behavior. The aim, however, should be to work toward intrinsic development of motivation, since children may no longer be motivated to participate if and when the rewards are no longer offered.

The child's joy of discovery as he or she develops a solution to a movement problem can encourage further exploration and discovery, hence self-motivation is developed. In movement education, the teacher primarily acknowledges the responses of children to movement tasks or problems. Because in movement education each child becomes personally involved with a task or challenge, the need for continual use of management techniques is minimized. The role of the teacher is to try to inculcate in children such values as cooperation, a willingness to share, consideration for people and property, a sense of working together toward a common goal, and concern for other children who may be less able to develop high skill levels.

If a program maintains the interest and involvement of children in what they are learning, and affords them the opportunity to share in decisions concerning what and the way they learn, then problems with antisocial behavior and discipline will tend to be minimized. It is doubtful that any system or program can eliminate completely disruptive behavior on the part of a child who seeks attention or who does not wish to participate. If the teacher has made some attempt to identify the children's needs, interests, and abilities, and then has planned the program around these factors, a better classroom climate and environment can be developed. Interactions between teacher and child will be more meaningful. This will necessitate that the teacher be well organized and gives some thought as to how each lesson can give attention to the individual characteristics of the children. Approaching teaching in this way obviously will take more work in terms of preparation than would a written lesson plan containing calisthenics, a relay race, and a couple of games which each class performs regardless of grade level.

Developing the right environment also will help tremendously. This means having apparatus that can challenge both the kindergarten and the sixth grade. The ability to provide each child with a ball, a jump rope, or a bean bag for use in a lesson would help considerably. In addition, having sufficient larger pieces of equipment, such as balance beams, climbing frames, and agility ramps, is a tremendous advantage for the teacher.

COMPETITION

When playing games which are fairly competitive, children sometimes are apt to get momentarily overexcited. If there are extra pressures on the children to win even the best cooperative situations may fall apart. Teachers sometimes are guilty of encouraging the kind of situation in which children scream and shout, while all the teacher does is to keep score. It then takes a long time for the class to settle down to work again upon returning to the regular classroom. This does not mean that children should not get excited occasionally or let off steam. The kind of situation that allows for this to happen does have a place in the program but requires careful management.

Another concern that may arise as a result of pressures brought to bear on children in competitive situations is that children may occasionally cheat in order to win. These situations frequently occur outside the school in agency-sponsored sports programs, or in school as a result of overzealous teachers who create both emotional and social situations that children find difficult to understand. Children may need help in learning to accept the emotions involved both in winning and in losing. Such situations can be eased if highly competitive team sports are de-emphasized during the elementary years. If children can participate in small-side team games which they have assisted in developing under the teacher's guidance, competitive pressures can be considerably reduced. Children also ought to feel that they are "winners" if they do their best. One is continually being reminded that society is based to some extent on competition. It is essential that children learn to understand and accept competition; however, winning is not everything or the only thing, it is only a part of our society that occasionally is overemphasized.

Some solutions and alternatives to highly competitive activities include using more self-testing activities, placing children into groups of compatible ability levels, and implementing activities that demand cooperation rather than competition. Competing with oneself allows a child to measure his or her own progress in order to improve individual performance. Grouping children so that their abilities are fairly homogeneous can minimize any frustrations that may be caused by wide variations in skill levels. The highly skilled child can become very frustrated by working with a child who has a much lower skill level. The move toward cooperation and collaboration can be fostered by setting tasks that encourage these behaviors.

LEARNING ATMOSPHERE

In movement education a basic ground rule for children to follow is that they should work on their own unless using a partner or participating in a small group. This means not interfering with anyone else's movement or practice. Children seem to accept this idea if it is clearly stated on the first class day and reinforced frequently. Children also should be asked to work quietly. This does not mean absolute silence, but it does require that the total noise level be low enough so that the teacher can use a normal conversational tone of voice. It is more conducive to a better learning atmosphere and social climate too if conversational interactions are possible. The teacher should rarely have to shout at the children and the children must learn to listen while moving.

ATTITUDES, VALUES, AND FEELINGS

By teaching the "why" as well as the "how" in movement education, children can receive a basis for understanding the function of exercise on bone, muscle, heart, circulation, and the other organic systems of the body, at the appropriate level of comprehension. The relationships between exercise and diet must be discussed in class. If children are able to experience and recognize the feeling or sense of well-being that follows exercise, they may be encouraged to participate in such exercise throughout their lives. For the young child, any effects of exercise will have to be fairly immediate for him or her to be aware of any benefits. Sometimes activity is overdone and rather than feeling good, the child gets hot and tired, and it will take some convincing talk to assure the child that exercise really is beneficial.

Learning to share equipment, taking turns in using it, and showing respect for property which may belong to others, are all values which children need to learn. Teachers can have a tremendous influence in reinforcing the positive aspects of such behavior. Viable relationships can develop but it will take time and perseverance. The respect developed between children and between teachers and children evolves as feelings are expressed and warm, friendly relationships are formed.

SUCCESSFUL EXPERIENCE

As the result of both maturation and practice, the level of children's motor skills will improve; however, there will be wide variations in both ability and physical development. The teacher must consider these factors when planning learning activities, as well as how the children approach learning in the early stages of acquiring motor skills. In fact, how children learn may initially be more important than what they learn. Children will be more inclined to learn if they are able to experience some degree of success.

Self-confidence in children can grow as a result of successful accomplishments in movement. Adequate teacher reinforcement will encourage children to accept their own limitations (discussed in later chapters). This can help them in accepting new and different challenges. Progress and improvement in motor skills will enhance peer group acceptance and self-confidence. Fear of failure can be eliminated by the teacher who recognizes different ability levels and does not set one standard that everyone must reach. Children also should not be forced into trying an activity for which they are not ready, either physically or mentally. Teachers occasionally have been guilty of forcing children into attempting a task beyond their capabilities, and it is then that accidents tend to occur. Some children, of course, do need a little push sometimes but the perceptive teacher will know when or when not to do this. In movement education the fear of embarrassment in front of one's peers is eliminated as children usually are not asked to demonstrate unless sharing an idea or their creative answer to a movement task.

SELF DISCIPLINE

Self-discipline can be encouraged in children in several ways. The ability to continue with an activity without the constant supervision of the teacher provides an indication that children are becoming more responsible for their own behavior. In the movement education approach, children are able to experiment in an atmosphere of relative freedom. This kind of freedom has to be introduced gradually. If children have been put through a system based on responding to commands, they often are quite lost when it is suggested that they come up with some ideas of their own about ways to move. They have become so accustomed to being told when and how to do everything that relying on their own resources takes a little time to accept. This problem not only occurs in the elementary school, but is indicative of the products of the total educational system as well. Many people have had nothing else but this type of education for most of their school years. Nothing much happened unless they were told exactly what to do, and also what was expected. They were told to buy the textbook, do the assignment, attend class, and so on. These individuals have not, in fact, learned how to learn. An overdose of spoonfeeding has seen to it that they do not seem even to know what is necessary for their own survival!

Freedom bears, of course, an associated responsibility. If children initially cannot handle freedom, the teacher will have to restrict the amount of freedom permitted, gradually allowing more as children are ready for it. With movement tasks and problems defined by the teacher, children are encouraged to work on their own, with a partner, or as part of a group. Goals are clearly established and understood. Children know what they are supposed to be doing or learning, without continuous instruction from the teacher. The teacher will, however, be providing support and feedback as well as serving as a resource person. Appropriate behavior by the children can be reinforced as they become more self-disciplined and responsible. It will be suggested later in the text that children can move into learning centers, implement contracts, and ultimately proceed into what might be called "open gym." Self-evaluative procedures can be introduced into the work gradually as children become accustomed to working more on their own.

SELF-DIRECTION

Closely related to the task of encouraging children to become self-disciplined is that of self-direction. The end product would be children who can decide what they want to learn and how they want to learn it. This cannot be achieved easily or quickly. Children learn best if they are interested in what they are doing, and the teacher can utilize this fact by finding out something about their interests. Obviously, there will need to be discussion and direction in terms of what skills should be learned, what games might be played, or which dances performed. As children begin to understand the structure of movement education they will be able to suggest the next step or formulate new ideas. If learning can be individualized, with children working on their own occasionally, there will be more opportunities for self-direction to develop. Intrinsic motivation, along with curiosity, can facilitate the joy of discovery and the satisfaction of successfully completing a task or solving a problem.

How individual children feel about themselves in relation to other children, particularly classmates, is important for the teacher to know. This self-concept can incorporate many different facets of development. To describe self-concept precisely is difficult because it is affected by such things as the child's appearance, body image, previous experience, peer group acceptance, and level of achievement. One's self-esteem might be said to be a measure of self-concept. The feeling can, of course, be positive or negative. Helping children to feel good about themselves is an important part of a teacher's role. Movement education, which encourages children to make choices, provides success experiences, and offers positive feedback about their responses, can help in development of a positive self-concept. (For the teacher who is interested in pursuing this topic further, several references are cited in the study guide.) The style of teaching suggested in this text encourages development of a positive self-concept in children.

3. Intellectual Aspects

We must recognize that when we encourage children to learn it is how the total child or organism reacts to the total situation which is important. That is, we cannot separate mind from body. There still is, in many quarters, the feeling that children's minds are nurtured in the classroom, while physical education classes take care of their bodies! Often physical education programs have tended to do only this, with many traditional programs offering few opportunities for any kind of thinking to take place, that is, discovering facts and principles, making comparisons or choices, solving problems, and so on. Most of these processes are part of the goals of education, and certainly are part of the goals of movement education.

Through movement a child can learn about the physical nature of the environment and about his or her own limitations with regard to the way the body can move in or cope with that environment. An understanding of the nature of force, gravity, momentum, acceleration, balance and stability, transfer of weight, and body mechanics, at the appropriate level for the child, can be gained through a well-planned movement program. There are many ways in which academic areas can be integrated with a movement program. For example, the opportunity to share in the decision-making process in a class, in terms of what, when, and how learning proceeds, is an important part of education for the student. Programs that fail to consider this function cannot be called successful in educating people, either in academics or in movement. In movement education, fundamentals of activity and skill learning will provide an important component of a movement program, in addition to supplying information relating to physical fitness, nutrition, health, and safety. In 1970 AAHPER published an outstanding book, *Knowledge and Understanding in Physical Education* (revised in 1973). Teachers and college students are urged to carefully examine this book for a better grasp of the possibilities in this area.

PROGRAM CONTENT

There are many different ways of classifying or systematizing the ways in which the body can move. Consideration must also be given to the ways in which motor skills have been developed for use in functional as well as expressive movement.

One way to classify body movements would be anatomically. This was the old Swedish Drill system and was used mainly for reasons of health and posture. In a sense, its value was meant to be therapeutic, with each joint and muscle group exercised systematically. This system did not lend itself readily to a total program which included skills.

The need here is to identify the parts of the body that can move, and where they can move, then look at how they move. The whole body then can be put into motion in moving in functional, creative and expressive ways. Program development is implemented by initially applying the movement factors to locomotor, non-locomotor, and manipulative activities. As children become familiar with effort factors and with learning by discovery, they will gradually become educated in movement to the point where they can proceed more independently and creatively, yet still under the guidance of a teacher. The fundamental movements then can be applied in games, gymnastics, and dance.

Locomotor movements represent the different ways the body can move or travel from place to place. Included are the functional skills of walking, running, hopping, galloping, and many other different ways of moving on the feet and on other body supports. These movements can be performed individually or in different combinations and sequences.

Non-locomotor movements are essentially activities which the body can perform without moving from place to place. Such things as balancing, bending and stretching, twisting, hanging, and swinging are included.

Manipulative movements include skills in which the body is manipulating or controlling an external object, such as a bat or ball. Such activities as throwing and catching, kicking, hitting, and bouncing are in this category as well as such activities as lifting and carrying, pushing and pulling.

Fig. 2-9 *A locomotor activity.*

Fig. 2-10 *Non-locomotor activity.*

Fig. 2-11 Manipulative activity.

In movement education, children often will produce movements in response to tasks set by the teacher that are difficult to categorize and name. Describing them may be possible in terms of the framework suggested earlier, that is, what, where, and how the body is moving. The description would include the body supports being used, the direction of the movement, the speed of movement, and so on. Thus, the classification of skills will have to be open-ended and flexible to allow for these different responses. The main purpose of such classification is to help the teacher in systematically planning a program and acquiring a sense of where to begin.

As the basic skills and their various combinations are developed, they can be applied to gymnastics, games, and dance activities. By the time a child reaches sixth grade, most of the skills and activities listed below will have been explored and developed. How to develop the movement program is described later in chapters 6 through 10.

The rationale for such a program can be explained in terms of why we move. The human being moves for a variety of reasons, one of which is to master the environment. Other reasons are to maintain flexibility and strength; to participate in a wide variety of physical activities such as games, play, sports, and dance; for functional and occupational movement; to maintain physical efficiency; to acquire a sense of well-being; for purposes of competition and cooperation, and for health, fitness, and recreation.

PROGRAM DEVELOPMENT

The child first learns to identify body parts and then how to move those parts separately and in different combinations. Explorations are made of the ways the body can support itself. Further progress is made as the child explores a wide variety of motor skills. A brief overview is given below of the main movement patterns developed in later chapters.

Locomotor Movements

Locomotor movements include such activities as walking, running, jumping and landing, hopping, skipping, sliding, and other ways of moving on the feet and on other body supports.

Walking is a fundamental motor pattern and is the most common locomotor skill. Children need practice in developing a good walking pattern.

Running is used in many different activities, such as chasing and dodging games, team sports, track, and jogging, and in combination with other activities. Children need a great deal of practice and opportunities to run.

Jumping and landing are important safety skills as well as elements of games and sports. Children need practice in jumping over things, jumping down from different heights, in the standing long jump, and in the high jump. The ability to land and roll should be taught early in the program so that children can learn to transfer the force of landing into a roll if necessary.

Hopping, skipping, and galloping often occur spontaneously in children, although more often children will perform these movements in response to a rhythmic beat or to music. These skills are required in many forms of folk dance and can be part of other dance or creative movement sequences as well.

Climbing is a different kind of locomotor skill. Children can still find trees and playground equipment on which to climb. Many schools now have challenging apparatus which invites children to climb. Climbing ropes, cargo nets, and geodomes, together with trestles and ladders, can be used indoors and outside.

Rolling is explored as children find different ways to roll. Rolling is another way for the body to transfer its weight onto different surfaces.

Non-locomotor Movements

A number of different activities fall within this category.

Balancing is an important skill to learn in early childhood. Children can balance on different body parts used either singly or in combination. They can balance on apparatus or on a partner. As the body counters the force of gravity, children learn to maintain stability.

Curling or bending and stretching form part of many different activities. These skills can be done simply for working on flexibility and stretching, yet they also are a part of many other movements in games, gymnastics, and dance.

Twisting and rocking movements need to be considered as movements that assist in development of flexibility and strength. Children can explore rocking that utilizes different body parts and requires the body to make different shapes. Both activities are important in gymnastics and other activities.

Hanging and swinging are both good exercises for the arms and shoulders and also for grip strength. Children can swing on a bar or on climbing ropes. They can hang from different body supports. Hanging and swinging can be combined with climbing and balancing.

Manipulative Activities

These activities include such everyday skills as lifting and carrying and pushing and pulling, together with many of the skills involved in sports and games that require the body to manipulate an external object such as a bat or ball. Children should learn about utilizing levers and leverage in relation to the body segments as well as about manipulating the body efficiently and safely.

Throwing and catching balls of different sizes, bouncing, kicking, heading, striking, volleying, rolling, and controlling balls with different body parts are important skills for children to master.

Lifting and carrying must be done correctly, and children need to learn these skills, especially how to lift heavy objects.

Pushing and pulling are useful skills which enable children to perform without straining the back.

Miscellaneous activities which are essentially manipulative in nature also include such tasks as skateboarding and learning to ride a bicycle.

Implementation of the Basic Skills or Movements

As children develop good body management and master some of the skills briefly described above, they can begin pursuing many different kinds of activities.

GYMNASTICS

Gymnastic movements developed in movement education evolve from the use of various combinations of activities, such as rolling, balancing, and transference of body weight on different supports, and can be performed on the floor or an apparatus. Through the use of the movement factors children can be encouraged to produce a wide variety of gymnastic movements. Themes can be used to facilitate work on various aspects of gymnastics. This kind of gymnastics is often called "educational gymnastics" and can be distinguished from olympic gymnastics, although many movements are common to both systems.

GAMES

Games develop from simple applications of the basic skills and can be classified in many ways. Learning to use a ball can lead to passing games using the hands and feet. Running activities can evolve into chasing and tag games as well as to team games. The use of small apparatus, such as hoops, bean bags, and jump ropes, can produce a variety of games which are primarily implemented by the children. As children grow proficient in throwing, catching, and striking, many other game possibilities become apparent. Children can be encouraged to develop games on their own as well as under the guidance of a teacher.

DANCE AND RHYTHM

Dance has played an important role in many cultures, whether primitive or more advanced. Many dances are part of our cultural heritage. Primitive societies often use dance as a form of celebration or ritual. Historical occurrences, battles, and other occasions are often recalled through elaborate dances and ceremonies.

The urge to dance lies within most people and yet it is often suppressed by the constraints and lack of spontaneity of modern society. We seem, in many ways, to have become more inhibited as we become more civilized. Young children, however, possess this basic urge to move and dance. They often run and skip simply out of sheer exuberance as they express their inner feelings through dance.

The development of dance will grow out of the children's responses to tasks or themes that require use of the movement factors and are built around locomotor, non-locomotor, and manipulative activities. The child's attitude to movement can be encouraged through a program that allows thinking and feeling through expressive movement. Dances can be developed which involve a wide range of movement. They can be quite simple or contain involved sequences. A dance can evolve from a piece of music, a poem, a story, rhythm, or other kinds of stimuli, including the use of imagery, a picture, or verbal cues.

Some discussion of the place of contemporary, folk, and square dance in the program is given in Chapter 9. This text suggests generally that children create their own kinds of group dance.

In conclusion, a movement program emerges from a broad base of competencies developed in the areas of locomotor, non-locomotor, and manipulative skills. The basic movement factors of time, weight, space, and flow are utilized to encourage children to become aware of their own movement capabilities. As children master these basic movements the skills can be used to develop games, gymnastic activities, and dance. Children should, of course, have many other opportunities for movement through aquatics, bowling, ice skating and roller skating, swimming, outdoor education activities (hiking, camping, cross country and downhill skiing) and many other sports and activities.

Successful Program Implementation

The success of any program will depend on many factors and their degree of accomplishment. The first essential is, of course, a statement of goals and purpose. The following components also are necessary for making a movement program successful.

1. The use by teachers of a flexible teaching approach which endeavors to match the methods of instruction with the individual learning styles, needs, interests, and abilities of children.
2. An approach to learning which, as far as possible, encourages children to explore and discover their own movement limitations and abilities as they learn and become proficient at a wide varicty of motor skills.
3. The creation of an atmosphere for learning in which the child can experiment freely without the fear of failure or of recrimination from the teacher.
4. An opportunity for children to share, within certain limitations, in the decision-making process affecting what and how they learn.
5. The provision of a challenging and stimulating environment that will encourage children to move, including sufficient apparatus and equipment, such as balls, hoops, jump ropes, climbing ropes, balance beams, and climbing frames, to enable children to make the most of the time available for movement and eliminate the need to wait for turns.
6. The development of quality in children's movement through the provision of adequate time for movement selection, practice, refinement, and mastery of motor skills.
7. An effort by teachers to ensure that the movement program is a vital part of the total school curriculum.

Summary

In discussing the place and purpose of movement education in the elementary school curriculum, the value of movement and its influence on children has to be understood. Children need to acquire essential knowledge, skills, and attitudes relating to movement.

Teachers need to develop their own personal philosophy as a foundation for writing goals and objectives. Such a philosophy will be based in part on the individual's personal values and beliefs about children, about education and learning, and about movement. Textbooks and position papers provide suggestions that can be used as guidelines in developing goals.

In this chapter, goals were broadly stated, as a basis for later discussion, in the sections on the physical, socioemotional, and intellectual aspects of goal development. Goal statements relating to the physical component considered vigorous exercise and the relationship of physical fitness to movement education. Other topics discussed included body management objectives and physical fitness testing. Socioemotional goals included the development of personal relationships, motivation, and the role of competition and cooperation as well as the development of a learning climate for movement education. Attitude development in children, including the acquisition of a good self-concept, self-direction, and self-discipline, were mentioned. Intellectual goals related to the child's opportunity to discover facts, principles, concepts, and solve problems relating to movement.

The chapter also focused on centering program development around the development of locomotor, non-locomotor, and manipulative activities and applying these factors to games, gymnastics, and dance. Additional elements which contribute to successful program development were listed.

Bibliography

American Association for Health, Physical Education, and Recreation. *Knowledge and Understanding in Physical Education.* Washington, D.C.: AAHPER, 1973.

______. *YOUTH FITNESS Test Manual.* Rev. ed. Washington, D.C.: AAHPER, 1976.

Thomas, Jerry, R., ed. *Youth Sports Guide for Coaches and Parents.* Washington, D.C.: Manufacturers Life Insurance Co., and the National Association for Sport and Physical Education, 1977.

Jarrett, James L. "I'm for Basics, But Let Me Define Them." In *Phi Delta Kappan,* December 1977, (pp. 235–239).

Study Guide

Objectives

AAHPER. "Essentials of a Quality Elementary School Physical Education Program." Washington, D.C.: AAHPER, 1970.

This excellent position paper (being revised in 1980) examines the objectives of physical education. The pamphlet discusses beliefs about the child, the teacher and teacher preparation, the instructional program, evaluation, and organization and equipment.

"Elementary School Physical Education: Beliefs, Goals, Objectives and

Activities." Ohio State Department of Education, Columbus, Ohio, January 1978.

This is another excellent resource pertaining to objectives.

Siedentop, Daryl. *Physical Education: Introductory Analysis.* 2nd ed. Dubuque, Iowa: Wm. C. Brown, 1976.

Singer, Robert N., and Dick, Walter. *Teaching Physical Education: A Systems Approach.* Boston: Houghton-Mifflin, 1974.

The book by Siedentop contains excellent discussions of goals and objectives. Singer and Dick present an interesting approach to planning and developing a program.

Bloom, Benjamin S., *et al. Taxonomy of Educational Objectives: The Cognitive Domain.* Handbook I. New York: David McKay, 1956.

Krathwohl, D. R., *et al. Taxonomy of Educational Objectives: The Affective Domain.* Handbook II. New York: David McKay, 1964.

Harrow, Anita J.A. *Taxonomy of the Perceptual Motor Domain.* New York: David McKay, 1972.

These three books have been influential in the development of ways to classify objectives in the cognitive, affective, and psychomotor domains. They provide an interesting way to develop objectives in any subject area.

The reader should try to develop a personal philosophy of physical education and a set of goals and objectives which include physical, socioemotional and intellectual components.

Corbin, Charles B. *A Text Book of Motor Development.* Dubuque, Iowa: Wm. C. Brown, 1973.

Siedentop, Daryl. *Physical Education: Introductory Analysis.* Dubuque, Iowa: Wm. C. Brown, 1976.

Rarick, G. Lawrence., ed. *Physical Activity: Human Growth and Development.* New York: Academic Press, 1973.

These books provide excellent discussions on developing a personal philosophy and goals and objectives pertaining to the physical component of physical education.

James J. Myrle. *Education and Physical Education.* London: G. Bell and Sons, 1967.

Johnson, David W., and Johnson, Roger T. *Learning Together and Alone: Cooperation, Competition, and Individualization.* Englewood Cliffs, N.J.: Prentice-Hall, 1975.

Felker, Donald W. *Building Positive Self-Concepts.* Minneapolis: Burgess Publishing Co., 1974.

The texts deal with the socioemotional aspects of physical education. James talks about aims, attitudes, and competition, and authority, responsibility, and freedom. Johnson and Johnson discuss goal setting, humanistic education, and open education. The third book by Felker presents ideas on helping children in their thinking and feeling about themselves.

AAHPER. *Knowledge and Understanding.* Washington, D.C.: AAHPER, 1970.

Mager, Robert F. *Developing Attitudes Towards Learning.* Palo Alto, Calif.: Fearon Pub., 1968.

______. *Preparing Instructional Objectives.* Belmont, Calif.: Lear Siegler/Fearon Pub., 1962.

The AAHPER publication deals with the intellectual component of instruction, while Mager treats the attitude toward learning and the development of instructional objectives.

Mosston, M. *Teaching Physical Education: From Command to Discovery,* Columbus, Ohio: Charles E. Merrill, 1966.

Mosston has some interesting points to make about all the developmental channels of growth and discusses the attainment of objectives in each of the four areas.

Torrance, E. Paul. "Seven Guides to Creativity." *In* The Journal of Health, Physical Education, and Recreation, April 1965.

In this article the author has presented guidelines for creative teaching. Torrance has written several other books on the subject, including *Guiding Creative Talent,* Prentice-Hall, 1962.

Seminar Questions and Activities

1. Suppose that the local school board decided to eliminate physical education programs at the elementary school level. Prepare a 10-minute speech in defense of elementary school physical education. Be sure that you can justify any statements that you make.
2. Examine the taxonomies of Bloom, Krathwohl, and Harrow and see if you can apply them in preparing objectives for a physical education program.
3. What can teachers do to improve or develop the self-concept and self-esteem of children in physical education?
4. How would you integrate some of the information about desirable knowledge and understanding of physical education into the physical education program? (See "Knowledge and Understanding in Physical Education," AAHPER.)
5. In what ways can children share in the decision-making process concerning what, when, and how they learn in physical education?

3 characteristics of the children we teach

Introduction

This chapter examines the physical growth, characteristic behaviors and needs of children at five different levels, including, preschool, kindergarten, first and second grades, third and fourth grades, and fifth and sixth grades. Implications for movement education are then presented based upon the descriptions given.

It is essential that, in addition to reading about children, observations be made of children in the five different groupings. Careful observation of individual children can provide a great deal of information about growth characteristics, posture, behavior, skill level, and socioemotional characteristics. Along with other professional experiences with children such observations will reinforce the fact that there are generally wide variations in most of these characteristics. The student will come to recognize that age, of itself, is a poor method of classifying children for movement education.

The chapter study guide provides some ideas for further study of children.

The Pre-School Child (Three and Four Year Olds)

Teachers and other professionals who choose to work with very young children need to have some ideas about what the three- or four-year-old child is like. Experience is, of course, the best teacher, and reading about children cannot be regarded as an adequate substitute for actually working with them. What happens quite often is that teachers who basically were trained to instruct children in elementary or secondary school find themselves working with pre-schoolers. Applying the teaching methods and strategies used with older children to this younger age group may cause problems due to the nature of the younger child. The teacher must start from the beginning with this child and understand his or her physical growth, behavioral characteristics, and needs as development proceeds. It should be stated at the outset that, although children generally proceed through a fixed pattern of development, they will be at different stages in that development since growth and maturation proceed at different rates. Teachers should be able to recognize these wide variations, not only in height and weight, but also in motor skill development, activity level, interests, attitudes, and maturation.

Each developmental stage that children pass through is different from all the others. Some of the differences are quite subtle, others more obvious. Age, in itself, is not the best way to classify growth and development, but as teachers generally work with children who are of similar age it is convenient to describe characteristics from this standpoint. There is considerable overlap in the stages children experience at different age levels. This is true for skill development also. For example, some children in second grade may be reading at about fourth- or fifth-grade level. The best second grader may be as good at throwing a ball as some of the poorer fourth graders, and so on.

In terms of sex differences in the learning of motor skills at the pre-school level, individual differences generally will be greater than those due to sex. (As they approach maturity, girls usually are ahead of boys, with a one-year lead by the age of five. This lead increases to two years by the time children reach the end of elementary school.)

The eyes are not fully developed and the pre-schooler tends to be far sighted. Eye and hand coordination is not very good in terms of the child being able to catch a ball or a bean bag. Reaction time and coordination slowly improve as maturation develops. Throwing and catching should probably be performed separately. The child will learn to catch a large ball more easily than a small one, while throwing is easier with a small one.

Gross motor or large muscle movements will be better than fine motor movements with regard to control mechanisms because of development proceeding from the brain out to the extremities.

As children of this level begin to develop motor skills, particularly locomotor movements, they are progressing from the wide-based, toes out, knees slightly bent stance of an earlier age when they first learned to stand alone and then walk. As muscles grow stronger more control is gained over balance and the child becomes more confident in maintaining an upright posture and in walking and running. The body's center of gravity is still relatively high compared to that of the sixth grader; hence, the pre-school child tends to be top heavy and falls over easily—but fortunately does not have far to fall! In addition to walking and running other locomotor skills are beginning to develop, such as hopping, skipping, and jumping.

CHARACTERISTIC BEHAVIORS

A wide range of behaviors are exhibited that range from extremely boisterous and noisy to very quiet and almost withdrawn. Most children are toilet trained by the age of four, although there may be an occasional relapse when the child is overexcited or under pressure.

The pre-schooler plays best alone, although they like to repeat activities, such as jumping off a box, with other children. They generally do not like to share apparatus or equipment. They are more likely to share if there is a good supply of equipment like balls and hoops. Children of this age resent interference with their play or any disturbance of the activity of the moment. With plenty of encouragement these children can learn to fasten buttons and tie shoes. Adults sometimes can offer too much help, delaying the children's attempts to do things for themselves.

Generally the young child is full of curiosity and eager for each new experience. Activities will be repeated if they are fun and enjoyable and the child is experiencing success in them. The sense of mastery which comes through practice, often communicated to the teacher by a cry of "Hey, watch me do this!" is evidence of such feelings. The short attention span typical of this age group demands a teacher who can provide a rich and stimulating environment. If a child is not successful at the activity he or she pursues it is quickly dropped and some other pastime is sought.

If given plenty of free space in which to move, the pre-school child will run with sheer exuberance. Young children enjoy running, jumping, rolling, and climbing activities. Imitative behavior is characteristic of this age group; these children like to copy adult behaviors, such as washing the car or sweeping the floor, or adult sport actions which they learn through their own observation and watching television.

Occasionally children will exhibit moody behavior and not want to participate. This probably is part of their search for identity and stems from the desire to have some control over their own activity. On the other hand, it simply could be boredom, loss of interest, or fatigue. A daily nap often helps to restore the child's disposition.

NEEDS

Many children today, at all age levels, do not experience all the love, affection, and sense of belonging that is necessary for their total development. Quite often they spend part of the day in a preschool, a nursery school, or a day care center. If the home is not providing security and love, the school may find that it has to compensate somehow for these deficiencies. In addition, children need daily periods of vigorous activity, with the opportunity to run, jump, crawl, climb, roll, and balance. They also need to manipulate things like balls, bean bags, and hoops.

It is a difficult and demanding task for a teacher to be a parent substitute in the midst of all the other activities and pressures of the school day. The teacher somehow must indicate to the child that someone cares and must be able to provide the hug or touch that shows this. Friendly guidance and help, together with the necessary patience to wait for things to happen, should be provided by the teacher. The teacher should carefully observe the child to ensure adequate supervision and the child's safety. Accidents are a leading cause of death and the environment requires carefully monitoring to eliminate safety hazards. Observation also will alert the teacher to the current needs and behavior of individual children.

IMPLICATIONS FOR MOVEMENT EDUCATION

A movement education program should provide at least two periods a day during which children may play in situations that are not totally teacher dominated. Children should be encouraged to explore the ways to move on large apparatus, such as climbing frames and benches, and to manipulate small apparatus such as balls, bean bags, hoops, deck tennis rings, and paddle bats.

The teacher should help children to master simple locomotor skills such as walking, running, chasing, dodging, jumping, hopping, skipping, and sliding. Learning how to land softly in association with running and jumping are important skills in which to develop competence. Activities chosen because they are essentially large muscle movements and presented through a wide variety of tasks and challenges will stimulate growth and strengthen bone and muscle. Other activities involving flexibility and balance will complete the basic skills in which it is essential for preschool children to achieve some competency.

A safely structured yet challenging environment will provide the opportunity to guide children toward learning about their own limitations and abilities. Careful supervision is essential at all times. Sometimes young children are not aware of certain dangers inherent to activities they think they can do. Vigorous movement can be interspersed with quieter activities. Children should not be coerced into activities for which they are not ready; however, the teacher should not be overly protective or stifle the opportunity for a child to try something challenging. The teacher often can pick up on what the child currently is doing and work with that activity instead of having the child switch to another task. It is often a mistake to perform the same activity with the whole group, rather activity should be centered on the individual or on a small group. Children will play side by side but no real cooperation or other involvement usually takes place to any great extent.

The Kindergarten Child (Five Year Olds)

PHYSICAL GROWTH

The child's growth continues fairly slowly but steadily. The legs lengthen quite rapidly, making the kindergartner still somewhat top heavy. Balance is improving, as evidenced by increasing ability in such skills as hopping, skipping, and walking the balance beam. Individual differences are more telling than sex differences, although, on the average, girls are about a year ahead of boys in physical maturity. A child of this age can run for longer periods of time and maintain vigorous activity longer than the preschooler, although the heart and lungs, along with bones and muscles, are still in a period of growth so short periods of vigorous activity should be interspersed with less physically demanding movement.

Hand and eye and foot and eye coordination is improving. There are wide variations in the development of skills involving such factors as coordination and reaction time. A readiness for learning skills is indicated by the interest shown by the child, together with the degree of persistence and success. Almost 90 percent of children appear to be right handed, although there currently seems to be some evidence of an increase in the number of left handed persons (Smart and Smart, 1973).

Gross motor movements are still more easily controlled and better developed than fine motor skills. If one looks at kindergarten children carefully some may appear to have postural defects such as being knock-kneed, having protruding abdomens, or round shoulders. These problems generally will disappear as the child ages. Many school districts have a screening program for children of this age that is usually administered soon after the child's entry in school. The purpose of the program is to identify major defects in gross motor and fine motor skills as well as in other areas.

CHARACTERISTIC BEHAVIOR

Like pre-schoolers, the kindergarten child is full of energy and is noisy and boisterous but still tires easily. He or she may still withdraw from activity at times for a variety of individual reasons. The teacher should accept this withdrawal and not force the child to participate too vigorously. Knowing the child one is teaching allows the teacher to decide when and how to interact. Kindergarten children can participate in activity for much longer than the usual 20 minutes provided in the class schedule; however, there should be variety and balance in activities, including vigorous and quiet play, discussion by the teacher, and dialogue with the children.

It is hard for young children to sit still very long, hence the teacher should plan to keep the class active and challenged as much as possible.

Five year olds may still need a little help with laces and buttons, but may resent interference and will insist on doing things themselves. Teachers need to be patient and let them try. Generally children are becoming more sociable and can understand the reasons for sharing as well as for rules of safety. Children in a movement program become aware of their own limitations and skill level fairly readily, which helps them appreciate the dangers and difficulties involved with certain pieces of equipment. They can do simple partner activities and meaningful circle games. Teachers should realize that it is the activity itself that is of concern to the child and not an objective that will be achieved later. The suggestion here is that the teacher avoid becoming too philosophical by offering lengthy explanations about intangible benefits that may be reaped tomorrow.

Motor skills are definitely much improved by kindergarten. Running, jumping, hopping, and skipping are eagerly attempted, along with climbing, hanging, and swinging, which are often done just for the sheer joy of moving.

Needs

Kindergarten children still need to feel that someone cares as well as to feel comfortable and secure. The first days at school can be traumatic for some children, especially if they have not been in a pre-school or other group situation beforehand. The teacher is still the child's guide, friend, and helper, and listens and provides comfort when things need a little sorting out. Children continue to need guidance in developing good health habits, satisfying relationships with others, and in learning to share, but they also need the chance to assume responsibility and share in the decision making that governs classroom behavior and learning.

Activities are needed that will assist in developing balance, coordination, strength, flexibility, agility, laterality, and directionality. The development of strength is particularly important for skill development. Kleinman (1975) has proposed that "the single aspect of physical activity most related to overall learning is one's capacity to direct and control motor output voluntarily." Activities are needed, Kleinman suggests, that stress conscious control of movement. Such activities as gymnastics, if taught through a creative approach entailing problem solving, fulfill the goal of integrating motor and ideational learning because thought processes and concept development are involved.

IMPLICATIONS FOR MOVEMENT EDUCATION

Some kindergartens have half-day sessions, while others meet for the whole day. In either case, time should be set aside for a movement period. Much can be accomplished in the regular classroom, but it is very advantageous to have available space outside and the use of a gymnasium or other large indoor space. Activity should stress exercise for the large muscle groups, including curling and stretching, jumping and landing, climbing, hanging and swinging, balance activities, and manipulative skills.

Through exploration and discovery, children can discover something about themselves and their own limitations. A rich and stimulating environment is necessary in order to provide variety and challenge. A very formal structure is not necessary because children can function through play which is at times free or has some teacher direction. Children need the opportunity for both types of play.

Young children need a lot of time to master the basic skills and so it must be scheduled to allow such practice. If the teacher is aware of individual needs and differences much can be done to prescribe suitable activities.

Safety training is important and children can begin acquiring responsibility for getting out and putting away equipment. They should learn how to land safely. Rolling should be emphasized as a way to absorb the momentum of a heavy or hard landing.

Kindergarten children can begin to understand simple ideas about exercise and the body. The teacher should utilize practical examples for this with verbal instruction kept simple. The teacher should note when the opportunity to teach movements arises during activity. Simple activities involving partners can be tried, and two or three children can share a piece of large apparatus. Periods of vigorous movement should be interspersed with quieter activity.

Young children need the teacher's frequent approval of what they are doing, and the teacher can respond to this need through praise and positive feedback as the children perform movement tasks. Good attitudes and behavior similarly can be reinforced.

First and Second Grade (Six and Seven Year Olds)

PHYSICAL GROWTH

During the early primary years children continue to grow slowly and steadily. Motor skill development improves, with gross motor skills still better than fine motor skills, although the latter improve with increased coordination of hand and eye. The ability to catch and track a moving object also is getting better. The eye itself is approaching its full size and with this comes the ability to focus on closer objects (near sight). Control of the smaller muscles shows improvement, thus allowing children to undertake more activities involving fine motor skills. Reaction time also has improved, enhancing those skills involving timing of a movement.

First and second graders seem to be perpetually on the move; however, this urge seems to be more satisfactorily dealt with than in younger children.

CHARACTERISTIC BEHAVIOR

As far as motor skills are concerned, all the locomotor skills are developing well. Most children will be able to hop, skip, and gallop. They can bounce and catch, and toss and catch a ball by themselves. The ability to throw a ball to a partner or against a wall is improving, although a considerable amount of practice is needed with ball skills. Differences will be apparent between the child who has older siblings or parents at home who encourage skill development and the child who does not have much opportunity to play with a ball, climb trees, or participate in games.

Six and seven year olds are able to keep time with a beat. They can clap or tap their feet and move rhythmically to a drum or music.

As described above, these children generally are very active, noisy, talkative, and restless. This behavior sometimes is coupled with a desire for attention or to show off, seemingly out of a need for frequent approval of their actions.

Children will persevere and can become completely absorbed and involved with an activity if they are being successful at it.

Differences in interests are becoming apparent; these differences can be based on sex as well as on the individual personalities of children.

Children this age begin to acquire a sense of right and wrong. Children can understand the need for rules and develop a sense of fair play. A novel environment is exciting to these children and they are highly motivated toward acquiring new skills and participating in activities that offer an element of challenge.

NEEDS

Children need an opportunity to pursue vigorous and purposeful activity that helps to satisfy the desire for movement and stimulate the growth of bone and muscle.

The encouragement, praise, and support of teachers and other adults are still necessary. Behavior can be channelled in the right direction by reinforcement of the desired actions and through simple ground rules, which the teacher must help the children to observe. These young children soon can take advantage of a teacher who is too lenient or who allows unacceptable behavior to go uncorrected. However, the teacher does not need to be overly rigid about behavior; in fact, the fewer rules the better.

Friendships are beginning to develop, usually between children of the same sex, although occasionally a boy and girl will develop a relationship. Children of this age enjoy working with a partner, providing that the activity is not too difficult.

The quiet child who also may be timid will need some extra help and support in order to encourage his or her participation. The child's fears must be allayed and a careful watch kept so that the teacher can provide the needed reinforcement.

IMPLICATIONS FOR MOVEMENT EDUCATION

A daily period for movement is desirable, with a variety of activities offered that are designed to help children acquire the basic skills. As skills are learned they can be applied in simple games that involve chasing and dodging, balance, and ball skills.

Activities designed for this age group should utilize all muscle groups, with special attention given to the upper limbs and trunk. Both indoor and outdoor apparatus is necessary to provide the opportunity for children to climb, hang, and balance. Ball skills can be practiced, together with simple activities involving paddle bats and balls. Scoops and balls also can promote hand and eye coordination. Children in the primary grades will begin to enjoy self-testing activities in which they are challenged to beat their own record in simple skills.

Time should be set aside for rhythms, dance, and creative movement. This area should not be considered by chance or relegated to rainy days. With careful planning the teacher can provide a great deal of activity in this area. Much of the work in movement education is creative or inventive because for a good part of the time children will be responding in their own way to the tasks presented by the teacher. Original responses should be encouraged in all skill areas, not only in the rhythms or dance portion of the program.

The child's curiosity can be encouraged through the movement challenge. This curiosity will lead the child to explore and discover his or her movement capabilities to the limits imposed by the teacher or the apparatus. The teacher can begin to develop activities around the emerging interests of the children. Different instructional strategies can be employed to match the children's preferred learning styles.

The teacher can utilize more frequently situations in which children work with a partner or in small groups. A rich variety of activities will still be needed, however, so that the children may be involved with a wide range of motor skills and activities. Instruction can be scheduled so that sometimes children work on their own and sometimes in large or small groups. The ability to make certain choices can be introduced gradually as children are encouraged to become more responsible for their own learning. This must be a gradual process but it should be introduced early so that children grow up with the idea of accepting this responsibility.

Teachers are urged not to become "hurry-up" educators but to allow plenty of time for practice and mastery of basics, especially for the slower learners.

Third and Fourth Grades (Eight and Nine Year Olds)

PHYSICAL GROWTH

During this period, growth proceeds much the same as it did in the previous group. Growth continues slowly and steadily, except for a few children, usually girls, who may experience a pre-adolescent growth spurt. These children who mature early may have certain advantages in learning skills.

This age group is one in which children are fairly stable in terms of health and attendance in school. It is a period during which postural defects again can become apparent. Teachers should refer any children who appear to have such problems to the classroom teacher, school nurse, or parent.

A variety of activities continues to be necessary, but children will spend longer periods of time on the same activity. Their attention span is increasing, as is their potential for more vigorous exercise as the heart and lungs increase in size and capacity. The child's strength is improving, and the center of gravity is a little lower so balance is better. There is a marked improvement in motor skills as well as a desire for successful performance.

CHARACTERISTIC BEHAVIOR

During this stage of development the child is becoming less egocentric and more interested in playing with others. Cooperation and collaboration are beginning to appear in games and other activities. The individual child still wants to score the goal or make the basket but can see reasons for passing the ball and cooperating in other situations. The "New Games" movement suggests that people should be playing cooperative and collaborative games rather than the usual competitive team sports, so the teacher may want to try these kinds of activities with children. Competition is a fact of life both inside and outside the school, yet learning to cooperate is a skill that teachers can develop in children over a period of time. Discussion about winning and losing and doing one's best can be introduced at the opportune moment.

Children are still quite noisy, although perhaps not quite as exuberant as at an earlier age, and they will play in groups more often or with a "best friend" who frequently may be replaced over the course of a few months. Arguments may develop over rules and who plays on a team. A teacher should be sensitive to this particular problem and form groups carefully. The children should share in making decisions about behavior as well as in formulating the rules of games. Being accepted by their peers becomes increasingly important to children of this age. Quite often physical ability is a key factor here, with the child who is poorly skilled frequently experiencing some rejection by classmates.

Children will continue to show preferences for certain activities as opposed to others. If the teacher is working toward enabling most children to achieve competence in a wide variety of skills more children will want to participate in activities if they can enjoy some success in them. This means frequent repetition of activities throughout the school year to enable children to review skills to which they were exposed earlier.

Many children are sensitive to criticism from adults. If such criticism is fair and not offered in a sarcastic way the children will learn to accept it. The teacher should keep any comments very positive, yet include suggestions for improvement. The children will sometimes be critical of adult behavior, yet they need the security that comes from knowing what the ground rules are and being helped to work within them. They can accept more responsibility and in turn are more responsible in their behavior.

NEEDS

From the above descriptions of growth and characteristic behavior it becomes obvious that children need to know that the teacher is there to provide support, acceptance, encouragement, and praise. The teacher must be aware of individual differences in interests, skills, aptitudes, and needs. Children can be grouped in several ways, such as by ability for certain activities, by social groupings for other tasks, and by more general criteria for activities in which everyone's ability counts. The important thing to remember is that the child wants to be assured of a position in the peer group, no matter how it is constituted.

Movement periods should be centered around activity and play. Concentration should still focus on mastery of the basic skills necessary for later participation in games, sports, dance, gymnastics, and other activities. Children are more interested in their bodies and in becoming physically fit. They can understand simple explanations of physiology and exercise. Health can be discussed in relation to exercise and nutrition. Children enjoy playing games with simple rules and small teams. Many games can be developed by the children under the teacher's guidance. The pressures of competition should be kept to a minimum, and self-testing can occasionally be used as a means of motivating children and evaluating their skills.

IMPLICATIONS FOR MOVEMENT EDUCATION

Classes in the elementary school generally are coeducational. Occasionally the girls may work separately from the boys, but this will be the exception rather than the rule. The movement program should continue to provide a daily period of exercise and activity. Locomotor, non-locomotor, and manipulative skills form the core of the program and should be applied to games, gymnastics, and dance. Other activities should center around individual skills such as riding a bicycle, skating, using a skateboard, or playing with a Frisbee. Aquatics may be included in the program if the necessary facilities are available.

Teachers can develop a balanced program to cater to an increasing range of interests and skills. Activities which help children develop strength, flexibility, agility, and coordination can be utilized. Teaching "why" as well as "how" should be an important part of each lesson.

The teacher must carefully monitor group work and games to ensure that all children are participating and that the atmosphere is one of acceptance and cooperation. Slower learners will need extra help and time to achieve competence. Children are interested in practicing for longer periods if they are being successful and are motivated to persist. An approach that enables all children to experience some degree of success should be used. Presenting challenges through verbal or written tasks which allow a variety of responses will facilitate achieving this goal. The same standard does not need to be applied to all children.

Competition can be introduced gradually through situations which do not overly emphasize the result. Often it is parents and teachers who over-emphasize the importance of winning. Children need to understand that not everyone can be a winner, someone will be a loser. The main point is that everyone enjoy the activity and do their best. Sometimes in physical education it is the same children who win every time. Teachers can watch for this and try to arrange activities so that other children may have a chance to do well.

Fifth and Sixth Grades (Ten and Eleven Year Olds)

PHYSICAL GROWTH

Growth generally proceeds as slowly as before; in fact, it levels off before the onset of the adolescent growth spurt. This growth spurt is likely to occur earlier in girls than in boys. Some girls may be taller and heavier than boys, although boys catch up and overtake girls during the junior high school years. Secondary sexual characteristics may develop as early as 9 years old for girls and about 11 years old for boys. The average age for pubescent physical changes is about 11 years for girls and 13 for boys. Of course, there will be wide variations in individual growth patterns. The physiological systems of the body (that is, the heart and lungs) that are important in exercise are nearing maturity. For most children the coordination of eye with hand and foot is quite good by this stage.

Small muscle development is much better at this age and children can become highly skilled in activities which demand fine muscle movement as opposed to gross muscle movement.

Individual differences, in addition to sexual differences, will become more apparent during these years. Some children may be a head and shoulders taller than others and there can be a weight difference of 30 or more pounds if extremes are compared. Some children may appear to be awkward if they are in a period of rapid growth. If a child appears clumsy most of the time the teacher should refer the child to the appropriate professional, following up when necessary.

CHARACTERISTIC BEHAVIOR

The character of individual children develops throughout the elementary years. In the fifth and sixth grades the teacher may begin to notice wider variations in growth, interests, needs, and abilities. Preferences for certain activities over others also will be apparent. The unskilled student may withdraw from certain activities or make excuses for nonparticipation. The teacher should watch for this and try to give the child extra help and time. Students may become self-conscious about the physical changes taking place as they move into adolescence. A diagnosis of the individual child's particular difficulties can be made and appropriate help indicated. This will mean discovering areas in which the child can attain some proficiency and success.

Behavior can be quite changeable at this stage. Children often can make themselves really useful and offer a lot of help to the teacher, while at other times they can be uncooperative, rebellious, and emotionally unstable if under pressure or stress. If things do not go well for them they can be easily discouraged and not want to participate. They will lose interest if they do not experience fairly immediate success; however, if they are experiencing success and are evidently enjoying themselves it may be hard to get them to stop.

Peer group and "best friend" connections usually are quite strong at this stage and may dominate other external influences on behavior. In forming groups the teacher can take this factor into account.

Quite often children in the intermediate grades will spend much time arguing over the rules of an activity, sometimes arguing more than playing. The teacher can do several things to alleviate such situations. First, the teacher must be firm about decisions involving rules and behavior and ensure the rules are fairly and consistently observed. In addition, the teacher should be sure the students understand the reasons behind the rules and possibly offer them the opportunity to share in developing them.

NEEDS

The teacher's firm leadership is essential with children in this age group, and the ground rules regarding acceptable behavior must be clearly understood by the children. The teacher also must be fair and friendly and maintain a sense of humor. These are the best years for children to learn motor skills since they have the ability necessary for becoming well skilled in a wide variety of activities. Individual preferences can be taken into account as programs are designed. Children want to succeed and excel, yet they also are interested in their personal appearance and physical fitness.

The teacher can help prepare children for both the physical and emotional changes that lie ahead as they enter adolescence. It is desirable to present health education units in the intermediate grades; however, these should not utilize time allocated to movement. Health topics might include growth and development, nutrition, disease, community and personal health, and guidelines for the formation of good health habits.

The children can be responsible for helping with equipment and officiating simple games. Older children also can assist children in the lower grades in acquiring skills.

If the teacher persists and reinforces appropriate behavior the children can become self-disciplined and assume more responsibility for their own learning. Children in this age group still need approval from an adult and to feel that someone is interested in what they are doing. The child who lacks feelings of love and security may seek to gain attention by disruptive behavior, forcing the teacher to find ways of handling this kind of attention seeking.

IMPLICATIONS FOR MOVEMENT EDUCATION

Much longer periods can now be spent on individual activities. A balance must be reached between activities that are developmental in nature and those that develop skill. More time can be spent on games which children can develop themselves and play in small groups. Individual differences must be recognized and the program arranged accordingly.

Increasing demands can be placed on the heart and circulation. This can be accomplished through running and chasing games, such as soccer and basketball, through activities on climbing equipment, and through gymnastics. Rhythmic activities can be specifically designed for developing aerobic fitness.

Children occasionally can be introduced to self-testing activities through individual tasks and challenges. In competitive activities the stress should be on developing good attitudes and feelings toward others, especially toward those who are less skilled. Respect for property, rules, and feelings can be emphasized throughout the program. Courtesy and fair play should be discussed. Intramurals might be introduced to provide an outlet for children who feel the need to compete. Many children will also participate in agency-sponsored sports occurring outside the school. The teacher should be aware of the extent to which children are participating in these activities, the type of activity, and the situations in which they are conducted.

The reasons for exercise and activity and the mechanics of movement can be discussed. Quite often a teachable movement will occur; providing the teacher with the opportunity to introduce related knowledge or information at just the right moment in an activity. The movement teacher can also develop health education units which may be taught by another instructor.

Finally, the teacher involved with movement education will need to discuss program continuity with the appropriate junior high school personnel. If the local school district has formulated a curriculum guide for grades kindergarten through 12, the teachers can work together on providing program continuity. If nothing is available to teachers it becomes important for elementary and junior high school teachers to agree on common goals and objectives.

Summary

This chapter has examined the characteristics of children at five different levels: pre-school, kindergarten, first and second grade, third and fourth grade, and fifth and sixth grade. These characteristics are divided into three areas: physical growth, characteristic behaviors, and needs. Some general implications for a movement program are drawn based on the descriptions of children's characteristics at the different levels. The wide variations in the characteristics of individual children are stressed, including differences in ability and interest. As children grow and develop they should progress through a curriculum that takes into account individual variables. No other subject repeats itself year after year in the way that physical education often does. A teacher who understands and knows children will recognize that different levels of knowledge, skill, and attitude development are appropriate to certain levels of child development.

Seminar Questions and Activities

1. Learn all you can about the readiness of children to learn motor skills. What factors should the teacher consider in deciding to teach certain activities to young children?
2. Compare the emphasis and/or information provided in two different elementary school physical education texts concerning the growth and development of children. Which one do you prefer and why?
3. Fundamental motor patterns seem to be important for the development of more complex movements. What does the physical education teacher need to know about motor patterns?
4. Discuss the developmental implications of teaching team sports to children in the elementary school.
5. How can physical education assist in the intellectual development of the young child?
6. Try to observe the behavior of children in each of the age groups described in the chapter. Develop a case study to share with the class.

Bibliography

Growth and Development

Gesell, Arnold, and Ilg, Frances L. *The Child from Five to Ten.* New York: Harper and Brothers, 1946.

Breckenridge, Marian E., and Vincent, E. Lee. *Child Development.* Philadelphia: W. B. Saunders, 1965.

Smart, Mollie S., and Smart, Russell C. *Children: Development and Relationships.* 3rd ed. New York: The Macmillan Co., 1977.

______. *Pre School Children.* New York, Macmillan, 1973.

Pikunas, Justin. *Human Development: A Science of Growth.* New York: McGraw Hill Book Co., 1969.

Kleinman, Matthew. "A Central Role for Physical Education in Early Childhood." *In New York University Education Quarterly.* Spring 1975.

Teachers should be experts in child growth and may develop some knowledge in this area from readings. The above sources are recommended to provide such background.

Study Guide

For more specialized information on motor development the following sources are recommended reading:

Espenschade, Anna S., and Eckert, Helen M. *Motor Development.* Columbus, Ohio: Charles E. Merrill, Inc., 1980.

Engstrom, Georgianna., ed. *The Significance of the Young Child's Motor Development.* Washington, D.C.: National Association for the Education of Young Children, 1971.

Fundamental Movement and Motor Patterns

Wickstrom. *Fundamental Motor Patterns,* Philadelphia: Lea & Febiger, 1977.

Wickstrom looks at the skills of running, jumping, throwing, catching, kicking, and striking, from pre-school levels to the mature adult patterns.

McClenaghan, B. A., and Gallahue, D. L. *Fundamental Movement: A Developmental and Remedial Approach.* Philadelphia, PA. W. B. Saunders, 1978.

These authors also examine fundamental patterns, provide ideas on program design and development, and offer suggestions for movement experiences. Remedial work is described for children who may have problems.

Kephart, N. C. *The Slow Learner in the Classroom.* Columbus, Ohio: Charles E. Merrill, 1971.

Kephart discusses the motor bases of achievement and perceptual motor training.

Godfrey, B. B. and Kephart, N. C. *Movement Patterns and Motor Education.* New York: Appleton-Century-Crofts, 1969.

The authors discuss motor patterns and deviations in performance and provide teaching suggestions.

Sinclair, C. *Movement of the Young Child.* Columbus, Ohio: Charles E. Merrill, 1973.

Sinclair describes the development of motor patterns and examines the differences in the movements of children. Case studies are provided, along with program ideas.

Diem, Liselott. *Children Learning Physical Skills.* AAHPER, 1978.
This resource is actually two beautifully illustrated books. The first deals with the period from birth to age three and the second with the period from age four to six. Translated from the original German, they are available from AAHPERD.

Developmental Psychology Today CRM Books, Del Mar, Calif., 1971.
This is an exceptionally well-illustrated and informative book.

Rarick, Lawrence. *Physical Activity: Human Growth and Development.* Academic Press, 1971.
Rarick's is a broad ranging book that deals specifically with physical activity.

4 discovery—an approach to learning

If the question, "How do children best learn motor skills and acquire attitudes and knowledge about movement, sports and exercise?" were asked, how would the question be answered? If the precise answer were known there would hardly be a need for much discussion in this chapter; however, because no such answer exists, some discussion is necessary.

In discussing learning, several applicable generalizations can be made and the teacher should be aware of these. Children must be intent on learning, be motivated and interested, and understand what they are supposed to learn. Knowing how well they are learning or performing also helps children. A knowledge of results usually is provided by the teacher or gained by the child through personal observation and feelings. Some degree of success should accompany attempts to learn in order for the learner to maintain interest and motivation.

Children learn at different rates, implying that some children learn faster or slower than others. Slower learners need more time to learn than do faster learners.

In order to develop quality in movement and to refine skills practice is necessary. During the early stages of learning practice should probably be performed in fairly short periods and take place over several lessons. This appears to be more beneficial than concentrated blocks of practice. There should be opportunities for experimentation and exploration in problem-solving situations. A wide variety of different experiences should be planned for young children.

Children approach learning in many different ways. Some may learn best by being told and shown exactly what to do, while others may learn best by discovering things for themselves. Of course, different things may be learned in different ways. In the area of motor skills, children are usually eager for activity and movement. They appear to have an insatiable urge to run, jump, chase, slide, roll, climb, hang, and swing. Children seek the challenges, competition, cooperation, and discoveries that await them in the area of physical activity. The teacher who recognizes this can constructively channel some of the child's energies by arranging challenging learning environments.

The joy, satisfaction, and sense of competence which most children gain from learning to move supplies the motivation and desire to participate which is necessary for learning to take place.

Just as children may learn in a variety of ways, so too must teachers be able to teach or facilitate learning in different ways. One of the problems in teaching is that there is usually more than one person to be taught at the same time. Individual students are unique beings, not only in the way they learn, pay attention, or are motivated, but also in their body build, interests, needs, and aptitudes. Thus, when a teacher works with a class or group of children the teaching task is much more challenging and difficult than that required in a one-to-one relationship.

The teacher is also a unique individual with different beliefs, feelings, and values relating to which teaching style or strategy will be used and what subject matter taught. Different ideas will be held by the teacher as to what will motivate or interest students. The teacher may question whether students can make responsible decisions concerning their learning and become self-disciplined and self-motivated. Resolving these questions often is ignored by many teachers who choose to teach all children on a sort of middle ability level, that is, the level at which most children can do something. The more capable children and the faster learners often are not sufficiently challenged by this approach and become bored, while the less capable never seem to catch up and so get left behind in the learning of skills. In addition, there are other discouraging features associated with learning, such as the lack of success on the part of the learners, failure by teachers to maximize equipment and facility use, large classes, and insufficient time for learning.

The teacher's recognition of each child as a unique individual does not imply that students cannot function as a whole class, within smaller groups, or even with a partner. Individualized instruction, in which material to be learned is modified to suit a particular student and allows each to proceed at his or her own rate, does not necessarily mean that a one-to-one relationship must exist. What it does mean, of course, is that the teacher has to be a skilled observer of children who is aware of individual differences in needs, abilities, and attitude. Monitoring children's responses and activities becomes an activity of prime importance for the teacher.

The teaching methods proposed in this chapter to facilitate and encourage children's learning are formulated on the premise that for young children, "finding out" should take precedence over "being told." The young child is very curious, especially during the pre-school, kindergarten, and primary years. No matter which grade level is being taught, if the teacher demonstrates and directs every move the children make the opportunity for exploring the possibilities of a movement task is missing. The opportunity to make choices and decisions also is missing, and creativity and originality are not encouraged if everyone must conform to the teacher's model. The child may be getting some activity but that should not be the sole objective of the exercise. What teachers then are looking for are ways to facilitate learning that will encourage or allow the development of the program's objectives.

DISCOVERY LEARNING

In discovery learning the teacher does not want the children to invent anew or develop from scratch every skill they learn. The teacher should start the process by presenting a task or problem for which children are invited to explore possible solutions. If the children are accustomed to a fairly traditional program and direct teaching, new ideas and methods must be introduced gradually, at first perhaps as part of a lesson. The younger the children involved the easier the transition will be.

The initial exploration of a task leads ultimately to the child's discovery of some aspect or solution pertaining to that task. The teacher can guide these discoveries toward a predetermined goal or accept all of the responses that the children make. The former process is known as *guided discovery;* the latter is a *problem-solving* approach. Each process will be examined in detail and some examples given to illustrate task description and development.

Before the teacher embarks upon the use of discovery methods with children, some knowledge is needed regarding the classroom climate which is conducive for such an approach. In responding to the task set by the teacher, children must feel free to

Fig. 4-1 *Reflecting an appreciative attitude.*

make a response in any way they deem appropriate. That is, the classroom climate must be such that the children feel the teacher will support their efforts. This support is provided through feedback from the teacher to the child and should be meaningful, supportive, and positive. The children need to feel that they are being carefully observed and that the teacher is, in the main, appreciative of what they are doing.

GUIDED DISCOVERY

In this process the teacher initially has an objective in mind, such as helping a student to develop a specific motor skill, acquire an attitude, or learn a fact. The teacher presents tasks or problems and carefully monitors the responses of the children. Inappropriate responses can be discarded and the children redirected toward the goal by means of other cues or tasks, the cues being different for different children. These cues represent a form of individual feedback and positive reinforcement.

One way for the teacher to develop the guided discovery process is to decide which skill is desired and then work backward through a series of prerequisite skills until a simple initial task can be presented to the class. This provides the teacher with a series of tasks to use in guiding children toward the final objective.

Each task or challenge must be presented in such a way that it encourages different responses from the child. Depending on the nature of the task, some responses will be alike and others will be different, but all should be in answer to the task. On the basis of what is observed, the teacher then can decide to work with individual children, a small group of students, or the entire class. Children can be invited to share their responses with the rest of the class. When presenting tasks for the first time, it may be advantageous to present the same task to the entire group for a period of time to allow the teacher to gain confidence in presenting tasks and cues that vary to meet the needs of individual children. This is where both the art and science of teaching are employed, the art in being able to think on one's feet and decide what the next best thing is for each pupil to do, and the science in applying the knowledge and understanding of subject matter, pedagogy, and learning theory.

Since children are free to respond to the task according to their own capabilities and limitations, no one is penalized for not being able to respond in a certain way. Accepting all the different yet appropriate responses and making decisions about what to do next at first is a difficult task for the teacher.

As an example of guided discovery, suppose the teacher wanted children to develop skill in the general area of supporting body weight on the hands. As a response children could perform cartwheels, handstands, round-offs, or other similar activities. The children will need to utilize many different elements such as the strength which allows the hands and arms to support body weight, inverted balance, the transfer of weight from feet to hands, and so on. The teacher has a great deal of latitude in this area to develop activities in which children support their body weight on their hands. Outlined below are suggested activities that children could perform for such development.

1. Find some different ways to move on four *body supports*.
2. Select hand and foot movement and placement from among various alternatives.
3. With the feet fixed, move the hands around to support the rest of the body weight.
4. Try the reverse. With the hands fixed, move the feet around or remove them from the floor, bringing them down somewhere else. Bring the feet down *softly*.
5. Try moving the weight from feet to hands and back to feet again.
6. With the weight supported on the hands, move the feet in the

air over a marked space. Try the same movement holding onto a bench and moving the feet over the bench.

7. Repeat the movements of activity 6, first with the body curled, and then with the body stretched.

The above ideas then need to be put into a question format and combined with the teacher's understanding of the mechanics of balance and Laban's movement factors. The tasks may be performed over a series of lessons and in combination with other activities. The ideas suggested above are now presented as tasks below:

Task 1. Students sitting down in their own space. Teacher uses conversational manner.

1. "Show me some ways that you can move by taking your weight on hands and feet. Remember as you move to keep away from others." (Teacher observes carefully and starts picking up ideas from the students.)
   "What *direction* is Susan moving in?"
   "What part of her body is providing the moving force?"
   (Similar questions can be used with other children.)

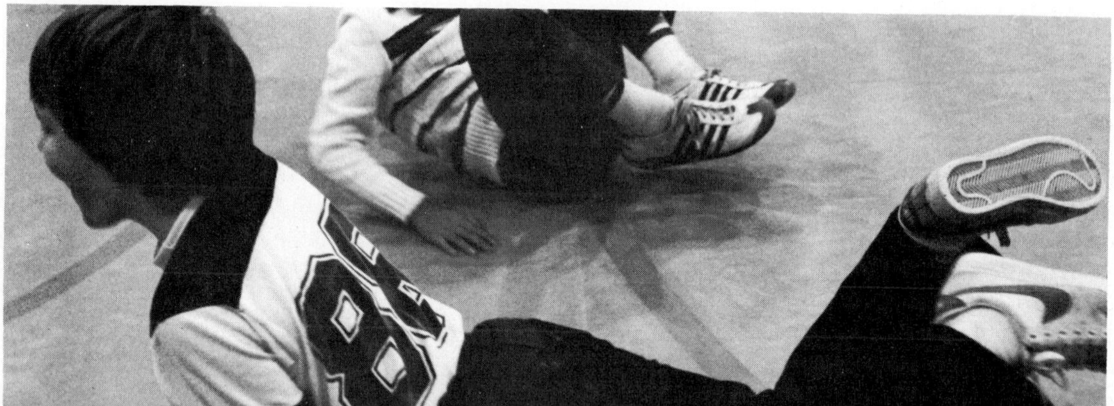

Fig. 4-2 *Moving on four supports.*

2. *Sub-Tasks:* In order to start the children thinking about how they are moving the teacher can feed in ideas such as "How *close to the floor* can you move?"
   "Have you tried moving in *different directions*"?
   "Don is moving quite *fast.* How *fast can you move on hands and feet?*"
   (Children may need to be reminded to keep away from others and learn to use the available space to the best advantage. Pick out different movement ideas or responses and share with the rest of the class.)

At this stage it is important that the teacher be able to provide some feedback, not only to individual children but to a small group or the entire class. By feeding in the movement factors of direction, level, and speed the teacher is expecting that over a period of time children will begin to understand what the factors are and be able to use them on their own, without the continual prompting or suggestion of the teacher.

The feedback does not have to be complicated. Sometimes a nod or a smile lets the children know that the teacher is appreciative of their performance. Instead of ordering children to do this or do that, the teacher often can ask other questions to make children think about exactly what they are doing or trying to do, such as "Are you really as close to the floor as you can get?" or "See if you can combine two or three different ways of moving into a sequence."

Task 2. Students listen to the following tasks as they are working on their own responses.

1. "Now I would like to see those children who can keep their hands fixed on the floor and find all the places that they can move their feet to."
   "Where else can you get your feet? Remember space is all around you, above you, and behind you."
2. *Sub-Tasks.* Be sure that children have tried moving their feet into different places in relation to their hands. "Have you tried moving both feet together?" Now try with your feet moving separately."
   "See if you can move your feet quickly sometimes."
   "See if you can find a way to bring your feet down softly."

Each time the teacher asks a question that suggests finding a way to do an activity, appropriate answers (movements) should be discussed. The answers will depend on exactly where the teacher is guiding the discovery. Children should be asked to repeat movements or sequences of movement that are compatible with the general direction of the task. With a task that involves continuous use of certain muscle groups or body supports, children may get tired. Different tasks can be used as a change. This series of tasks could be picked up again later in the same lesson or in a later lesson.

Task 3.

1. "See if you can *find a way to move* so that you go from feet to hands and back to feet again."
2. *Sub-Tasks.*
   "Move your hands as supports at *different distances* from your feet, sometimes *close* to your feet and sometimes *farther away.*"
   "Try doing this at *different speeds.*"
   "Can you move *sideways* or in a *twisting* pattern?"

Task 4.

1. "From a crouch position, see if you can take the weight on both hands and move your feet to another position."
2. *Sub-Tasks*
   "Can you bring your feet down together? Now try bringing them down one at a time—be sure you try this *softly.* How *slowly* can you do this? Can you keep your feet up in the air a long time?"
   "Let's see who can jump their feet over the space chalked on the floor."
   "Perhaps you could hold onto the bench and jump your feet over the bench."
   "Try and get your 'tail' up as high as possible."
   "What other *shape* could you make when your feet are off the ground?"
   "Who can get their toes up really *high?*"

Task 5.

1. "Find a way to move so that your hands take your weight one at a time and your feet come down one at a time. The pattern will be hand—hand—foot—foot."
2. *Sub-Tasks.*
   "Try doing this with your body stretched and feet as high as possible."
   "What helps you to keep balanced when you are upside down?" (Position of the head, and where child is looking.)
   "Is it possible to put all your supporting parts down in a straight line?"
   At this point there will be many different ideas coming from the class.

The above outline of tasks and sub-tasks has been presented in some detail so that a teacher can get a feeling for the guided discovery process. As children develop and refine their responses the teacher can have different children demonstrate their solutions to the tasks. Each lesson will develop differently and the teacher should be flexible enough to pick up certain responses of children and discard others.

Gradually children will become accustomed to applying Laban's factors and will gain an understanding about the mechanics of movement as the teacher introduces different concepts of balance, force, momentum, and so on. The development of the tasks and sub-tasks can be fairly systematic and will be discussed later in this chapter.

THE DISCOVERY PROCESS

The complete process entails these elements: *explore, discover, analyze, select, repeat, refine,* and *consolidate/implement.* Getting children to explore movement possibilities is not the difficult part of the process, the difficulty may arise with the third step, analyzing the movement responses. Many teachers have tried to implement movement education but have never been able to get beyond the discovery stage, since the process seemed to stop at that point. Their students often performed numerous activities, but without much evidence of quality. In using guided discovery the teacher and student interact to decide which responses will be developed further, or whether the responses need to be repeated and refined.

Sub-tasks can be thought of as limitations imposed upon the original task (Bilbrough and Jones, 1968). They help to refine the task response and can apply to the use of body parts or equipment.

Analysis, therefore, is a critical part of the teaching and learning process as developed in this text. But how does the teacher analyze movement responses and develop them further? The movement responses or aspects of the responses that are selected for development or repetition can be chosen based on several criteria. At a very simple level of selection, children may be encouraged to develop or repeat a movement mainly because it feels good or they enjoy doing it. The joy of discovery itself can be the motivating force for additional exploration and discoveries, or the teacher may be looking for the most efficient way of performing a certain skill. There may well be a "best" or most efficient way of responding that the teacher seeks to encourage through guided discovery. Another criterion may be that the children must develop a repertoire of two or three different ways of responding to the task.

At a greater level of sophistication, analysis is related to a knowledge of the physical laws of motion, the mechanics of movement, and Laban's movement factors. The teacher must critically observe all the different movement responses and then draw the attention of the children to the various aspects of the movement. In addition, tasks can be developed in the cognitive and affective domains. The "what," "where" and "how" of the movement needs to be examined. This can be accomplished as follows:

"What" is the body actually doing?

Which part or combination of parts is moving?
On what supports is the body moving?
Is the body making a particular shape or series of shapes?
How is the body weight being transferred?
Are any body parts leading the movement?
Are any body parts initiating the movement?
Is an object being manipulated?
Is a specific recognizable skill (running, jumping, throwing, balancing, etc.) being performed?

"Where" is the body moving?

In what direction?
In what kind of a pathway?
At what level?

"How" is the body moving?

How much force or effort is being used?
Is the movement heavy or light?
Is the movement fast or slow, or does the speed change?
Which parts of the body are providing the force?
Is the movement continuous (flowing)?
Is the movement rhythmic?

"Effort," a term used by Laban, can be described in terms of force and speed and whether the movement is direct or indirect. Different combinations of these factors produce different kinds of effort. Relationships also can be examined in terms of how the body is moving relative to other people or objects. Practical applications of the preceding process are developed in Chapters 6 through 9. The reader who is interested in reading more about Laban's use of effort is referred to the references in the study guide. For another description of the guided discovery process see Mosston (1966).

PROBLEM SOLVING

This term is used in movement education to describe situations in which students are given tasks or problems without the teacher defining a particular skill to be achieved as an end product. The tasks usually will be presented in a definite program area, such as locomotor, non-locomotor, and manipulative skills, and their application to games, dance, or gymnastics. Both teacher and child can cooperatively develop movement ideas and skills, or children can be encouraged to develop them on their own. As suggested earlier, the teacher can help children clarify their responses by looking at the what, where, and how of the particular movement being performed. For example, the teacher might ask the children to find a way to move while sitting on the floor, show some different ways to balance on any three parts of the body, or develop three different kinds of bridge shapes with a partner. The teacher may make such comments as: "Susan is making an interesting shape." "Which parts of your body are providing the push, John?" "Can you make your landing a little softer?" "Did you mean to do that so quickly?"

Children can be invited to share their ideas with the rest of the group. This will be important later on when the teacher must make decisions about what to practice or repeat. If the children get accustomed to the notion of sharing ideas they will have a number of tasks to try rather than one model to follow. The teacher must also be prepared to accept the large variety of different responses produced. This approach will encourage solutions that vary from textbook solutions or one's own preconceived expectations.

In the process of discovery learning, whether the learning is being guided toward a particular goal or is more open, the child is reinforced by the process itself. The discovery that a successful response has been made is self-reinforcing and will encourage further exploration and further discoveries, and will elicit more creativity and originality. Discovery strategies, according to Kagan (in Shulman and Keislar, 1966), foster arousal and promote maximum attention. These strategies also require more involvement and thus a greater likelihood of learning than those which may take place under the more traditional teacher demonstration and practice model.

As children become accustomed to the movement education approach to learning skills they often can proceed without any prompting from the teacher. A person who is educated in movement is able to choose the movements appropriate to any situation, that is, the person becomes aware of his or her own effort. This degree of assimilation and integration of Laban's movement factors, together with an understanding of biomechanical principles and a clear idea of what the task is, does not happen overnight. Laban indicated that this type of body awareness could be achieved only after a protracted course of study and an in-depth knowledge of effort (Thornton, 1971).

Mauldon and Layson (1965) indicate that "this is not a matter of applying Weight, Space, Time and Flow to a particular activity but the reverse, that is, appreciating how the activity can be considered in the light of the fundamental principles." It appears, therefore, that what legitimately might be called movement training, or training in the use of the effort factors, must of necessity precede the possible development of movement education.

Problem solving implies using the knowledge or skill one already possesses to solve new problems or gain fresh insight into ways of learning different skills. Naturally, students will need to have developed some of the basic tools before this can happen. It has been suggested by Severs (1969) that teachers use the movement factors proposed by Rudolf Laban as "key words." Severs pointed out that in elementary school physical education programs in England, "The majority (of teachers) have only a vague idea of how to develop their material from the basic stages to more advanced levels." In addition, continues Severs, "they lack a conception of what sort of answers to expect and how to utilize them further in the general framework."

One of the stumbling blocks to the development of movement education both in England and the United States has been the inability on the part of teachers to develop the work beyond a rudimentary stage. Setting simple movement tasks produces a *quantity* of movement, but attaining *quality* has been a missing component of the teaching/learning process. As Severs (1969) states, "The work by its very nature is difficult to develop, requiring a high degree of experience and persistent application before the necessary powers of analysis and knowledge of developmental stages can be required." Many teachers did employ the concept of key words in the form of questions based on the "find another way" method. The key words used included almost all of the Laban movement factors. Children were asked to move slowly, quickly, at different levels, sideways and backwards, heavily and lightly, and so on. After all the terms had been exhausted the process came to a stop. The program became a short unit of movement exploration.

Development was suggested by Severs through the use of the *key word* system, followed by *sequence* development and *activity* lists. The key words contributed to variety and quality of movement and were fed in as cues while children were developing their movement responses to tasks. Sequence development involved joining, linking, or adding different kinds of movements. This was achieved by providing additional key words through such statements as "*join together* . . ." or "*add to your movement*. . . ." The concepts were applied to movements on the floor or on apparatus. The children might work alone, with a partner, or as part of a large group. Gradually, through repeated use, children become able to apply the movement factors in appropriate ways as the situation demands and the teacher does not always need to direct the work or use the keywords so often.

In conclusion, the preceding discussion and examples of discovery learning, together with an appreciation of the use of Laban's principles, must be related with other aspects of children's learning mentioned at the beginning of this chapter. Teaching the reason why certain movements or activities are performed as they are can be integrated into the process at appropriate times as tasks are developed. Cognitive aspects are involved as children learn to make choices and decisions and think about what they are doing.

Basic skills can be systematically developed through directed discovery by using key words and sequences. More creative and open-ended concepts can be developed through problem solving.

In movement education learning progresses systematically, utilizing and building on the skills which individual children already possess. The learning climate is such that children feel free to explore and experiment. The creation of a stimulating and challenging environment also encourages exploration and children discover that learning can be an exciting and satisfying experience.

It may be necessary occasionally for the teacher to take a direct approach to teaching. Instructing children in exactly what to do and how to do it may have its place; for example, a difficult class may need firm management or the teacher may feel that everyone should do a particular movement. The flexible teacher will be able to decide when direct teaching is necessary.

Chapters 6 through 9 provide the teacher with many examples of discovery learning and how to utilize this method with the children for mutual satisfaction.

Summary

In discussing the learning of children this chapter has concentrated on discovery learning which builds on the child's natural curiosity and is based on the premise that children can be encouraged to "find out" rather than always being told what to do and how to do it. Naturally, children learn in a variety of different ways—the teacher's job is to find ways of matching teaching strategies with children's different learning styles.

Children are unique individuals with different interests, abilities, and needs. Instruction should be individualized as much as possible so that children can learn at their own rate and to the level of their own ability.

Guided discovery and problem-solving approaches to learning were stressed in the chapter. Using guided discovery techniques the teacher may shape or guide learning based on the careful observation of the responses of children to the tasks set by the teacher. There is usually a predetermined goal in mind in guided discovery. Problem solving as an approach is more open-ended in terms of developing the movement responses. Children are free to make choices and develop their own responses. Examples are given in the chapter of both processes.

The learning sequence for both guided discovery and problem solving is explore, discover, analyze, select, repeat, refine. The key to developing quality and making progress is the teacher's ability to decide which of the child's responses to tasks should be repeated. Through observation of *what*, *where*, and *how* the body can move additional opportunities for developing movement can be provided. The process entails that the child goes through a form of training in the use and understanding of effort qualities. At first this work is developed through the use of keywords which are based on Laban's movement factors.

Seminar Questions and Activities

1. Describe some of the ways in which children learn motor skills. Compare and contrast "discovery" learning with the other methods you describe.
2. "Learning to move and moving to learn" is a phrase used by many people as a rather simplistic description of a movement program. What are the full implications of this idea for child development?
3. In what ways can a teacher analyze children's responses to movement tasks? Give examples of your suggestions.
4. How might a teacher encourage children to become self-directed learners?
5. What are the main criticisms regarding "discovery" learning when it is used as the sole approach to teaching motor skills?

Bibliography

Bilbrough, A., and Jones, P. *Physical Education in the Primary School.* London: University of London Press, Ltd., 1968.

Kagan, Jerome. "Learning, Attention and the Issue of Discovery." In *Learning by Discovery: A Critical Appraisal.* Edited by Lee S. Shulman and Evan R. Keislar. Chicago: Rand McNally and Co., 1966.

Mauldon, E., and Layson, J. *Teaching Gymnastics.* London: Macdonald and Evans, 1965.

Severs, J. "A Planned Approach to Educational Gymnastics." In *The Leaflet.* London: The Physical Education Association of Great Britain and Northern Ireland, July, 1969.

Thornton, S. *A Movement Perspective of Rudolf Laban.* London: Macdonald and Evans, 1971.

Study Guide

Gilliom. *Basic Movement Education for Children: Rationale and Teaching Units.* 1970.

This book provides a good introduction and discussion of the learning theories underlying movement education. Chapter 3 considers the commonalities in different learning theories and examines discovery learning and problem solving.

Bruner. "The Act of Discovery," (1961).

Bruner discusses how discovery learning can aid intellectual functioning, assist in developing intrinsic rather than extrinsic motivation, help people learn how to discover, and aid in the retrieval of stored information as well. The article by Bruner, and many others relevant to this chapter, are to be found in the following text.

Sweeney, Robert T. *Selected Readings in Movement Education.* Reading, Mass.: Addison-Wesley, 1970.

Kleinman, Matthew. "A Central Role for Physical Education in Early Childhood." *In New York University Education Quarterly,* Spring, 1975.

It is suggested in this article that the capacity to direct and control motor output voluntarily can be gained through movement education in which motor and ideational learning can be integrated.

Mosston. *Teaching Physical Education: From Command to Discovery.* Columbus, Ohio: Charles E. Merrill, 1966.

Probably more than anyone, Mosston has mapped out the guided discovery and problem-solving processes and proposed a spectrum of teaching styles, as the title of the book indicates.

Hellison, D., ed. *Personalized Learning in Physical Education.* AAHPER, 1976.

Personalized learning strategies and concepts are discussed by numerous authors.

Roberton, Mary Ann and Halverson, Lolas E. "The Developing Child—His Changing Movement." In *Physical Education for Children: A Focus on the Teaching Process.* Logsdon, Bette J., *et al.* Philadelphia: Lea and Febiger, 1977.

AAHPER. *Motor Activity for Early Childhood.* Washington, D.C., 1971.

Riley, Marie, ed. *Echoes of Influence.* Washington, D.C.: AAHPER, 1977. (See especially pp. 48–61.)

Flinchum, Betty. *Motor Development in Early Childhood.* St. Louis: C. V. Mosby, 1975. (Discusses learning modes.)

Department of Education and Science. *Movement: Physical Education in the Primary Years.* London: Her Majesty's Stationery Office, 1972. (Children's learning of motor skills.)

Corbin, C. B. *A Textbook of Motor Devevelopment.* Dubuque, Iowa: Wm. C. Brown, 1973. (Chapters 23 and 24 by Aileene S Lockhart.)

These references contribute to the theories of learning movement. Summaries of conditions which improve motor learning and an examination of the principles of motor learning are included in this book.

Kerr, Robert. "What Does Movement Education Mean?" In *Motor Skills: Theory into Practice.* Vol. 3. No. 1. Fall 1978.

This is a stimulating article on the entire question of the purpose of movement education.

5 planning for effective teaching

Classroom Climate

The beginning teacher may at first be quite involved and concerned with managing the behavior of children, sometimes to the detriment of what is being taught. If the teacher can get the children actively involved and absorbed in a task as soon as possible the need for intensive behavior management will be minimized. It is when children are bored and disinterested in what they are doing that inappropriate behavior may occur. Managing learning should be the main concern of the teacher rather than managing behavior. It is important to realize that the greater the involvement on the part of the child, the less need there should be for a great deal of time being spent on class control and behavior management. Of course, experience is a great teacher and the suggestions discussed below are intended to supplement the teacher's personal experience by providing additional points to observe.

If a learning atmosphere is to be created in the gymnasium, or in any other space available for movement, the space should be regarded as a classroom or learning laboratory. Children must learn to work quietly, to listen, and to move and listen at the same time. This does not mean that children cannot or should not talk to each other, but rather that screaming and shouting are discouraged. This is especially important if the teacher is speaking in a conversational tone.

As the teacher communicates both verbally and nonverbally with the students, the kind of classroom climate that develops will largely depend upon the kind of interactions that take place between teacher and student and between student and student. The teacher needs to be firm, yet friendly, with the students enjoying some degree of freedom in their participation and in their responses to tasks. However, the children must be able to assume associated responsibilities to create the desired open atmosphere. These responsibilities include working quietly, not interfering with others who are actively and purposefully involved, and demonstrating respect for others. Children must also learn to respect apparatus and equipment.

The fact needs to be stressed that teachers too are people with feelings. The ability of the teacher to share feelings with the class and with the individual child, as well as the children's ability to share feelings with the teacher, needs to be developed. A sense of warmth and caring, if developed between teacher and child, can help to humanize relationships. Such an atmosphere can contribute to accommodating the needs of children, such as the need for acceptance, recognition, security, and a sense of belonging. Learning children's names is an important step toward enabling the teacher to make more personal contacts with children.

Positive reinforcement and praise, setting tasks, and presenting questions in a nonthreatening manner will encourage children to respond in their own way. Teachers generally have been dominant in verbal interaction occurring between themselves and the children. They often have talked too much out of a concern to give directions, to admonish children displaying deviant behavior, and to criticize and manage such behaviors. Children usually have had very little chance to develop any kind of interaction with the teacher. Part of this problem resulted from the fact that the time allocated for physical education often was limited and the teacher felt the need to move the lesson along; however, the primary cause was that the teacher did little to encourage any interaction whatsoever.

If the teacher becomes involved with discovery learning a great deal of interaction will be necessary between the teacher and children. The teacher becomes the center of operations and guides, suggests, and directs children to facilitate their learning. Verbal communication is the means whereby the teacher presents tasks, asks questions, adds cues, and provides feedback to children. While the approach focuses on the individual learner and may be said to be child centered, the teacher provides the key to developing the work.

Grouping Children in Movement Lessons

Because of individual differences in children's learning patterns, needs, interests, and abilities, the teacher has to consider different ways for children to work on their own, such as with a partner or as part of a small group. Teachers often divided a class into ability groups based on skill or rates of learning. For activities such as gymnastics this idea usually worked quite well. In games and sports, however, teachers often distributed the more highly skilled performers among the other groups to "even out" the teams. For other activities where skill level did not count so much groups were constituted arbitrarily. Groups were not often formed on the basis of children's learning preferences.

Teaching the class as a whole certainly made things more convenient for the teacher. If the learning environment was well structured and there was enough equipment to eliminate the need for children to wait for turns, much could be accomplished. However, since children learn at different rates and have different skill levels, the faster learners tended to become bored and lose interest while the slower ones fell behind. In trying to accommodate different rates of learning the teacher can utilize the methods of guided discovery and problem solving, which enable children to respond at their own level and allow a teacher to take into account individual learning rates in children. Two serious problems exist in using these approaches, however, and they occur in the lack of continuity in many school programs in which classes may meet only three times a week, and in association with this is the difficulty presented in record keeping or remembering the stage each child is at until the next lesson. In addition to using discovery learning methods with children the teacher occasionally can place them in groups and provide different kinds of learning opportunities. Children of almost any age can be placed into groups on the basis of:

1. Their ability to work on their own. Such children generally are self-motivated, show some degree of responsible behavior, and are capable of self-direction and self-discipline. They also may be capable of some self-evaluation.
2. A preference to work with a partner or as part of a small group.
3. A need for much teacher support and direction.

Children who fall into the first category may be given work to do on their own as soon as they can read. They can work from task cards or utilize a contract or learning center. (These alternative learning strategies are described with examples in Chapter 10). Similarly, children in the second category can use the same concepts. The last group will need to work under the guidance of the teacher until such time as they become more independent. By using groups the teacher can spend time with individual children who may need more help and attention.

Getting to Know Children

How can a teacher really get to know children and develop some feeling for a child's individual characteristics? The classroom teacher who is responsible for a single class or group of children will get to know the children in that class quite well during the year. The specialist teacher, on the other hand, may very well see several hundred children a week across all grade levels, but may see them over several years' time. It may take much longer in this situation to just learn everyone's name!

Children who seek attention for some reason through disruptive or inappropriate behavior will become known fairly quickly. The teacher will become familiar in similar fashion with the highly skilled as well as the poorly skilled child. One way for the teacher to collect information about individual children is to compile an anecdotal record. Fairly typical behaviors can be listed, with incidents involving these behaviors noted in a grade book by a child's name. The items listed could be coded to save time. Such facts as characteristic behavior, degree of involvement, skill levels, and rate of learning could all be included. Over a period of time the teacher will have collected quite a lot of information about many different children. Examples of behavior and abilities a teacher might want to note are:

Prefers to play alone/or learn alone.
Able to work on own.
Likes to work with a partner.
Enjoys group work.
Makes friends easily/or does not make friends easily.
Does not get involved easily.
Self-confident, talkative, aggressive.
Shy, withdrawn, quiet.
Natural leader/or follower.
Slow/or fast learner.
Highly skilled in. . . .
Poorly skilled in. . . .
Early maturer.
Always asking questions.
Evidence of creativity.
Emotionally stable/or unstable.
Persistent with tasks/or easily discouraged.
Appears to have motor problems.
Seems to need a lot of support.
Exhibits responsible behavior/or is irresponsible.

Fig. 5-1 *Withdrawn or time-out?*

Demonstrates continually disruptive behavior.

Teachers can develop their own lists and modify or add to them as necessary. Entries should be made as soon as possible and dated.

Many teachers do, in fact, store information relating to particular children in their heads. Much of this information could be recorded before it is forgotten. Recording this information might also help to eliminate some of the biases that can occur in regard to individual children.

Other teachers can be a useful source of information about children. The specialist teacher should always find time to talk to the classroom teachers about different children.

Simple questionnaires can be given to children to gather information about learning preferences, preferred activities, and attitudes toward the movement program. Younger children can respond to questions presented through pictures or in cartoon form. Happy or sad faces can be used by the child to indicate particular feelings. It is important for the teacher to know how children feel about the movement program, since these feelings may not always be what the teacher had imagined.

Skill levels should be pre-assessed by having the children perform simple activities which the teacher observes. Such activities as jumping and landing, skipping, throwing and catching, or bouncing a ball will give the teacher some idea of the number of children who have mastered particular skills, which will assist the teacher in deciding where to start.

Developing Different Teaching Strategies

For the teacher who is accustomed to a fairly traditional approach and has always taught the same activity to all children at the same time, the preceding discussion may have provided some ideas for other ways to plan for a change in teaching methodology.

Any transition or move toward initiating change should be undertaken carefully and fairly slowly. A belief that change may be beneficial is essential, and the teacher must be prepared to give different ideas a chance to develop. This may mean at least a semester or two in terms of time, not just two or three weeks. Changing or adapting to a different style of teaching may, at first, feel quite uncomfortable. The teacher should not feel too upset or discouraged if plans do not work out perfectly immediately. It does help if there is someone with whom to discuss planned changes. If a group of teachers are trying to implement some new ideas the group can be mutually supportive.

The children themselves also will have to be involved in the changes or new approaches right from the start. The total program and its goals can be discussed with each class at the beginning of the year or quarter. Input can be obtained from the children about what they are going to learn, what they would like to learn, how they may be able to learn, and what choices are available to them.

As teachers move away from whole class teaching they should experiment carefully with the alternatives. For varying and usually short amounts of time children may be encouraged to work in groups using task cards or may be presented with verbal challenges. It may be desirable to conduct practice sessions as children are introduced to small group work. Responsibilities should be given gradually and with fairly close supervision and feedback. These changes can begin at the kindergarten level.

The feelings are sometimes expressed that as soon as the teacher allows some choice of activity, or permits children to participate in the decision-making process, anarchy will follow. Nothing could be further from the truth. If, as teachers, we want to inculcate in children the qualities of self-direction, self-discipline, and responsibility, along with the ability to make intelligent choices, we must provide the opportunity for these qualities to develop. Naturally, such development will be a gradual process. As children are introduced to other ways of learning they must show that they can handle themselves in the new situations.

What the teacher has to attempt is to match appropriate teaching strategies to the different learning styles of children. Learning thus can be personalized for an individual child. In simple language, this means doing for Tommy what Tommy needs—hence the earlier discussion about the teacher getting to know the children he or she teaches. Individualized instruction can be attempted for some children. This does not mean that there necessarily must be a one-to-one relationship between teacher and child, since several children can be working either on the same or different tasks at their own rate and at their own ability level in a group situation. Instruction can be humanistic if there is a genuine concern on the part of the teacher for children and the way they learn. Teaching and learning should take place in a fairly relaxed and informal setting in which children can be successful and thereby feel good about themselves and the program.

If mastery of certain skills is achieved at some level, with all children learning something and acquiring desirable attitudes toward learning, the process by which this is accomplished may be more important than the actual products of such learning.

Naturally, the manner in which the other components of the school are functioning will have some influence upon the way movement is taught. If the school utilizes self-contained classrooms, a fixed schedule, and teachers are not very "open" in their methods of operation, the movement teacher will need to proceed carefully and sensitively. The task will be much easier if the school utilizes individualized instruction, learning centers, continuous progress, and differentiated staffing patterns. If parents and aides also are available to assist with the program, so much the better. Integration of the movement program into the body of the school curriculum will be easier if both philosophies of procedure are mutually compatible. No matter what approach is utilized in the school, however, the movement teacher has a tremendous opportunity to work in different ways with children, either independently or in conjunction with other curriculum areas.

PLANNING AND TEACHING A LESSON

Good preparation is the key to good teaching, with individual lessons being developed from a unit plan. Lessons will be aimed at some aspect of helping children learn a skill, acquire knowledge, or develop positive attitudes toward a wide variety of different physical activities. Actual program guidelines are provided in chapters 6 through 10. This section will examine some ways to plan and teach a movement lesson.

Individual teachers should always feel able to plan a movement program and lessons in their own way. The text suggests methods for developing lessons that teachers may use as presented or modify to suit their own purposes.

Quite simply, a lesson usually has a beginning, a middle, and some kind of conclusion. Different labels can be given to these sections; in this text these lesson sections will be referred to as:

1. Introduction.
2. Lesson focus.
3. Applications.

The introduction to a movement lesson is often regarded as a kind of warm-up exercise and usually takes the form of a class activity. The form an introduction to a lesson takes will depend on the overall theme of the lesson. It can be a vigorous and demanding activity or an opportunity for quiet, individual learning. The teacher may have the children do some stretching activities, participate in a chasing game, participate in a short period of directed or free practice with small apparatus (ball, hoop, bean bag, jump rope, etc.), or possibly develop some movements to music. Examples will be given later in the chapter.

The lesson focus contains the main instructional part of a lesson. The teacher can use guided discovery or problem-solving methods that are structured around the theme of the lesson. (These processes were discussed in chapter 4.) The lesson may require that the children work individually, with a partner, or in small groups.

The final part of the lesson should offer an opportunity for children to further develop the skills they have begun to learn or for some form of implementation or application of the skills. Usually children will be working in small groups in this portion of the lesson.

Depending on the amount of time available, the three parts of a lesson can be conducted over different lengths of time. The introductory part generally will be quite short and lead into the main focus of the lesson. These two parts together may account for about half the available time, leaving the other half of the lesson for implementation or application activities. If periods are very short, possibly 20 minutes, the teacher may want to distribute the material of a complete lesson over two periods. A lesson plan should include a statement of objectives, which may be broken down into psychomotor, cognitive, and affective components. Generally, development of such qualities as positive attitudes that the teacher may be trying to encourage in children can be stated at the beginning of a unit or series of lessons.

The material presented in the text in Chapters 6 through 9 provides the teacher with ideas from which to create lessons. An example of a lesson is given below:

Lesson example: 30-minute period, 30 children, Grade 4.

Objectives: Children should be able to demonstrate several different ways of jumping and show they understand what is involved in landing lightly.

1. *Introduction*

   Walking and Running

   Keywords—change of speed and direction. Awareness of others as they move (relationships). Keeping as far away as possible.

   Jumping:

   Over lines painted or taped on the floor

2. *Lesson Focus*

   Explore/discover—Jumping over the body shape made by a partner and landing in different ways.

   Keywords:

   Using one foot, both feet.

   Directions—sideways, backward

   Force—discuss and stress soft landings.

   Notes:

   Partners change roles frequently, with one jumping over the other, who makes a shape over which to jump. Discuss words that describe the body's action in landing softly.

3. *Applications*

   Divide the class into six groups and assign to stations for the following activities:

   a. Standing long jump. Experiment with how the arms can help in jumping farther.
   b. Run, jump, roll. Develop a sequence that includes a change of direction.
   c. Jumping. Hoop is held horizontally by one partner while the other jumps in and out. Stress directions and take off from one or both feet.
   d. Jumping. Forward and backward jumps over a rolling hoop.
   e. Agility ramp. Run up then jump off. Land softly and roll.
   f. "Hop scotch." Develop this type of game for children.

Groups may rotate every 5 minutes or whenever the teacher feels a change is necessary. If the children are accustomed to group work they may change activities on their own, after demonstrating successful accomplishment of the task.

The teacher can work from this outline and provide feedback and additional cues and challenges as necessary. The teacher and children can share ideas, with the teacher praising good performances as children show quality and originality in their work.

Phrasing Questions

The essence of the teaching methods proposed in this text is the art of asking questions. This process entails drawing out rather than pouring in children's responses, that is, teachers should ask questions rather than provide answers to questions. As the teacher poses a question or task for children, most of the responses will be in movement, although occasionally the teacher may ask for a verbal answer. Good questions or tasks will be challenging and yet will permit some choice of response on the part of children. The tasks must also be phrased in such a way that all children have a chance to respond successfully. Creativity and originality can be encouraged if the teacher asks questions that demand a divergent rather than a convergent response.

The usual method for presenting tasks is to ask the kind of question that begins "Find another way to . . ." or to preface a fairly direct command such as "Jump sideways" with the phrase "Can you. . . .?" However, this does not necessarily alter the command so that it becomes a suitable task that encourages a variety of responses from the children. By combining these two types of approaches into a question form which asks "Can you find a different way to jump sideways?" a variety of responses will be elicited from the children. "Can you . . ." implies that there is a possibility of answering yes or no! Other ways can be found of saying the same thing, for example, "Who can. . . ?" "How else could you. . . ?" or "See if you can. . ." offer the same challenge to children, although perhaps a little more indirectly.

THE TEACHING CYCLE

Continually asking questions over a period of time is a demanding teaching task. The questioning process might be called a teaching sequence, or cycle, in that the teacher presents an initial task, monitors the responses of individual children, and then must be ready with more questions, keywords, or cues in order to develop children's work. Naturally, the teacher may make comments to children to offer praise or other positive feedback as well as to present additional tasks. Some children may produce responses which the teacher may feel are inappropriate to the particular kind of movements desired. The teacher must be ready with questions or cues that will redirect these particular responses. Learning to observe all the children and supply the necessary feedback can be a complex teaching task. The teacher must first develop the habit of scanning the whole class. The focus may then shift to those children who may be ready for a further challenge, who need help in responding to the initial task, or who are ready to repeat and practice their response. The teacher may decide to have the entire class work on similar tasks for part of the lesson. Gradually, because of the differing rates of learning, the need will arise for the teacher to recognize these differences and begin to develop activities with individual children.

The cycle of questioning and observing repeats itself, with the teacher providing feedback, presenting new tasks, and suggesting appropriate cues. As the lesson develops it is the children who actually set the pace. The teacher picks up ideas from the children and utilizes them according to the direction desired, that is, whether the teacher has a definite goal in mind or activities are to be more open ended. At the end of the lesson it will be important for the teacher to record the events which actually occurred.

THEMES AS ORGANIZING IDEAS FOR LESSONS

A theme, as used in movement education, denotes an organizing idea around which the program may be organized or structured. Lessons then can be developed around the organizing focus of a theme.

Laban originally proposed 16 basic movement themes which could be used as the core of a movement program. The themes consisted of different aspects of movement, such as body awareness, awareness of space, the shape of movement, awareness of weight and time, relationships between effort and shape, and elevation (jumping and flight in the air). As a total framework, the themes primarily were used to develop movement in drama, mime, and dance. Other people became interested in themes and their possibilities when applied and adapted to gymnastics and games as a way to develop skills and body awareness.

Themes are developed by using the movement factors to explore the possibilities of what, where, and how the body is moving in terms of practical, functional, and expressive movement. When used in this way movement factors can be thought of as sub-themes or tasks. The teacher may evolve other ideas which can be used as themes and arranged in many different patterns.

The activities described in this text generally are organized around themes developed within the categories of locomotor, non-locomotor, and manipulative activities. Concepts also are explored, such as the nature of balance, creating and applying force, and absorbing force. Finally, the skills and movements so developed are applied where appropriate to gymnastics, games, and dance.

The themes should be explored systematically from the lists developed for each grade level. After choosing one or more themes to work on the teacher should decide which sub-themes are to be used to develop the theme. Themes are explored at increasingly sophisticated levels in terms of children's understanding and performance. As the teacher develops different ways to group children the themes can be presented on task cards, in learning centers, and in contracts. Task cards can be used by individual children or by small groups. Tasks or problems are written on a card and children respond to them at their own rate. A learning center is a more sophisticated form of task card wherein objectives are clearly stated, learning activities are prescribed, and some form of self-evaluation usually is included. Contracts are a form of agreement between teacher and child that states a certain activity will be attempted and completed within a specific time limitation. (See Chapter 10 for examples of task cards, learning centers, and contracts.)

CONCEPT DEVELOPMENT

The development of concepts in children is one of the key goals in education. In movement the teacher can help children integrate isolated pieces of information by encouraging insight and the discovery of relationships. The ability to abstract a commonality or assimilate a generalized idea means that the children have perceived a relevant relationship and are beginning to think on their own. The teacher can facilitate the process of conceptualization as illustrated in the following examples.

Task:

Find a way to jump over the taped line on the floor and land softly.

The teacher moves around the activity area to suggest that he or she is listening to the children landing. Soft landings are quiet landings! The teacher suggests to the class that everyone sit down to discuss the question "What helps us to land softly?"

Typical Responses:

"Try landing on your toes."

The teacher can demonstrate landing with very little "give" and making a hard landing. The comment can be made that landing on the toes does not seem to soften the landing very much.

"Try bending your knees."

The teacher again bends the knees but keeps them fixed or fairly rigid—again producing a hard landing. If the teacher exaggerates the force of the landing and indicates that such a landing is quiet painful, the children usually get the message. The next step might be for the teacher to combine landing on the toes and bending the knees—another hard landing. The teacher may now choose a student to demonstrate a soft landing. The teacher then can ask the class if they noticed any difference between the two landings. Sometimes it is difficult for children to verbalize what they see so the teacher may need to help here. The teacher has to elicit the idea that the hips go down on landing to produce a kind of squashing or squatting movement, a "going with" the flow of the movement. The children may talk about springs or shock absorbers in the discussion of what happens to make a soft landing. The

Fig. 5-2 *Does landing on the toes really help?*

Fig. 5-3 *Bending the knees—still a hard landing!*

children should then practice all kinds of jumps and concentrate on landing softly. The teacher again can make a point of listening to each child land.

The next step is for the children to develop different styles of jumping, with the teacher's guidance. (This facet is given more attention in later chapters which describe the development of practical activities.) The children's responses may include jumping down from different heights, running and jumping, landing and rolling, jumping over obstacles, and so on.

The teacher could have presented this skill to the class by saying "Watch me, this is how you land softly," and after a demonstration had the class practice. The method described previously requires a different approach. The teacher focuses the children's attention on what is actually happening so that they can begin to develop the concept of how to absorb force. This idea can then be transferred to ways of catching a ball softly. The question can be asked, "What happens if we catch a ball and try to stop it instantly, without any 'give' in the hands and arms?" If the ball is fairly hard, it can hurt. The teacher may ask the children how catching a ball softly is like landing softly on the feet, with a discussion following on the concept of movement being slowed down gradually rather than stopping all at once. The teacher may illustrate the principle by describing the result of applying the brakes on a bicycle or a car. Next, the teacher may reverse the concept to discuss how force is imparted to the body or to an object by the body. Throwing a ball would be a good example. How far can a ball be thrown if the arm cannot be moved? A question such as this would start children thinking about the problem. Of course, the teacher must understand the level at which the children function intellectually and should modify the concepts according to the level of the particular class. Sometimes "Who can show me. . . ?" is better than "Who can tell me. . . ?"

Children can understand the relationship between distance and the absorption or application of force. This concept then can be applied to the principles of transferring body weight, such as walking softly or lightly, running quietly, accelerating and decelerating, stopping and starting, and changing direction. The teacher can discuss how overcoming the inertia of the body at rest, that is, getting started into motion, requires more force than is necessary to keep it moving. An analogy to use here is that of trying to push a car: It takes a lot of force to get the car rolling, but once it is moving (on a level surface) it can almost be pushed with one finger. The teacher can provide other illustrations of the mechanical and effort principles involved in movement, such as starting a 50-yard dash, putting the shot, jumping for height and distance, and throwing for distance.

Task:
Children are to learn about balance

The teacher can introduce the concept of balance in many different ways. Most children will say a person is balancing who stands on one leg and wobbles about a little, although they may not believe a person is balancing who stands steadily on two feet! Walking is a series of over-balances; as we start to lean forward we begin to lose our balance, thus we move a foot out to support the weight of the body and regain our balance. Generally a balanced position implies that one can over-balance or lose balance and perhaps fall.

Children can be asked to find different parts of their bodies on which to balance (suggest small surfaces at first). The teacher can gain ideas from the children and may indicate body parts they may not have tried or suggest balancing on more than one part. At this point it may be necessary to clarify the difference between being balanced and being stable. One simple way to describe this is to suggest that a person who is balancing can be pushed over easily, while it is difficult to push over someone who is very stable (or the opposite of balancing).

At this point a demonstration by the teacher can be of use. The teacher stands with feet apart and asks someone in the class to try to topple him or her over with a push on the side at about waist level. Generally this is quite a solid position from which it is difficult to move anyone. The teacher may then suggest a push from the back (being ready to over-balance). A discussion can follow centered around the question of why it is so difficult to be pushed sideways but so easy from the back. Children enjoy this type of discussion and usually will suggest that the body does not easily topple to the side since one leg is braced or supports the body against the force of the pusher while there is no such support against a push from the back. The children then can be asked if there is a way that the teacher could place the feet so that it is not too easy to push the teacher over from either direction. Often the children will suggest a position with the feet still spread apart but with one in front of the other. The pushing process is repeated so that the children can see that it is still difficult to push the teacher over sideways and not as easy to do it from behind.

The teacher may then ask, if a person who desired to be in a very solid position bent over and placed a hand on the floor, where should the arm, or third support, be placed for maximum balance? The teacher can assume a position with the arm in line with the feet and ask the children if this is a good place. After various suggestions, the teacher should arrive at a position in which the feet and arm form a triangle. Someone in the class may try to push the teacher over and afterwards the shape made by the hands and

Fig. 5-4
Try and push me over.

Fig. 5-5 *It's easier this way!*

feet can be discussed. The teacher may ask if the children know of or can think of anything that has three legs (a tripod), and why is a support for a camera made with three legs rather than four. The students should make shapes in which they are as stable as possible. What is the best way to do this? (The children will discover the best position is as close to the floor as possible, with the supports as far apart as possible.)

Fig. 5-6 *A solid "tripod."*

The teacher may next ask, "If I now want to do a headstand, that is, balance upside down on three supports (my two hands and head), how shall I place my supports?" The children should utilize the same idea of a triangle, with the head at the apex.

The teacher can discuss the idea of the center of gravity of the body and of other objects with those children who are ready.

Task:

Children learn about the transfer of weight

A person moves the body from place to place by transferring weight onto different parts or body surfaces. The teacher should have the children explore some of the different ways they can travel and classify the ways in which they can move. The usual movements will be suggested, such as walking, running, hopping, skipping, and galloping. Rolling, jumping and sliding also may be mentioned. Of course, moving can be accomplished on parts of the body other than the feet. Children can crawl, move like inchworms, or leap from feet to hands. Essentially, most ways of moving can be classified as a process entailing steps, some type of rolling, as in tumbling or gymnastics, or sliding

Fig. 5-7 *Sliding along.*

as in ice skating, skiing, or simply in moving across a smooth floor. The children should discover that the body can move by putting out a support such as an arm or leg, and body weight may be transferred onto that support; the most frequently used locomotor skills involve these three types of movement. Rolling movements usually are employed in tumbling and gymnastics. Children can find ways to combine different ways of traveling, for example, by utilizing a run together with a roll and a sliding movement.

Teachers need to be aware of exactly how much value children derive from a demonstration or from observation of movement. For example, few children below fourth grade will notice anything wrong in a demonstration of walking when the demonstrator moves the arm and leg on the same side of the body forward together. When asked what they notice about such walking the children usually will say that the teacher is taking big steps, or the arms are stiff. They do not notice that the forward arm is not opposite to the forward leg. This should indicate to the teacher that it is necessary to direct the child's attention to particular parts of a movement. Children could be asked to describe what the teacher is doing with his or her arms and then asked to see if they can

Fig. 5-8 *Transfer of weight—rolling.*

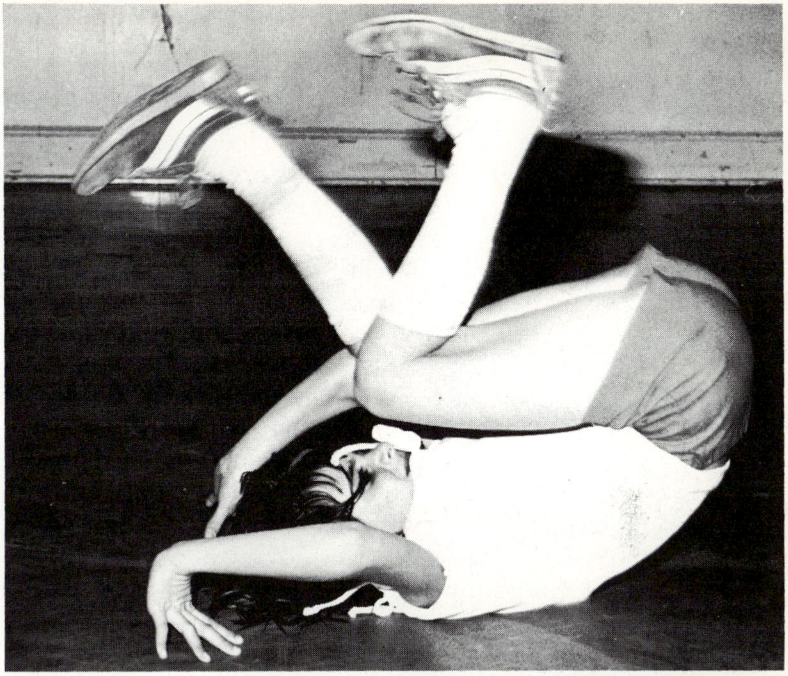

Fig. 5-9 *Transfer of weight from apparatus.*

walk like that. Questions could be asked about why the arms move in opposition to the legs and if the children could run fast without using their arms. The difference between a walk and a run also can be examined.

As the teacher begins to work with movement concepts, many other ideas will present themselves that can be developed through the use of themes. These ideas may include work on levers and leverage, center of gravity, the laws of motion, and momentum. Additional material on this subject can be found in *Knowledge and Understanding in Physical Education* (AAHPER, 1973).

Summary

This chapter examined some of the relationships between teaching methods and facilitating learning, and indicated the importance of establishing a suitable learning climate wherein children feel free to explore and experiment under the teacher's guidance and with his or her support. In such a learning situation children learn to work quietly, and the teacher uses a conversational manner and offers a great deal of positive feedback to individual children.

Methods of grouping children were discussed and ideas on how to get to know children were suggested, including the use of anecdotal records. Developing different teaching strategies was discussed, as was the planning of a movement period based on a framework consisting of an introduction, lesson focus, and application.

The art of asking questions was described, along with the concept of a teaching cycle. The use of themes as organizing ideas for a curriculum and individual lessons was suggested.

Finally, concept development was discussed and examples provided pertaining to teaching balance, transfer of weight, and absorption of force.

Seminar Questions and Activities

1. Describe some methods a teacher could utilize to learn about children's individual needs and interests.
2. As a teacher, how would you group children for: (a) apparatus work in gymnastics, (b) practicing basketball skills, and (c) working at a learning center?
3. From your readings, can you define personalized learning? How might a teacher develop personalized learning in the gym?
4. Choose a movement theme from those suggested in Chapter 5 and show how you would develop it.
5. In what ways can children participate in the decision-making process regarding the activities they learn? How might they approach the way they learn such activities?

Bibliography

Bilbrough, A., and Jones, P. *Physical Education in the Primary School.* London: University of London Press, 1968.

Kirchner, G., Cunningham, J., and Warrell, E. *Introduction to Movement Education.* 2nd ed. Dubuque, Iowa: Wm. C. Brown, 1978.

Laban, R. *Modern Educational Dance.* 2nd ed. Revised by L. Ullman. New York: Frederick A. Praeger, 1963.

Study Guide

Anderson, William G., and Barrett, Gary T. *What's Going on in Gym.* Monograph 1, Motor Skills: Theory into Practice. 24 Taunton Lake Drive, Newtown, CT: 1978.

Cheffers, John. "Observing Teaching Systematically." In *Quest* Monograph 28, Summer 1977. National College Physical Education Association for Men.

Locke, Lawrence F. "Research on Teaching Physical Education: New Hope for a Dismal Science." In *Quest* Monograph 28, Summer 1977. National College Physical Education Association for Men.

Siedentop, Daryl. *Developing Teaching Skills in Physical Education.* Boston: Houghton Mifflin Co., 1976.

This material discusses interactions between teacher and student.

Hellison, D., ed. *Personalized Learning in Physical Education.* Washington, D.C.: AAHPER, 1976.

Gilliom, Bonnie Cherp. *Basic Movement Education for Children: Rationale and Teaching Units.* Reading, Mass.: Addison-Wesley, 1970. (See Chapter 4, pp. 29–32, and teaching units in Part II.)

Blackburn, Jack E., and Powell, W. Conrad. *One at a Time—All at Once.* Pacific Palisades: Goodyear Pub. Co., 1976.

Dreikurs, R. *Children the Challenge.* New York: Hawthorn, 1964.

Bechtol, W. M. *Individualizing Instruction and Keeping Your Sanity.* Follett, 1973.

These books are of value in providing information on individualizing instruction.

Howe, Leland W., and Howe, Mary Martha. *Personalizing Education: Values Clarification and Beyond.* New York: Hart Pub. Co., 1964.

This is a good source of information on values clarification.

Blosser, P. *Handbook of Effective Questionning Techniques.* Worthington, Ohio: Educational Associates Inc., 1973.

The author discusses various practical questioning techniques.

For development of an elementary school physical education attitude scale and other references see:

Cheffers, John T. F., Mancini, Victor H., and Zaichowski, Leonard D. "The Development of an Elementary Physical Education Attitude Scale." *In Physical Educator,* Vol. 33, March 1976.

In addition to developing an attitude scale, this source offers information on additional references. The reader also is referred to the study guides for Chapters 10 and 11 in this text for further sources pertaining to teaching methods, evaluating children's progress, and assessing needs and interests.

Stanley, Sheila. *Physical Education: A Movement Orientation.* Toronto: McGraw Hill, 1969. (Especially pp. 197–205, 210–213, 269–292, and 224–242.)

In addition to this source, the text by Kirchner (listed in the preceding bibliography) provides ideas on lesson planning.

Lenel, R. M. *Games in the Primary School.* London: University of London Press, 1969 (pp. 44–48).

Broer, M. R. *Efficiency of Human Movement.* 3rd ed. Philadelphia: W. B. Saunders Co., 1973.
The author discusses body mechanics.

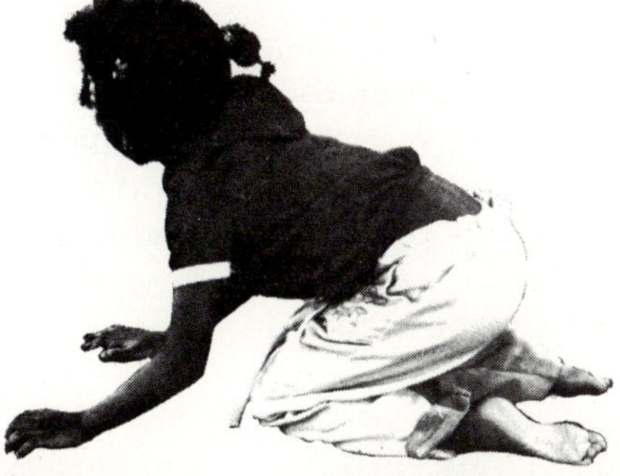

6 the program for pre-school children

The pre-school child, typically between the ages of three and five, presents an interesting challenge to the teacher. These young children characteristically have a natural and spontaneous desire to move, and they are very curious and eager to try everything. (The reader is urged to read the sections in Chapter 3 on the growth and behavioral characteristics of pre-schoolers and the implications for program development.)

Preliminary Considerations

The first consideration in planning a program is to examine the space that will be available for movement. The only indoor space available might be the classroom, therefore it will be necessary to clear some floor space each time the teacher desires to conduct a movement session. Teachers tend to get lazy after awhile, but it is worthwhile to make the effort to move tables and chairs. Other areas also should be examined as possible locations for the teaching of movement. If a large space is available, a clearly defined smaller area should be marked off within it and the children encouraged to stay within this area. The boundaries can be marked by chairs, benches, or cones. Clearly defined boundaries are necessary for outdoor areas as well.

The teacher should then assess the equipment and apparatus available for both indoor and outdoor use. Much can be improvised in terms of equipment. The teacher should develop a list of equipment that is not immediately available and plan to gradually acquire whatever else is needed. (See the Appendix for a list of suitable equipment.)

CHILDREN'S DRESS

As long as children are comfortable in the clothes they are wearing, dress generally does not present a problem; however, long dresses and restrictive, tight pants sometimes prevent free movement. This problem can be discussed with parents. Footwear also can present problems if children wear heavy shoes or boots, but they can be encouraged to work in bare feet if the floor surface is clean and not too cold. Even sneakers will look clumsy after observing children moving in bare feet.

Working in socks is not recommended since children can become sloppy in their movements and can easily slip if allowed to run around in their stocking feet. In certain communities the teacher may encounter difficulty by requesting children to remove their shoes and socks.

Fig. 6-1 *The problems with a dress code!*

LEARNING TO LISTEN

It is a good idea for the teacher to have a signal that will alert children when to start or stop activity. Teachers may clap their hands, beat a drum, or simply say "Stop," or "Go," or "Begin"; however, whichever signal is used, children should understand its significance and it is worth spending a little time to practice the appropriate response. A whistle is not recommended as a signal.

Instructions should be kept to a minimum, and if the ground rules for expected behavior are established during the first few sessions, the job of working with the children will be made so much easier. Teachers can formulate their own ground rules as they begin teaching, but they probably should develop rules pertaining to an acceptable working noise level, appropriate footwear and dress, and observing the working area of other children and not interfering in it.

It is important that the teacher develop a working vocabulary and list those words and phrases that may be new to the children and gradually introduce them. The children will soon grasp the

Fig. 6-2 *Who is listening?*

Fig. 6-3 Over the top.

concept of discovering different ways to do things once they understand the meaning of words like over, under, next to, behind, facing, in and out, through, circle, far away from, near to, shape, and space.

Organizing and Planning

The motto of teachers who deal with children of about three or four years of age might well be "Teach a little and play a lot," since formal instruction is contrary to the nature of the child at this stage. The teacher should allocate plenty of time for practice and play. It is much better to develop activities based on what the children are actually doing than to say "Put that away now," or "Come here and do this."

Children can be involved happily in movement activities for as long as 45 minutes or more, providing that the teacher is prepared to offer a wide variety of activities that range from vigorous and challenging tasks to those which are quieter and less demanding.

The way in which the total program is designed will vary considerably depending upon a variety of factors, including the number of children involved, the space and equipment available, and the teacher's ability and interest in teaching movement. Rather than prescribe daily lesson plans, the teacher can select activities or themes from among the suggestions given later in this chapter. A balance of locomotor, non-locomotor, and manipulative skills, together with some rhythmic and expressive movement, should form the basis of the program.

Depending upon the size of the space available, the teacher (and aides) may designate an area for active movement and for practicing ball skills. The rest of the space may be utilized for equipment for climbing, hanging, swinging, jumping, and balancing. Children may be allowed to play with equipment at different times during the day; it is not necessary that the entire group participate in a single movement period. The teacher should attempt to schedule at least two opportunities during the day for movement if children are in school all day.

It is a good idea in the early stages of a program to avoid putting out too much equipment too soon. Children gradually can be introduced to activities that involve the use of balls, hoops, jump

Fig. 6-4 *Working with hoops.*

ropes, and bean bags as well as work on the larger pieces of equipment. Safety is an important consideration for the teacher, who will need to ensure that the environment is free from hazards and that equipment is set up properly. The young child is not always aware of dangers and may try such stunts as "flips" unless cautioned against them and carefully observed. The teacher must closely supervise children when they are using apparatus, particularly for climbing and hanging. In the movement education approach, children generally will not attempt to do things they feel they cannot do; however, they may attempt to imitate an activity they saw performed by an older child.

At first the teacher can structure a few activities for short periods of time, and thereby allowing the children to become accustomed to listening, stopping, and starting. The main concern at this time is for the teacher to establish the ground rules and initiate a routine to which the children can become accustomed. Working with children without using a highly structured program may at first worry some teachers. However, experience is a great teacher, and actually trying some new techniques often proceeds much better than one would expect from reading about teaching in a book. The thoughtful and perceptive teacher who works with pre-schoolers will quickly learn to adjust methods and materials to correspond with children's abilities and interests.

The teacher's ability to enter the world of the child and see things from his or her point of view will require careful preparation and familiarity with the young child's environment. The teacher will be rewarded for his or her efforts through the cries of "I can do it!" or "Watch me!" that come from excited children who are successfully developing a repertoire of motor skills that will help them cope with their environment, develop self-confidence, and build strong, healthy bodies.

Children gradually will acquire knowledge about movement and about their own limitations and abilities through a carefully planned program. In a similar fashion, they will acquire positive attitudes through a program that encourages feelings of caring for people and property and sharing successful, happy learning experiences.

Program Outline

It is suggested that a movement program for pre-schoolers include the following topics:

1. Identifying body parts.
2. Understanding relationships and developing a movement vocabulary.
3. Developing locomotor skills.

Fig. 6-5 *"I can do it!"*

4. Developing non-locomotor skills.
5. Developing manipulative skills.
6. Rhythmic and expressive movement.

The role each of these components plays in a movement program and methods of instruction are detailed in the paragraphs below.

PROGRAM CONTENT

1. *Identifying body parts.*
   The teacher will ask children to identify body parts by touching them. This activity can be repeated until children are familiar with body parts, including the head, nose, ears, eyes, chin, shoulders, neck, elbows, hands, stomach, back, side, hips, knees, ankle, and toes.
2. *Relationships.*
   a. Far away from, next to.
      Examples
      "Move your hands on, off, over, under, near (next) to your knees."
      "See if you can move your hands far away from your feet."
      "Find some ways to move your hands (or feet) far apart."
      "Find all the different places where you can bring your hands close together (clap)."

"Can you sit next to one other person (partner)?"
"Let's see if we can walk around the room and stay as far away as possible from everyone else."

b. In front of, behind.
c. In front of, behind someone else.
Examples
"Stand behind your partner."
"Put the ball behind you/in front of you."

The teacher can formulate other exercises in order to develop an understanding of all these relationships.

Fig. 6-6 *Make a shape over your ball.*

3. *Developing locomotor skills.*
   a. *Explore and discover.*
      (1) Walking and running.
      These two activities should be explored on a fairly regular basis.
      Examples
      "Let me see you walk around our space."
      "*How else* could we walk?"
      "*Where else* could we walk?"

The teacher can obtain ideas from the children as the activity proceeds and share these ideas with the rest of the class or introduce them through the use of key words.

"Susie is walking *backward.* Who else thought of doing that?" "John is walking really *quickly.* That's good, John."

"Let's all try to walk *quickly.*"

Children at first may need prompting until they begin to understand the purpose of keywords (described in Chapter 4). Appropriate movement factors that may be introduced here as keywords could include:

Directions—forward, sideways, backward.

Pathway—straight, zig-zag, crooked.

Force—heavy, light/soft.

Speed—fast, slow, faster, slower.

As children work on these concepts the teacher should stress that they should be aware of other children as they move around and keep as far away from them as possible. This is a better way of getting children to move about without colliding with one another than for the teacher to say: "Don't bump anyone else," because that would merely give them the idea to do just that!

(2) Moving quietly/softly

Examples

"Let's make a lot of noise with our feet when we move around. Do not stamp so hard that you hurt your feet though!"

"Now let's move so softly that I won't be able to hear anyone moving."

"Let's see if everyone can freeze or stop when I hit the drum. Good—most people stopped right away."

The teacher may not have the attention of all children, so it would be a good idea to check this by occasionally asking children to hold up their hands if they are listening, with the teacher reinforcing those who are listening.

The teacher can develop these movement ideas over a series of lessons, depending upon how well the children grasp them. There must be many opportunities for repetition and work with individual children.

(3) Other ways of moving on the feet.

Children can be asked to show some other ways of moving on their feet, for example, "If we couldn't walk or run, how could we move on our feet?" This will elicit many different ideas which can be developed and shared. Again, the keywords suggested previously can be applied to aid skill development.

The teacher must remember to praise the responses of children in a real and meaningful way in order to provide encouragement and motivation.

(4) Different ways of moving on other body parts or supports.

The teacher could begin developing this theme by utilizing a sitting position or by asking the children to find a way to move while keeping their hands and feet on the floor. Keywords would include direction, pathway, speed, and level.

(a) Other variables.

The teacher could direct children to move on certain specified supports, such as hands and feet, hands and knees, seat and feet, on the front of the body, on the back, etc. Also, the children could utilize different parts to provide the force to push or pull.

Examples:

"Lie on your tummy and find a way to move so that your hands are pulling or pushing you along." "Can you lie on your back and find a way to let your feet push you along?"

Each idea can be utilized for individual children or for the group by using keywords. The teacher may ask individual children to demonstrate their movement responses with the group. The teacher can discuss in a simple way the type of movement being observed and perhaps suggest that all the children try to do it.

Example

"Look at Tommy. In which direction is he moving? Is he moving fast or slow? Which parts of his body are holding him up?"

It is useful to apply the what, where and how framework described in Chapter 4. In the example given above the teacher is trying to determine *what* Tommy is doing, *where* he is going (direction and level), and *how* he is moving (that is, effort quality, whether heavy or light, fast or slow, moving in a straight or crooked direction).

(5) *Miscellaneous ideas.*

Children gradually develop the ability to hop, gallop, and skip, and as maturation proceeds, more children become able to enjoy these movements. Children should develop correct motor patterns in the basic locomotor skills. (For references pertaining to the fundamental motor patterns, see the study guide at the end of this chapter.)

The movement factors can be applied singly, or children can combine them to build sequences. These sequences should be very simple as movement at this age is more spontaneous than structured.

Fig. 6-7 *How else can we move?*

Fig. 6-8 *See if your hands can move you along.*

Examples
"Let's see who can run *quickly* but very *softly.*"
"Who can find a way to walk backward in a curving pathway?" "As you go backward, you should be careful to do what?" (Look out for others!)

(6) Different ways of jumping and landing.
The simplest kind of jump is to jump in place, although it helps to have an object to jump over. This is where the teacher's collection of boxes, milk cartons, and canes will prove useful. Through tasks the children can be invited to find different ways to jump over lines painted or taped on the floor, tiles or carpet squares, a jump rope laid on the floor in various shapes, hoops, bicycle tires, or chalked or taped circles.

Fig. 6-9 *Jumping in and out of the rope shape.*

Children should be asked to try landing softly. Initially all obstacles or objects which children jump over should be at floor level, with jumps made from a stationary position or from a walk or run. Everyone should be able to find something to jump over, and children can be encouraged to move around and jump over or down from different kinds of obstacles. The following suggestions may help the teacher to further develop this activity.:

- Have children jump using *one* or *both feet*, jump in *different directions*, jump with a *twist*.
- Gradually increase the challenge by having children jump *in and out* of a hoop that is held a few inches off the ground (to begin). Children can jump over wands or canes resting on blocks, boxes, or milk cartons. The crossbar can be placed in a sloping position so that children can choose the height with which they feel most comfortable. Children can jump *down* from low wooden boxes or chairs (check for stability).
- Have children jump *in and out* of car tires, *over* milk cartons or foam shapes, *down from* an agility ramp.
- Children can jump over a wriggling jump rope or jump up to touch an elastic rope held just above reach height.

Many other ideas for jumping and landing will present themselves to the teacher as the activity proceeds. (Mats generally will not be necessary for children to land on at this stage.) Various shapes, such as circles, triangles, and stepping stones, can be taped or painted on the floor for jumping in and out of or

Fig. 6-10 *Up the agility ramp.*

Fig. 6-11 *Jumping down from the steps.*

over. Diverging lines (widening creek) also can present a challenge.

- Jumping can be combined with rolling.

(7) Different ways to climb on available apparatus.

(8) Different ways to roll.

Children can begin rolling from a rocking position or by utilizing the "log" roll, which requires the body to be extended, or various other ways of rolling. Forward and backward rolls are difficult at first for children to perform, and the teacher should supply mats if possible. The teacher should direct children to start from a crouched or squat position, with their hands on the floor in front of them, about shoulder-width apart, and fingers pointing forward. The teacher may ask, "Who can find a way to tip or roll over going forward? Sometimes this is called a somersault."

The teacher should discuss what shape one needs to make in order to roll, and must think of ways to get the children to tuck their heads ("Look at your tummy," or "Hold a bean bag under your chin.") For some children who are doing a roll for the first time the sensation of being upside down can be disorienting. The teacher may even need to manipulate the child through the first roll; however, once they get the idea the children will discover all kinds of rolls and will want to repeat them. A wedge-shaped tumbling mat that allows children to roll down a slope under the force of gravity is useful at this stage. (Children do this quite naturally outdoors where there is a sloping bank of grass.)

Children may develop other rolls through the use of Direction keywords, such as "Who can roll in a *different direction?*" Children can run, jump, land, and roll, especially if they jump down from the agility ramp or from a box.

Young children find the backward roll rather difficult because the head gets in the way. This roll can be started by rocking forward and backward and then attempting to go right over backward by taking both knees over one shoulder; however, they may come out of the roll sideways because the head gets in the way.

Fig. 6-12 *Climbing and sliding.*

Fig. 6-13 *High enough?*

4. *Non-locomotor skills.*
   a. *Explore and discover.*
   These essentially are skills which are performed in place and mainly concern flexibility, strengthening, and balancing activities. They can be practiced individually as themes or regarded as developmental activities. Basically, the activities to explore include balancing, spine flexibility (curling, stretching, twisting), rocking, hanging, and supporting weight on the hands.
      (1) Balancing on different body parts.
         (a) *Balance*
         Examples
         "Show me how you can balance on one foot."
         "Can you think of any other parts of your body on which you could balance?"
         "Can you find a way to balance on three parts of your body?"
         Cues for development.
         The teacher may suggest a body part or parts children can balance on, such as on the seat (no other

Fig. 6-14 *A balance on two parts.*

body parts touching the floor), tummy, heels, and knees. The children can change the body shape by stretching or bending while balancing. They may run, then freeze in a "statue" balance on different body parts, or walk on a line drawn on the floor, on a low balance beam, or on a "two-by-four" laid on the floor. The teacher may have the children sit, kneel, or stand on a rocking board, balance on a balance board, or try different ways to cross the balance beam. Greater challenge can be provided by using a higher balance beam.

(b) *Spine Flexibility*

This entails curling, stretching, and twisting. The spine can flex, extend, and twist, and activities that produce these movements can be developed.

(2) Different ways to curl and stretch.

(a) Thematic approach:

"Let me see you make yourself as small as possible—smaller than that—I can still see some noses and knees." (The teacher can praise tight, curled-up shapes.)

"Now see if you can stretch out and make yourself big."

Fig. 6-15
The rocking board.

Fig. 6-16
One kind of a stretch.

Keywords for this activity would include direction, speed, and level.

(b) *Other variables.*

Different starting positions may be used, such as sitting or lying, or on the feet, back, or knees. The teacher should encourage sequence development of curls and stretches.

(c) Bridge shapes. The teacher can have the children make bridge shapes over a hoop or small carpet square, generally using four supports (hands and feet). The activity may be varied by having children make high, long, or twisted bridge shapes. The teacher may pose such questions as "Who can make a different kind of bridge?" (The teacher will look for face-down and face-up bridges.) "Make any kind of a *high* bridge. Now change to a *long* bridge."

(3) Different ways to suspend the body.

(a) Hanging

This seemingly is a natural activity for young children, since they love to hang upside down using their knees. Suitable equipment will be necessary, such as a horizontal ladder or turning bar set at heights ranging from waist, shoulder, and head to stretch high. Mats should be underneath the apparatus. The teacher may offer clues such as hang upside down from *different supports,* hang by the hands and arms and find ways to swing, explore ways to *turn around* the bar, and travel *along* the bar or ladder while hanging.

(4) Different ways to support the body weight on the hands.

Acquiring the ability to support the body weight on the arms will help develop strength in the arm and shoulders as well as in the trunk musculature. The keywords for this activity would include move on four supports (hands and feet) in different directions, at various speeds, and on different levels and pathways.

Children may move from feet to hands and back to the feet in different ways. They may move their hands and feet alternately, make moving bridge shapes, and go over and under a partner's bridge without touching. They may fix the hands in one place and move the feet around, then fix the feet and move the hands. Gradually the children will gain the confidence and strength needed to support their weight on their hands

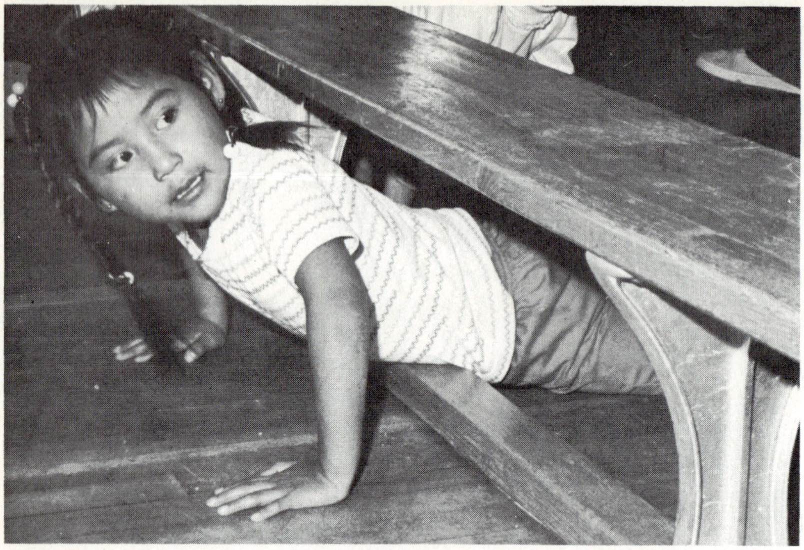

Fig. 6-17 *Under the bridge.*

Fig. 6-18
"Manipulating" the ball.

for jumping their feet over a rope, in and out of a hoop, and over a bench. These activities can be explored with the body curled or stretched.

5. *Manipulative skills*
   a. *Ball skill development.*

   At first children simply can "play" with balls of different sizes. They will enjoy rolling a ball and chasing after it, and many will be able to bounce and catch a large ball. Some children will even try to kick a ball and throw it with two hands. The teacher can assist by suggesting that the children work on keeping their eyes on the ball since their attention often will be elsewhere. The teacher should remember that children of this age can learn to throw a small, tennis-size ball with one hand but usually need a larger ball (6 to 10 inches) in diameter in order to catch with two hands.

   Examples

   Start by having children work individually with a ball.

   "Find some ways to move the ball around the space."

   "How many different parts of your body can you use to move the ball?"

Fig. 6-19 *How far will it go?*

"Can you keep the ball close to you?"
The teacher may have the children sit facing a partner several yards away, with feet spread apart. The children should roll the ball back and forth with the hands, then with the feet. Next, each child may take a ball and bounce and catch it from a sitting position, then toss it up gently and catch it. They can roll a ball away, chase after it, catch it and bounce it low and high.

Fig. 6-20 *Partner work.*

The children may roll a ball against a wall and try to retrieve the rebound, roll a ball to hit a milk carton, catch a rolled ball in a plastic scoop, and later, after gaining more skill, catch a thrown ball in a scoop. The teacher can have children throw a tennis ball for distance. The teacher may be able to help by asking if stepping forward helps the throw, and if so, which foot is best. Children may also be asked if they can start a throw by standing sideways.
The children may stand and bounce a ball to a partner. The range of skill development will be wide and the teacher needs to provide assistance when needed and allow plenty of free play time with the balls. Young children can throw and catch a large (6- to 10-inch) ball with a partner. The teacher should have plenty of fleece or yarn balls available as well as balloons and frisbees. Children can try to keep balloons up in the air by using different body parts or hit them over a net which is about head high. Pre-school children also enjoy playing with a small cage ball. Other manipulative skills can be gradually introduced, such as:

Fig. 6-21 *Some free play.*

Manipulating a ball with the feet.

The teacher should encourage children to find different ways to move a ball using the feet. They can try to keep the ball close, change direction, pathway, and speed, and find ways to stop the ball using the feet. They also may try to pass the ball to a partner using the feet only or to kick it against a wall or at a target such as cones or milk cartons. The class can share the ideas developed.

b. *Striking Skills*

Using light paddle bats and fleece balls or badminton shuttle cocks, children can be encouraged to try to hit the ball or shuttle up in the air. Using plastic hockey sticks, they may hit fleece balls, plastic pucks, or small milk cartons. Children may also be encouraged to hit Whiffle balls from batting tees by using light plastic softball bats.

c. *Large apparatus activities*

Very often the equipment needed to challenge pre-school children, such as climbing apparatus, has not been made available to them on the playground, in school, or in other facilities. However, many novel pieces of equipment now are appearing in parks and on school playgrounds. The teacher again is responsible for careful supervision and safety.

Fig. 6-22 *One way to move the ball!*

As part of a movement program for pre-schoolers, children should be able to play on climbing frames, horizontal ladders, turning bars, swings, and slides. There should be enough equipment available so that children do not need to wait for a chance to use it. The teacher can present the children with verbal tasks and challenges pertaining to the apparatus. For example, the teacher may ask children to find different ways to cross the ladder, or explore different ways to hang from the bar. Again, the teacher is responsible for carefully supervising and ensuring the safety of the children.

6. *Rhythmic and Expressive Movement*

Because of the unifying framework intrinsic to movement education, the teacher should have little difficulty in developing the expressive component of movement. Many of the tasks and themes will be similar to those utilized for the functional component; however, the way in which children's responses are used will vary. Determining what is an expressive response, as compared to a functional response, will depend on the way the movement is interpreted by the teacher and the child. The child's responses will need to be evaluated from a different perspective since the teacher is seeking to encourage the development of the child's inner resources as well as his or her movement vocabulary.

Fig. 6-23 *Half way across.*

7. As the pre-schoolers' coordination, sense of timing, and rhythm improve they can begin to participate in activities that utilize rhythm. Using a drum or other percussion instrument, the teacher can encourage children to respond to a beat by moving a part of the body. Children can tap or clap in time, and they can learn to listen and control the movement of different body parts. Music can be added after the children have shown some mastery of the basic concepts.

The following paragraphs present an outline that can assist in developing a program for pre-school and kindergarten children.

PROGRAM OUTLINE

1. Identification and movement of body parts.
2. Locomotor activities.
3. Non-locomotor activities.
4. Manipulative activities.
5. Action words and singing games.

PROGRAM CONTENT

Explore and discover—The identification and movement of individual body parts.

What can move?—Head, shoulders, arms, elbows, hands, fingers, hips, trunk, knees, ankles, feet, and toes.

Keywords: Where—In different directions, at different levels, in different pathways.

How—Quickly—slowly. Rhythmically, to a beat. Heavily—lightly. Directly—indirectly. Using flow.

Relationship—Near to, far away from. Move toward, move away from.

Implementation

Teacher begins with children sitting down. This activity essentially involves individual work at this stage.

Examples

"Let your head move in any direction you like. Good! I see forward and backward and side to side movement. Can anyone find another way to move the head? Experiment with slow and fast movements. Try moving the head to the beat of a drum."

The teacher may have children explore movements of other body parts.

"Where can you move your hands in the space around you? Try high above you, behind you, or right out in front. Try moving your hands and arms really slowly (or quickly).

"Touch your shoulders. Now see if you can move one shoulder. Now try both shoulders. How can they move?" (Children may move the shoulders up and down, forward and backward, in a circle, etc.)

"What other body parts can we move? Where and how can they move?" (Children can share their ideas.)

"See if you can tap the floor with your hands or feet, keeping time with the drum beat. Try with feet together . . . now far apart . . . far away from your body . . . now close to you."

"Try clapping. Clap loudly, then softly. Clap in different places. Build a simple sequence using clapping and tapping."

The teacher can work on developing children's control, that is, stopping when the drum stops.

"Can you shake your fingers? Your feet?"

"Can you make your arms (legs) shiver (shake)?"

"Find some different ways to make your arms (legs) move smoothly (jerkily)."

"Curl and stretch your fingers (or arms)." (Children may use different speeds and directions, and may move both the fingers and arms together or alternately.)

"See if you can make your hands and arms bounce."

"Make different patterns or shapes in the air. Describe shapes, letters, or numbers using different body parts, such as the nose, hands and arms, or feet."

The teacher can pick up ideas from the children's responses and develop them. The teacher should allow children to share their ideas and should reinforce and praise original movements. Wide variations in children's movement responses are to be expected, and the teacher should permit children to repeat movements in order to develop more quality. Remember to present tasks in question form rather than as direct commands.

Explore and discover—The wide variety of possible ways to move on the feet, using simple combinations and sequences.

What movement?—Walking, running, hopping, skipping, leaping, jumping, or other activity.

Keywords:

Where—Direction, pathway, level.

How—Quickly or slowly, heavy or light.

Body shape, relationship, floor pattern.

Implementation.

The teacher should utilize all the floor space possible in order to develop the child's movement.

Examples

"Explore all parts of the available space by moving any way that you like." (The teacher should monitor and reinforce good ideas.)

The teacher may use cues or questions to encourage the children's use of direction, pathway, speed, and variety of movement. Children should be aware of others in the class who are also moving and should try to stay far away from them.

The teacher may bring the children's attention to the difference between heavy and light movements.

"How does your body feel when you are heavy (light)?"

Let the children move in different ways, freezing in different shapes on a signal. Use shape words such as wide, big, spiky, straight, thin, long, round, small, and twisted.

"Find a way to move by taking very big steps." (Emphasize direction.)

"Lay your hoop on the floor and find some different ways to jump around it. Let's move around all the hoops, and on the signal, find an empty hoop and make a shape in it."

"Try to run and jump. Make sure your landing is soft."

"Jump and turn. Jump high in place."

"Hop on one foot."

"Skip forward, side-slide, or side gallop."

"Move stiffly (loosely)."

"Who can find a way to bounce like a ball?"

"As you move about, what are your arms doing? Can you move without using your arms? Can you make some different shapes as you move?"

"Emphasize different body parts as you move. Show me your elbows as you move (or hands, head, knees, feet, etc.)."

"Develop simple sequences of walk—run—walk—run, or walk—hop—walk." (Children can develop other sequences.)

The teacher may have children make floor patterns.

"Pretend you were moving in new snow. Make some straight tracks (discuss straight). Make circles, triangles, zig-zag tracks, spirals. Write letters in the snow."

Observing movement

The careful observations of the teacher can produce suggestions concerning the children's movements that will help obtain quality of movement. The teacher may make such comments such as:

"Try that movement again, only a little lighter this time."

"Could you do that a little slower?"

"Did you mean to do the movement that way?"

"Let's do that again and really stretch those fingers this time."

Rhythms

The teacher can use a drum or other percussion instrument to pick up the rhythm of the children's movements as they walk, run, hop, and skip. Music also can be used to encourage or stimulate different kinds of locomotor movement; however, the use of music too soon in the program can sometimes hinder the development of expressive movement. If used, music should be carefully chosen for its clarity of phrase and rhythm. Children can also accompany themselves with percussion instruments.

Use of Imagery

Asking children to move like frogs or rabbits has probably been overdone as a stimulus for getting children to perform different kinds of movements. If we want to develop creative and expressive movement in children, it is much better if they learn to respond to movement tasks based on the framework of what, where, and how the body can move. Instead of saying, "Be a frog," the teacher can focus on how a frog moves, where a frog lives, or what sounds they make, in terms of the kinds of effort qualities the teacher wishes to elicit.

Explore and discover—Non-locomotor activities.

What:—Curling and stretching (bend/stretch, open/close, rise/fall), twisting, turning.

Keywords:

Where—Direction, pathway, level.

How—Heavy or light. Firm or fine touch.

On different body supports.

With different body parts leading or initiating movement.

Change of speed, fast or slow. (Sudden/sustained.)

In dance, the qualities inherent in the movement factors of time, weight, and space often are referred to as sudden and sustained, firm and fine, and direct and indirect movement, respectively.

Implementation.

- Curling and stretching.

From different starting positions on the feet, back, side, hands, knees, etc., children may practice curling and stretching. The teacher may introduce the idea of going up and coming down (rising and falling, opening and closing).

"Which body parts are leading or initiating the stretch? Try stretching at different speeds or while changing the speed of the stretch. Make a quick or sudden stretch. Make a slow or sustained curl."

Children may explore rocking movements, supporting body weight on different parts. This utilizes the factors of direction and level. The children may explore twisting movements in sitting, standing, and lying positions. The teacher may choose some ideas to develop and repeat.

- Action words.

Words that suggest movement can be used as the child's movement vocabulary expands. At first these words should be used singly, and then two at a time. Examples of action words are stiff, loose, spin, turn, shake and shiver, explore, collapse.

Explore and discover—Manipulative activities.

What?—Children may use a balloon, newspaper, ribbon on a stick, crepe paper streamer, lummi, rhythm sticks, or mimetics.

Keywords: Where?—Direction, level, pathway.

How?—Heavy/light, sudden/sustained.

Body supports, body parts.

Implementation

Examples

"Find some ways to keep a balloon up in the air. Can you move as slowly as the balloon? Can you touch the floor as softly as your balloon? Can you grow and stretch as I blow up the balloon? What happens to the balloon when I let it go without tying the end? Can you move like the balloon did?"

"Try to keep the balloon up when you are sitting down."

"Try hitting the balloon up very softly. Now hit it harder."

"Can you move about and keep the balloon up in the air?"

"What different body parts can you use to keep the balloon up?"

"Use half a sheet of newspaper. Put it on the floor and find some different ways to jump over it. Hop around it." (The teacher may use other movements as well.)

"Hold the paper up in the air and let it float down to the

floor. Can you move like your piece of paper did?"
"Roll your paper up into a ball and see how far you can throw it. Pretend you are having a snowball fight."
"Use your ribbon on a stick to make some different patterns in the air by waving the stick about." (This explores levels, pathways, speeds, and direction.)

Mimetics

Children can mime such actions as sweeping, washing the car, shoveling snow, sawing wood, using a screwdriver, using a hammer, mowing the lawn, driving a car, pushing the car, using different sports skills, walking in space, and pretending to be robots. These actions may be exaggerated and accompanied by sounds. Actions can be explored using the movement factors. Children also enjoy singing games such as *Mulberry Bush, Looby Loo, Farmer in the Dell,* and other similar songs or nursery rhymes. Teachers also can use their own ideas based on poems and stories.

Expressive movement also can be developed in response to words that convey emotion or feeling such as happiness, sadness, or fatigue. Different kinds of movement words can elicit a response, for example, move stiffly or loosely, shake, shiver, twist, or collapse.

Dance and rhythmic activities can be tried as children work toward developing basic locomotor, non-locomotor, and manipulative skills. Sequences can be formulated and functional and expressive movements combined.

Music, speech, and drama teachers often are willing to work with the movement teacher to develop activities for pre-school and kindergarten children.

Study Guide

To begin, the reader should look at the references in Chapter 3 by Smart and Smart (1977), Sinclair (1973), and Espenschade and Eckert (1980). These deal with the pre-school child.

Gesell, Arnold L. *The First Five Years of Life.* New York: Harper and Brothers, 1940.
This is a classic text pertaining to the young child.

Gallahue, David L. *Motor Development and Movement Exploration for Young Children Ages 3–7.* New York: John Wiley and Sons, Inc., 1976.

Flinchum, Betty M., and Hanson, Margie R. "Who Says the Young Child Can't." *In Journal of Health, Physical Education and Recreation.* June 1972, pp. 16–19.

Seminar Questions and Activities

1. Outline a curriculum for three- and four-year-old children that a teacher who had very little background in physical education could use.
2. How important is it to work toward the development of correct motor patterns when children begin learning how to run and jump and throw and catch?
3. Observe pre-school children at play. Concentrate on one child for about 20 minutes and list all the activities of the child during this period. Comment on your observations. (Making a videotape is a possibility here!)
4. Find a school or other facility in which you actually can work with pre-school children and try out some of the suggestions made in this chapter.

7 the program for kindergarten, first, and second grades

Kindergarten

It is suggested that a teacher who is planning to study this chapter should first read the previous chapter on the program for the three and four year olds as well as the description of kindergarten-age children found on pages 53 to 56. This will provide the reader with background material and a feeling for what the five year old is like. If the teacher of kindergarten children then reviews fairly systematically the activities suggested in Chapter 6 for pre-school-age children, an indication of the kindergartner's physical and intellectual status and skill levels can be obtained. The kindergarten child is about five years old and ready for all kinds of movement experiences.

Many kindergarten children must adjust to a new situation as they make the transition from home to school, but many children already will have had exposure to a day care or pre-school setting. In some schools physical education or movement is taught by the kindergarten teacher, while in others instruction is provided by a specialist teacher. Quite often the children are in school for half a day, but it is recommended that at least 30 minutes be set aside for a movement period if the day is fairly structured, otherwise children can participate in movement activities at different times during the school day. Because of the childrens' urge to be active, teachers may find it beneficial to provide at least two opportunities in addition to recess and lunch-time play during which children may participate in activities. More time can be devoted to involving children in movement exploration as well as providing time for free play.

SPACE AND EQUIPMENT

If kindergarten classes are conducted in the regular school, the movement period may be scheduled in the location normally designated for the school movement program; however, the primary and intermediate grades usually use separate outside playground areas. There may also be climbing apparatus and a blacktop area located outside. A list of equipment suitable for kindergarten children is given in the Appendix.

One of the difficulties encountered in providing equipment in the elementary school is the problem of acquiring equipment that can be utilized by both kindergartners and sixth graders. For indoor work, having the necessary equipment for climbing, hanging, swinging, balancing and so on is a high priority. The apparatus needs to be versatile and challenging for all grade levels.

Fig. 7-1 *Apparatus stations.*

Much can be improvised, but the space used for movement often appears very sterile compared to the usually rich and stimulating environment of the classroom setting.

Getting equipment out and putting it away can be a problem, especially with large pieces used for climbing and balancing. Generally equipment cannot be left out and must be stored and locked away. Small equipment such as balls, bean bags, jump ropes, and milk cartons can be kept in sturdy cardboard cartons or plastic laundry baskets. It is probably better to distribute such equipment among several containers rather than store everything in the same container in order to facilitate access to and distribution of the equipment. Children can learn to collect and put equipment away in the proper box or container.

ORGANIZATION OF MOVEMENT PERIODS

Twenty minutes is commonly allocated for teaching physical education or movement to kindergartners. This amount of time is rather unrealistic in terms of conducting a satisfactory program, especially if the class meets only three times a week. The first priority for the teacher then becomes to try to schedule a daily class period of at least 30 minutes. Of course, the classroom teacher can supplement the physical education program by providing opportunities for additional movement during the day.

PROGRAM CONTENT

The program should center around teaching locomotor, non-locomotor, and manipulative movements, rhythmic activities, and dance and games. Before embarking on a program the teacher should outline the scope and sequence of program activities for the year. (Readers might now want to examine Chapter 10, which elaborates on many of the problems associated with planning a program.) The key at this level is to remember that children may have a short attention span if not interested, and can tire fairly easily if one activity is pursued for too long a time. Successful experience is very important. (See Chapter 2 for a review of program objectives.)

The teacher should formulate a list of themes which can be utilized over several periods. Probably more than one theme will be used each time; however, a balance of activities from the three main areas of program content should be maintained, with vigorous activities interspersed with those which are quieter. Frequent review of all skills should be included in the program.

Developing the Program

It is important to remember again that there will be wide variations in children's abilities and in their degree of maturation and readiness to learn motor skills. Often teachers merely teach games and expect—or hope—that all the children will somehow learn the necessary skills. Some children do develop skill in such a way, but many others do not make much progress and fall farther and farther behind. The teacher's primary responsibility, however, is to ensure that all children learn, not just those who are gifted or talented.

Sample lesson plans are provided following the description of program ideas. The teacher may wish to utilize part of the time in structured exploration, with the rest used for practice and supervised but free play.

Program Themes*

LOCOMOTOR THEMES

Different ways of moving on the feet.
Moving and learning to be aware of others.

Fig. 7-2 *Moving on different parts.*

Moving on different body parts.
Different ways of jumping and landing.
Different ways of rolling.
Supporting the body weight on the hands.
Exploring climbing apparatus.
Building sequences of locomotor movements.

NON-LOCOMOTOR THEMES

Exploring range of movement at the shoulder, spine, hip, and ankle joints.
Different ways of twisting.
Different ways of rocking.
Balancing on different body parts.
Different ways to cross a balance beam.
Exploring hanging and swinging on apparatus.

MANIPULATIVE THEMES

Exploring manipulating a ball using different body parts.
Exploring manipulative activities using bean bags, frisbees, balloons, whiffle bats, hoops, scoops, and deck tennis rings.

Locomotor Skills

The teacher describes themes and gives keywords to aid in developing the themes. He or she provides ideas for implementation. In moving on the feet, the skills of walking, running, hopping, skipping, galloping, and other ways of moving are to be developed. Jumping and landing are explained in a later theme. The process the teacher should utilize is: Explore and discover, analyze, select, and repeat.

1. *Explore and discover*
   Theme:
   Different ways of moving on the feet.
   Keywords:
   Where (space)—*Different directions. Different pathways.*
   How (speed)—*Changing speeds, stopping* and *starting.* (force)—*Different amounts of force, e.g., heavy, light/soft.*
   Discussion

   The teacher will start the children moving by asking questions or setting tasks, generally for the entire group. Teacher–student ratios at the kindergarten level might be 1 to 12, but by using the ideas presented in this book the teacher will be able to work with larger groups. Of course, the larger the group the less the amount of individual attention that will be possible.

   Note: Early lessons for children to learn are to listen while moving and also to work in one's own space. As children start moving about it is important that they avoid collisions and learn to adjust their movements to the movements of others. As discussed earlier in the section on pre-school children, the students should learn to work quietly in their bare feet or sneakers, and not interfere with others.

Implementation

Further tasks, based on themes, can be developed.

Examples

"Show me some ways that you know of moving on your feet."

"Good. Susan is running and Jennie is skipping. Who else can skip?"

"As you move, remember to keep far away from other people."

"Everybody seems to be moving at the same speed. Who can move more quickly or more slowly sometimes?"

The teacher should continuously move around the class to pick up ideas from the children and relay them back to the class again. In observing children the teacher should look at the quality of the movements. Are the children moving with control? Are they moving lightly? Are they aware of other people? Do they respond well to a signal to stop?

The teacher's goal is to develop most of the more usual locomotor skills as well as various other ways of moving. The teacher may say "How could you move if your feet were tied together?" or "Find some ways to move on different parts of your feet." In order to acquire an awareness of others the teacher should have the children move, but within a smaller space, that is, using half the gym, then only a quarter of the gym. The teacher should suggest changes of speed and direction as the children move and praise them for moving without contact.

- The teacher can have the children stand on the four sides of a fairly large square or rectangular area and suggest they find different ways to cross to the other sides. At first the teacher can suggest walking across, running, hopping, or skipping, going straight across, or weaving about. Children may move across on different body parts or go in different directions. The teacher should stress that children are to avoid any collision or contact.
- After the children have had plenty of practice in

moving using the variables of speed, direction, pathway, and relationship, the teacher can have them play simple tag and chasing games. For variation, the children may chase a partner, play tail tag (everyone has a tail except two or three chasers), or couple tag. (For this game, two people join hands and chase the rest. Everyone who is caught joins hands to make one long chain, or joins hands with a partner as others are tagged, with each new pair also chasing the rest of the children.)

Children also may play any kind of game in which some children (the dodgers) must cross a space and get past children who are chasers. The teacher should stress that the good dodgers *do not* get caught, but should avoid putting too much pressure and stress on them in the early stages of the game.

- The teacher should encourage the development of *sequences,* such as a combination of running, hopping, and skipping. Sequences may include a change of speed and direction, but variations should be added one at a time.

Children also may follow the leader in groups of two, three, or four, changing the leader frequently. They also may move to a beat or music. The teacher may ask children "How does the beat tell you to move?"

The teacher must remember to avoid eliminating children from games and other activities. Usually the children who are eliminated are those who need the most practice!

2. *Explore and discover*
Theme: Different ways of moving on other body parts. Children can be encouraged to explore ways of moving on the hands and feet, front, back, and hands and knees.
Keywords:
Same as for component 1. Different ways of moving on the feet.
Discussion

The children will discover all kinds of ways to move in response to tasks. If they move on their hands and feet as they explore the possibilities of moving at different speeds, in various directions, and on different levels, they will also be developing strength and agility. Many of the movements will not have any real functional value or immediate application, although much of the work will involve supporting the body weight and perhaps pushing or pulling the body against resistance as it slides along the floor, which will benefit arm and shoulder muscles and help in later activities that require use of these muscles.

Implementation

Tasks will again be based on the main theme. The teacher may need to provide certain cues or keywords to get the children started, but they will soon understand what is expected if they are presented with a challenge and creativity is encouraged.

Examples

"Who can show me a way to move on his or her tummy?"

"Look at Jane. Which part of her body is moving her along? That's good, Jane. Now see if you can move like that in different directions (or at different speeds)."

"How else can you move if your body stays close to the floor (low level)?"

"See if you can find three different ways to move on your hands and feet."

The teacher must provide the children with an opportunity to repeat their movement responses. Sometimes half the class may watch while the other half works through their ideas. The question might be asked as to which responses children should repeat. In answer to this, the first thing a teacher should look for is whether the responses answer the problem the task presented. The teacher may want to be sure that all children practice moving on their hands and feet or watch as someone performs an activity that they all could then try. Most responses can be repeated and developed by using keywords. This is especially important at the kindergarten level, as children are beginning to learn about their own limitations and abilities.

3. *Explore and discover*

Theme: Different ways of jumping and landing. *Note:* The suggested activities for pre-school children should be reviewed.

Keywords:

Direction, force (heavy or light).

Note:

The five basic ways of jumping are:

- Take off on two feet, land on two feet.
- Take off on two feet, land on one foot.
- Take off on one foot, land on two feet.
- Take off on one foot, land on same foot (hop).
- Take off on one foot, land on the other foot (leap).

Soft landings should be stressed.

Through guided discovery the teacher can direct children toward discovering these basic jumps. Jumping can be explored using different directions or with a twist. The teacher can acquire ideas from the children, for example:

"Look at Jimmy. He's jumping off on two feet and landing on two."

"Who can think of or show me another way to jump?"

Implementation

Generally the teacher should start jumping activities on the floor. It does help, however, to provide an object for children to jump over or down from. Lines can be taped or chalked on the floor, and boxes, milk cartons, canes, or broomsticks can be laid across the lines or on blocks. Children can work individually or with a partner.

Examples

"Arrange the equipment so that you have something to jump over. Don't forget the soft landings."

"Did you try to jump sideways yet?"

"That was a good landing, Susan. So nice and soft."

As with pre-schoolers, the children can start their jumps at floor level, jumping in and out of hoops or shapes made by a jump rope, or over tiles or lines. As the children become ready for more challenge, the teacher can set up cross bars (positioned in a sloping

Fig. 7-3 *Using a hoop for jumping.*

fashion to allow for individual differences), raise the height of objects to be jumped over, or increase the distance between two lines. Children will soon let the teacher know if the object they are jumping over is not high enough or if it is too high. The children may work with a partner and take turns at making a shape by holding out an arm or leg which the other partner may jump over. One partner may hold a hoop at different heights as the other explores ways to jump in and out of the hoop.

The teacher may stand in the middle of a circle of children and swing a long pole or stick around the circle; as the stick goes around, the children jump over it in turn. The same idea can be tried utilizing a bean bag tied to a rope. Children may also practice the standing long jump, if possible on a mat or carpet.

Children can combine different kinds of locomotor skills with jumps in sequences. Rolling is important and should be encouraged after various jumps. A sequence might include a run, jump, roll, and balance. Other combinations may be tried. Children enjoy the idea of stepping stones, which can be made of hoops, tires, or chalked circles. Hop scotch can be introduced gradually. Children also will enjoy using the agility ramp and doing a variety of jumps and landings, followed by a roll. They also can be encouraged to make different shapes in the air as they jump.

Fig. 7-4 *Jump the stick.*

When the apparatus for jumping is used, the children may also find ways to go under it rather than over it. They can also place their weight on their hands and try to jump their legs over the bar.

Non-locomotor skills

Kindergarten children need to participate in a wide variety of movements that utilize the large muscles and include activities to develop flexibility of all joints (a full range of movement), and strengthen the major muscle groups. Activities such as curling, stretching, twisting, rocking, climbing, hanging, swinging, and supporting weight on the hands all provide the movement needed and may be developed as themes through the use of the movement factors. Formal calisthenics are not the best way to develop positive attitudes in young children about exercise and activity. Balance skills, using static balance (in place) or dynamic balance (on the move), need to be developed.

1. *Explore and discover*
   Theme: Rolling in different ways.
   Keywords:
   These are italicized in the following paragraphs.
   Implementation
   In developing non-locomotor skills children may practice the following:
   Rolling with the body *curled* up.
   Rolling in different *directions*—forward, sideways, backward.
   Rolling *stretched* out—"log" roll.
   Rolling *forward* with a bean bag tucked under the chin.
   Balancing then rolling.
   Rolling then balancing.
   Rolling *smoothly* and *softly.*
2. *Explore and discover*
   Theme: Activities in which the weight is partially supported on the hands.
   Implementation
   The activities can help children acquire the skills of this component:
   Moving in different ways on hands and feet (face down, face up).
   Changing *direction* and *speed.*
   Using hands and feet alternatly.
   Moving from feet to hands to feet, etc.
3. *Explore and discover*
   Theme: The possible range of movements at joints, especially the shoulder, spine, and hip joints.
   Keywords:
   What—Moving body parts (arms and legs), by curling,

Fig. 7-5 Supporting the weight in different ways.

stretching, and twisting, in different shapes.
Where—Direction, pathway, level.
How—Slowly, quickly

Discussion

Children can explore all the possibilities of hand and arm movement using circling movement, bends, or stretches. The same can be done with the feet and legs. Arms and legs can move singly or together. Activities can be tried in standing, sitting, and lying positions.

Curling and stretching movements can be done from different starting positions, for example, sitting, lying, or kneeling.

Examples

**Dance and rhythmic activities suitable for kindergarten are discussed in Chapter 6.*

"Let's sit down. Now show me all the different places you can reach and stretch to using one hand." (Repeat using two hands.)
"Remember, space is all around you—above, below, behind, and in front."
"Have you explored all the possible places in space you can reach?"
"Try doing this with your foot and legs—slowly at first, then more quickly."
"Let me see who can make a 'bridge' shape with their body by using four supports. Make a high bridge. Now make a long

bridge. Try a wide bridge and a twisted bridge."

"Make a sequence of some different kinds of bridges."

"Hold a ball in both hands above your head. Now see if you can make the ball move in a very big circle, first slowly, then quickly."

Analyze and select

As the responses of individual children are observed the teacher may comment on them and discuss them. In conjunction with the teacher, children can select activities they should repeat and refine. Such activities may include those which the teacher wants all children to be able to do (guided discovery), or tasks which the children are developing on their own (problem solving). Children at the kindergarten level can be asked to practice activities which they enjoy, or those which the teacher may see as appropriate, original, and creative. The paragraphs below describe which can be developed.

4. *Explore and discover.*

   Theme: Different ways of twisting the body using different starting positions.

   Keywords

   Twisting on the feet. Sitting with body erect.

   Sitting with body bent forward.

   Lying down, twisting upper or lower half of the body.

   Speed—Twisting is best done slowly.

5. *Explore and discover*

   Theme: Different ways the body can rock.

   Different ways to rock the body:

   Stretched out, curled up.

   On different surfaces and lying on the front or back.

   On hands and knees.

   On the feet.

   In different directions—forward and backward, sideways.

   Create and Develop—A sequence of different kinds of rocking movements can be developed. Children may practice the sequence.

6. *Explore and discover*

   Theme: Balance on different body surfaces. Explore ways to cross a balance beam.

   Keywords: Keywords or phrases are italicized.

   Implementation

   Children may balance on different body surfaces, such as on one foot, on the back, front, hands, or knees.

   Examples

   "Use any two, three, or four *supports* to balance."

   "While balancing, *change the body shape.* Make a big shape. Make a small shape."

   "Stretch out a jump rope and try to balance walk along the rope."

Fig. 7-6 *Some different balances.*

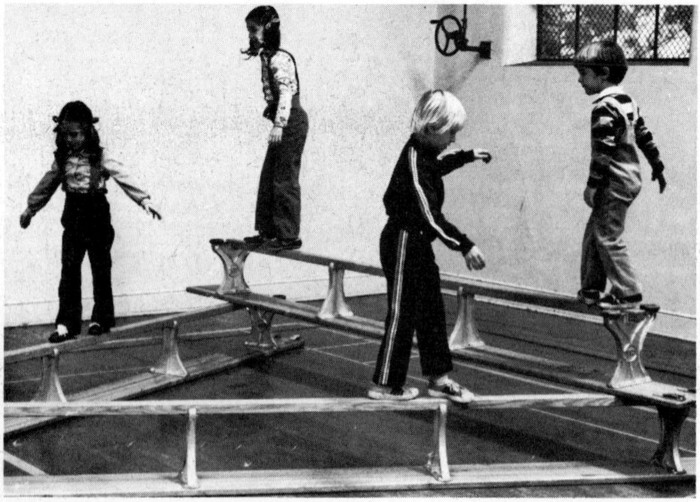

Fig. 7-7 *A balance course.*

"Find some *different ways to cross* the balance beam." (Employs the factors of *direction* and *level).*

The teacher should attempt to *create a challenge*

Examples

"While crossing the beam, step through a hoop or over a milk carton (or other obstacle)."

"Try crossing the beam with your arms held out sideways. Now put them at your sides. Which way is easiest or helps you to balance?"

"Try to balance on a rocking or balance board. Stand up on the board. Sit down on the board."

7. *Explore and discover*

Theme: Activities on apparatus that involve climbing, hanging, and swinging.

Implementation

The teacher may develop the theme on available apparatus, including climbing frames, trestles with ladders and planks, turning or horizontal bars, parallel bars, etc.

Examples

"Find some different ways to climb or cross *over* (or *under*) the apparatus."

"Find some different ways to hang from a bar."

"Find some ways to *get on* (or *move along, move over,* or *move around*) the apparatus and then *get off.*"

"Hold tightly to a climbing rope or sit on a knot tied in the rope. *Swing* gently."

"Hang from a bar and let your body swing *forward (backward, sideways).*"

Discussion

The teacher can look at the lesson plan given at the end of this section for assistance in developing a program. Merely making lists and mechanically going through each item generally will produce dull teaching and boring movement periods. Knowing when to present another task, provide a cue, or wait for things to happen may not be easy for the teacher to decide. Also, the teacher's desire to demonstrate to children exactly what should be done may be very strong, especially if the teacher feels time is short and the class should be moving along more quickly. However, being patient and allowing the children to develop their skills gradually are important aspects in the art of teaching.

The teacher essentially must mentally review the framework of what, where, and how an activity is to be conducted in order to be prepared to inject the appropriate cue or question at the right movement. Each teacher then will be prepared to develop children's movement responses in his or her own way.

Manipulative Skills

The kindergarten child enjoys playing with a ball and will happily spend a lot of time chasing, bouncing, throwing, or catching a ball. Kicking and striking skills present a challenge to the five year old. It is essential that children have plenty of time to practice as well as for periodic review of skills.

1. *Explore and discover*

   Theme: Manipulating a ball.

   Keywords: Direction, level, pathway.
   Fast, slow, getting faster, slowing down.
   Heavy—light/soft/gentle.

   Implementation

   "Each child should have a 6- to 10-inch playground ball in order to practice the skills of this component.

   Examples

   "Move the ball around the room on the floor with any part of your body (hands, feet, nose, knees, etc.). Keep the ball *close to you.*"
   "Change direction. Change speed."
   "Go in a *straight* line. Move in *different pathways.*"
   "Roll the ball away. Now chase after it and catch or stop it."
   "Bounce the ball using two hands."

Fig. 7-8 *Bounce—and catch?*

"Bounce the ball using one hand." (Children may do this in place or moving around, using different body supports, that is, sitting, standing, kneeling, etc.)

Self testing

"How many bounces can you make without losing the ball?"

Toss and catch

"How softly can you catch?"

With a partner. "Sit down facing your partner and roll the ball to him or her."

"*Bounce the ball* to your partner."

"Move the ball to your partner using only your feet."

"Stand up. Now toss and catch the ball with your partner."

"Roll a ball against a wall and stop the rebound."

"Roll a ball and try to hit a milk carton."

Balloons

"Try to keep a balloon up in the air using your hands and feet." (Children may use other body parts as well.)

"Hit a balloon to your partner over the net." (The net should be almost head height.)

Using a ball

"Children may throw a ball against a wall where there is sufficient space available, either indoors or out. They may try both underarm and overarm throws. Children may try stepping forward with the opposite foot, with the body turned sideways. (See the discussion on page 154.)

Analysis and selection

The teacher may assist those children who are developing the skills and correct patterns by directing his or her attention to the various components of the skill, such as arm, body, and leg action, and visual concentration.

2. *Explore and discover*

Theme: Miscellaneous manipulative activities.

Implementation

Children can practice with these skills using plastic hockey sticks and a fleece ball or plastic puck. They also may use light paddle bats to hit a fleece or foam ball and keep it up in the air. (A badminton shuttle could also be used.) A Whiffle (plastic) softball bat may be used to hit Whiffle balls off a batting tee.

The teacher may ask children to find different ways to play a tug-of-war with a partner.

Children may use plastic scoops to throw and catch fleece balls.

Children may throw and catch deck tennis rings and Frisbees.

The teacher can have children slide and toss bean bags into targets.

Discussion

The teacher should review the ideas suggested for pre-schoolers and also look ahead to the chapter on activities for first and second graders.

Each child must have a ball. Some balls can be of about tennis ball size (for throwing) but most should be about 6 to 10 inches in diameter. Remember to have available fleece or yarn balls as well as Nerf (foam) balls and "All" balls (a commercial name for a bouncing foam ball). Kindergartners will enjoy a cage ball (a 30-inch ball) and also balloons.

For much of the time the children can work (play) individually with a ball. The teacher can present tasks for the whole group, for smaller groups, or for individual children. They will need a lot of time to practice. As their coordination, reaction time, and eye and hand coordination mature, so will their ability to work with balls.

The teacher can help individual children, especially with catching. An activity for children who need assistance is to have them hold their hands up in front at about eye level, with the teacher gently tossing the ball into their arms at about the same level. Catching at first will be a kind of clutching movement. Generally children will turn their heads away as the ball approaches, and consequently they are not watching the ball at all. The teacher can emphasize that they need not be afraid of the ball (providing adult-sized, hard basketballs are not used but rather beanbags or yarn balls) and that they should try to keep their eye on the ball. A few successful 'clutches" will help develop confidence and a "can do" feeling. Moving the ball around is a natural extension of the work with locomotor skills that uses the movement factors of direction, speed, level, and pathway. In addition, responding to signals to stop and start and using force (how softly the ball can be caught or how hard it can be thrown) can be introduced.

Guided discovery can be used to develop the proper throwing action (*i.e.*, stepping forward with the opposite foot, standing sideways, rotating the trunk,coming through with the elbow, and following through). The teacher cannot become too technical and occasional demonstrations may help in this area. Differences between throwing underarm and overarm can be discussed, and the teacher may ask questions such as "What happens when you bounce a ball close to you? Where does the ball go?" "What will happen to the ball if you bounce it farther away?"

Examples

The teacher may use such cues as shown below in developing ball skills using the feet:

"Show me some different ways you can move the ball around with your feet. Who can find a way to stop the ball?"

"Look how Tommy can stop his ball. Lori has another way. That's

good, Lori! What might happen if we stepped on the ball too hard?" (Overbalancing or twisting an ankle may result.)
"As you move the ball around, which part of your foot seems to help you control it best?" (There may be a difference of opinion, but the teacher should strive to have children agree on the use of the *side* of the foot. The teacher may ask how many sides of the foot can be used.
"Can you make the ball change direction as you are moving around?"
"Who can move faster with the ball sometimes?"

The teacher should remember to apply the skills developed in the lessons at this time, especially those skills relating to the use of space, that is, staying away from others and not interfering in their activity. (Generally, each child is so involved with the task that he or she is too busy to "goof off" or create discipline problems.)

Simple games can be introduced, such as kicking a ball between a partner's legs or rolling (bowling) a ball to knock over milk cartons. Circle games are usually not too exciting at this level. Children can be given a ball and another item of equipment, such as an open box, milk carton, hoop, or jump rope, and asked to invent a "game." The teacher also can supply footballs with which the children may practice (soft foam and plastic footballs—the type with holes—are available). Self-testing activities are popular, and children can be challenged to break their own record. Children may be placed in groups of two or three for simple passing activities that are performed both in place and while children move around.

Dance and Rhythmic Activities

Program suggestions pertaining to this area are given in Chapter 6.

SAMPLE FOR KINDERGARTEN CHILDREN

The following sample lesson format consists of an *introduction*, a *lesson focus* (in which themes selected from among those presented earlier are developed), and *applications* (skills developed and derived from the main theme).

Locomotor skills

These skills will emphasize the theme, "change of direction."

1. *Introduction*
   Children will have free practice with a ball, jump rope, or a hoop, and should be encouraged to perform activities that involve a change of direction. (The teacher should move around the class and talk to individual children, offering them suggestions and praising and reinforcing appropriate movements.)

2. *Lesson Focus.*
   a. *Explore and discover*
      (1) *Theme:* The children will move about on their feet and demonstrate changes of direction (guided discovery).
      Examples
      "Let me see you walk using all the space in the gym. When I clap my hands I want you to go in another direction." (The teacher will clap at appropriate intervals.)
      "Don't always turn the same way. Which other ways could you go?"
      "Stop as quickly as you can when I clap twice." (Children practice and the teacher provides feedback as necessary.)
      "Remember to watch out for other people as you change direction and be ready to stop if necessary."
      "That's very good. Now let's try the same thing as we jog."
      "Watch the space around you. When it is crowded, slow down."
      "Now let's see if you can change direction on your own."
      "Keep walking or jogging, but always into an open space." (The teacher may provide additional practice time and offer cues to individuals or to the group.)
      "Stop! All children with blue eyes should sit down in their own space. Now I would like all the children with brown eyes to walk around those with blue eyes. Let's go in and out and around. Watch out for others. Good! Now let's try that running around." (The activity may then be repeated with the brown eyed children sitting. The teacher should make sure the children are spaced well apart.)
   b) Partner Tag. Playing in pairs, one child will chase the other and try to tag him or her. This game should not go on too long. The game may be repeated with the children moving around on their hands and feet. (This requires a much shorter activity time because it is quite tiring.)
3. *Application.*
   a. *Group Work*
      Children are placed in groups of three or four. The teacher will present tasks for the following five equipment stations:
      - Balance beam—children cross using different directions.
      - Tumbling mats—children roll in different directions.
      - Hoops or tires—children hop or run through hoops or tires in different directions.
      - Boxes and poles—these can be arranged for jumping in different directions.
      - Bench—children move along the top in different ways and show a change of direction.

Children should be free to change stations whenever they wish. (The teacher may have provided more structure for this procedure through earlier lessons, that is, the children learned to rotate groups upon a signal from the teacher.)

4. *Conclusion*

Children will put away the equipment and afterward the teacher will talk to them as they are sitting down. The teacher will ask what they have learned and briefly discuss how changes of direction are accomplished, such as by a car or airplane. The teacher may ask which animals can move sideways. A discussion of what the children may do the next period is also useful.

Responding to a rhythmic beat.

1. *Introduction*

The children should be seated in their own space, and the teacher will have a drum.
"See if you can tap your feet on the floor in time with the drum. Stop tapping when the drum stops." (Children practice this activity.)
"Now see if you can tap with your hands and feet."
"How else could you make a tapping or clapping noise?" (Teacher varies the rhythm and picks up ideas from the children and shares these ideas with the class.

2. *Lesson focus.*

a. *Explore and discover*

(1) Theme: Using rhythm sticks to explore ways to respond to a beat. The teacher will distribute two sticks to each child. (The sticks should be half an inch in diameter or slightly larger, and about 12 inches in length.)

Examples

"Find some different ways to tap your sticks together."
"Good! Now try to keep time with me." (The teacher uses drum, the children sticks. The activity is practiced.)
"How else could we tap the sticks? Maybe on the floor, or with your partner?" (Teacher interacts with the children, praising and commenting on their responses)

For the activity, *keywords* pertaining to *where* and *how?* a task is accomplished may refer to the *space* around you, behind, and above the child, or to hitting sticks *softly* or *loudly.*

Examples

"Try to make a pattern of the way you tap, such as

on the floor first and then hitting the sticks together."

"All right. Now let's sit with a partner and make up some patterns as we hit the sticks. Look at Mary and Tim. They have the idea."

"Practice until you can do it smoothly. Make your own rhythm." (Teacher moves around and provides feedback, praise, cues, and help, if needed.)

3. *Application.*

"Can you stand up and move about while tapping your sticks?"

Show me all the places in the space near you where you can tap." (Children may tap their sticks above their heads, behind their backs, at their sides, and at different levels.)

"Find a partner and play 'Follow the Leader.' Copy the patterns made by the leader." (Switch leaders frequently.)

"Now have a rest. Sit down facing your partner. One of you can still be the leader and make some patterns with the sticks. The other partner will try to copy the patterns." (One child will mirror the other.) The teacher can superimpose a rhythm or let the children set their own.

4. *Conclusion*

The teacher may ask the children if they can think of anything that moves to a beat or rhythm, such as the trotting of a horse. Do people move to a rhythm? (The teacher may discuss such activities as walking, running, the beating of the heart, or skipping.) Does music always have a beat?

Judging the force necessary to throw a beanbag different distances.

1. *Introduction*

The teacher should provide a beanbag for each child and plenty of open boxes or cartons of various sizes as well as tires and hoops.

Examples

"Find a space and see how high you can throw your beanbag. Did it go straight up?" (Children should avoid hitting the ceiling) "Did it come down close to you?"

"Try to throw the beanbag up gently so that it comes down close to you."

"Now try throwing the beanbag away from you." Be careful that you do not hit anyone!"

"When did you let go?" (These are not meant to be rhetorical questions and should involve the children in some discussion.)

2. *Lesson focus*

a. *Explore and discover*

(1) *Theme:* Tossing and sliding beanbags at targets and determining the amount of force necessary.

The children should stand behind a scratch line and with an underarm motion try to toss the beanbag so that it lands between two lines approximately three or four yards away and about three feet apart. The teacher will make up tasks and provide cues on the degree of error based on observation. Children can develop skill by tossing the beanbags into boxes of various heights and having different sized openings. The beanbags also may be tossed into tires, hoops, or chalked circles. The children also may slide the beanbag into the target area. The teacher should remember that some children may need more challenge than will others.

3. *Application*
   a. *Group work in stations.*
      - Toss a beanbag into a hoop.
      - Slide a beanbag to knock over a milk carton.
      - Toss a beanbag so that it lands on a chair.
      - Toss or slide a beanbag into a target composed of concentric circles. Bull's-eye scores three points.
      - Toss or throw a beanbag over a rope which is at about head height so that it lands in a target area.
   - Toss a beanbag into open boxes or containers placed at varying distances from a scratch line. The boxes should have different sized openings. Children will rotate on the teacher's signal. Some children may begin to lose interest in this activity, especially if they are not being too successful at it. The teacher can watch for this and be ready with a change of activity.
4. *Conclusion*
   The teacher can discuss with the class what helps in throwing straight. Questions which the teacher may want to ask could include: "Why does the beanbag sometimes go too far or not far enough?" "Was it easier to throw with your right or left hand?" "Would you like to do this again?"

The program for the First and Second Grades

Each section of this text may be considered separately in terms of the teaching material it affords; however, it is recommended that teachers study and understand the information found in the preceding chapter as well as in the chapter that follows since children will exhibit wide variation in skill development, maturity, and in other behavioral characteristics. Some first graders will still need to work on those activities suggested for kindergartners, while others will be ready for activities considered suitable for second graders. It is therefore too simplistic to label activities as being suitable for a certain age or a certain grade level and why it is suggested here that teachers regard this chapter as merely one part of a continuing curriculum.

In comparison to kindergarten children, first and second graders generally are becoming more proficient with most of the locomotor skills. Hand and eye coordination is improving, as is reaction time. Six and seven year olds are ready for more vigorous activity and more challenge than are five year olds. They are capable of more sustained involvement and more readily play together in small groups.

Activities in the program center around developing competence in the basic movement skills, including locomotor, non-locomotor, and manipulative movements. Creative and expressive movement is increasingly important, and simple games can be added to the program. The children can begin to acquire knowledge and understanding about health, exercise, and movement.

PROGRAM THEMES AND ACTIVITIES

The movement program should incorporate the elements listed below.

Locomotor.
- Walk.
- Run.
- Jump.
- Roll.
- Climb.

Non-locomotor.
- Balance.
- Curl, stretch, twist.
- Hang and swing.
- Supporting weight on the hands.

Manipulative.
- Ball skills—throw, catch, roll, kick, bounce, pass.
- Ball games.
- Striking skills.
- Use of large apparatus.

Dance and Rhythms.
- (Activities suitable for use with Grades 1, 2, and 3.)
- Activities suggested for kindergarten.

Moving body parts, both individually and in combination.
Locomotor activities.
Non-locomotor activities.
Manipulative activities.
Developing combined sequences. (Involves individual, partner, and group work.)
Creating dances.

Locomotor movement development

It is important to include some locomotor movements in each lesson. The children of today's society tend to get less and less exercise as many are bussed or driven to school or live in environments that are not conducive to play or vigorous physical activity. The teacher should systematically select certain movement themes or activities to be developed throughout the year and must allocate time for practice and regular review of all the skills developed. Skills to be developed in this age group include walking, running, hopping, skipping, galloping, and jumping while other locomotor movements should emphasize ways of moving on the feet and on other body supports.

The teacher has a choice of approaches in developing the locomotor movements of children. Activities may be developed by asking the children to find different ways to move on different body supports (feet, hands and feet, or other body parts), and their ideas then can be developed through the use of the movement factors. The teacher may use the methods of guided discovery to lead the children toward specific skill development or may encourage development of a broad spectrum of locomotor skills by utilizing children's movement responses in a more open-ended fashion. Alternatively, specific skills, such as walking or running, can be selected and the movement factors applied to the skills to produce variety and allow the child to fully explore the skill.

The activities described in this chapter utilize all of these approaches. Once a teacher understands the possibilities presented by the different approaches he or she will be able to make a well-reasoned choice of the method he or she most prefers to use.

The teacher should understand that in formulating tasks for development of skills, he or she may follow a pattern of applying appropriate keywords and other cues to the children's responses to the initial task. The cues should not be employed mechanically, with little thought or consideration given to why the cue was offered. Different cues should be given to different children based upon the teacher's interpretation of the individual child's particular need. At first this is not an easy task, but if the teacher perseveres he or she will discover that teaching actually becomes easier through this approach.

Explore

Walking. Stress good form (head up, appropriate arm swing from the shoulder, proper heel—toe action with feet straight forward).

Keywords

Where—Moving in different *directions*, moving in different *pathways*.

How—Walking with different step *size*, walking on different *parts* of the feet, walking with changes of *speed*.

Relationships—Walking *far away* from others, walking *close* to others, walking *behind* (*beside*, *in front* of) someone.

Discover

Different ways of walking through application of the keywords and other variables.

Analyze and select

Walking generally is combined with other skills in its application. Selection and analysis can be fairly open ended, but deviations from the normal walking pattern should be noted. Information on fundamental motor patterns can be found in the study guide at the end of the chapter.

Implementation

The teacher can include some walking activities as part of a movement period, or combine walking with another activity. Activity is initiated through tasks and/or cues.

Examples

"Let's walk around the gym." (The children start walking.)

"Does anyone notice anything about the way we are walking?" (For instance, are all the children going in the same direction around a circle?)

"What could we change in our walking?" (This would be an attempt to get the children to start thinking about what they are doing, as well as how they are doing it.)

The direct approach would merely have had the children change their direction and speed, if it even required that much. The teacher usually just made children walk or run, without offering any additional development. However, with the approach suggested in this text, the teacher will want the children to become familiar with the movement factors as well as with other variables. Questions or cues can help in developing the children's skills. It may be difficult initially for the teacher to start the children thinking in terms of direction, speed, force, and the various other aspects of movement, but they gradually will grasp the concepts the teacher is presenting to them.

The teacher can draw ideas from the children rather than tell them exactly what to do and when to do it. For instance, the teacher may say something such as "Mary suggests that we are all going in the same direction. What could we do about that?" After several lessons the children should be able to apply most of the variables themselves when given the opportunity.

The next step would be to develop sequences of walking patterns. The children should select certain aspects to practice and combine.

"Join together three different ways of walking and try to include changes of direction and pathway." The children can explore this idea on their own, then share their ideas. They may try moving in a smaller space, or work on relationships, such as moving far away from (or close to) other children.

Children can play tag games at walking speed. The teacher may place a group of four of five children in each corner of the space, and the group can walk diagonally across the space to the opposite corner. Each group would move in a different way. Groups can move across alternately or singly or even all at once.

Explore

Running. Children can explore running by using all the variables. There are many applications for running in games and in dance.

Discover

Children should discover the ability to run at different speeds and utilizing changes of direction and pathway. The teacher should stress lightness. Children should be able to dodge and swerve, accelerate, and stop and start. They should be aware of others and avoid collisions.

Implementation

After the activities for running and walking have been completed, the movements elicited by these activities can be used in many ways. Children will be able to demonstrate the agility required for chasing and tag games as a result of their work in the movement activities suggested above.

- Chasing and tag games
- One-on-one. Children are in pairs. One person chases and tries to tag the other.
- One against three. This is played in groups of four. Three children join hands to make a small circle, while the fourth child tries to tag a particular child in the circle by going around the outside of the circle. He or she must not go under the children's joined hands.
- Tail tag. All but about five children tuck a "tail" in their belts or pants. Those children without a tail try to get one.
- One against the class. The class lines up at one side of the space. One or more "catchers" try to tag the children as they run across to the other side of the space on a signal from the teacher. *Variations.* In order to decide who will run across, the teacher may call colors (all those who are wearing blue should run, etc.). At Halloween the class may be divided into groups such as ghosts, goblins, witches, etc. Children who are tagged stay in the middle to help catch the rest. *Swim, fish, swim.* Children are "fishes" who try to avoid being caught by several "fishermen." If caught, they sit down in place and can catch others who run by. Children cross on the instruction, "Swim, fish, swim."
- Couple tag. Two children join hands and chase the class. As they are caught the children join on to either make one long chain or new pairs.

Other Kinds of Running Activities

Children can develop endurance for running if taught to jog easily through alternate periods of walking and running. The teacher should gradually decrease the distance walked and increase the distance run, although long distance racing or competition should be avoided at this stage. "Run for fun" should be the slogan for children of this age.

Shorter distances, such as the 30-, 40-, and 50-yard dash, gradually can be introduced. The outdoors is preferable for most running. The teacher should remember not to set the same standard in running activities for everyone!

Explore

Other ways of moving on the feet and on different body parts.

Discover

Different ways of moving on the feet, including hopping, skipping, sliding, and galloping, and on other body parts, especially the hands and feet.

Implementation

One of the reasons for teaching children to skip, slide, and gallop is that these activities often form the basis for folk dance and may possibly be used in dances created by the children themselves. These movements can be combined in a variety of different patterns and used in conjunction with a drum or other percussion instrument or music. Children can invent circle dances for groups of four to six.

Explore

Jumping skills, with a stress on soft, safe landings. Included here will be jumping or skipping rope, and jumping combined with other skills.

Discover

Children will learn their own limitations. They will learn how to set up equipment for jumping, the preferred take-off foot, and how to land softly by absorbing force. They will acquire the essentials for good standing long jump, and jumping with a rebound. Different ways to skip rope can also be emphasized.

Implementation

Teachers should look at the sections on jumping for kindergarten children. As a review, children should progress through:

Jumping over lines on the floor.

Jumping in and out of hoops or tires, or shapes such as circles or triangles made by laying ropes on the floor or with chalk or tape.

Jumping over hurdles made from boxes, milk cartons, canes, broomsticks, or wands.

Jumping over shapes made by a partner.

Fig. 7-9 *Using a hoop another way.*

Jumping down from boxes or other equipment placed at different heights.
Jumping in and out of a hoop held at different heights.
Running and jumping over low hurdles.
Jumping over shapes made by two people.
Standing broad jump.
Running high jump.
Jumping to catch a ball.
Jumping to volley or bat a ball or balloon.

Keywords

Directions: Forward, sideways, backward.
Force: Landing quietly (softly).
Jumping with a *twist or turn.*

Review the five basic jumping patterns discussed earlier, that is, two feet to two feet, two to one, one to two, one to one (hop), one to one (leap). Build sequences using *combinations* of walk, run, hop, skip, jump and land, roll, balance, and leap. Make different body shapes in the air.

Examples

"Share a hoop with a partner. One of you will hold the hoop

about knee high, while the other tries some different ways to jump in and out of it."

"I see some really good ideas. Don't forget to try jumping with one foot and remember the soft landings."

"See if you can find some different ways to jump off the ramp."

"When you land, do some kind of a roll and try to finish standing up on your feet."

"See how far you can jump with a two-to-two kind of jump. How can your arms help you to jump farther?"

"Set up the boxes and poles so that you can jump over the poles at different heights. Try to find a way to go under the crossbar instead of jumping over it. Put your hands on the floor on the other side of the bar and see if you can take your weight on your hands and jump your feet over. Try to bring your feet down softly."

Mats should be used if children are coming off high apparatus. When children use the agility ramp they may try flips off the end, so before allowing children to work on the ramp the teacher should stress that they must come down on their feet first. Avoid situations where children may bruise their heels by landing hard on them.

Jump rope

Children can practice rhythmical jumping on both feet until they can do it consistently for a sequence of several beats. This is done without the rope. They then can hold the rope folded in half in one hand (the rope should be long enough to pass under both feet and reach to about the armpits) and swing it around vertically. If they tap the rope on the floor, they can jump in time with the taps.

The teacher should now show the children how to swing the rope using both hands, keeping the wrists at about hip level and swinging the rope back and over the head. Children should learn to time the jump, jumping just before the rope hits in front. The children may try "jump the shot," jumping over a rope which is turning horizontally. (This requires tying a bean bag or old sneaker to the end of a piece of rope about 10 feet in length.) Children will learn to skip rope at different rates. They can learn a variety of different steps (hopping on one foot, astride jumps, alternating feet, etc.) and also to run while turning the rope.

Explore

Different ways to roll.

Discover

Different body shapes necessary for rolling. Rolling curled up and stretched out. How to use a roll in landing after a jump from apparatus.

Fig. 7-10 *A first attempt.*

Implementation

Children generally should use tumbling or individual mats for rolling and should be encouraged to make efficient use of the mat area (*i.e.*, they should not need to line up and wait for a turn.)

Rocking can be used as a preliminary activity to rolling since it requires that the body weight be transferred onto different parts. Rocking vigorously can lead to a backward or sideways roll. (The front or forward roll usually is approached from a crouch position.) Ask children what shape they have to make in order to roll. (They must be round like a ball.) The teacher may ask the children how they can get themselves into a ball shape. The answer would be to place the hands down first—to break the force of the roll—with the head tucked under. In order to tuck the head properly, the teacher may suggest that the children look at their tummys or tuck a bean-bag under the chin. Many times children will open out in the middle of the roll, but they should be encouraged to stay tucked up. The class may observe the rolls of two children and suggest how they could improve their rolls or make them smoother. The children's attention can be focused on certain parts of the roll, for instance, is the head tucked, is the roll smooth, and is it finished on the feet? Tasks can be presented for reaching and rolling, and for diving and rolling over a rolled-up mat or someone laying across the mat (this must be performed carefully). Jump and roll, and roll and jump are the beginning sequences.

Explore

Climbing activities.

Discover

Children learn about their own limitations with regard to climbing activities requiring use of the hands and arms only and use of the hands and feet.

Implementation

Climbing activity requires climbing ropes, peg boards, climbing frames, cargo nets, etc.

Climbing ropes

Children should find different ways to hang and swing on the rope, including the following:

Swinging on one or two ropes across a marked space, landing and rolling.

Finding some activities to do while holding onto two ropes. (*e.g.*, "Skin the Cat." The feet are kicked up and back over the head to touch the floor, then returned to the starting position. The ropes are held at about eye level.)

Experimenting with different kinds of foot grips. Children should curl and stretch as they climb. (The basic foot grip is

Fig. 7-11 *A climbing challenge.*

Fig. 7-12
Let's swing together.

to cross the legs and catch the rope between the outside edges of the feet.)

Peg board

(See Appendix on equipment for details.) Children hold onto pegs which fit into holes on a board mounted on the wall and climb by moving the pegs.

Climbing frames, trestles, ladders, cargo nets.

Children may find different ways to climb by using the hands only or the hands and feet.

Safety.

The teacher is responsible for seeing that climbing equipment is erected properly, mats placed under equipment. Children should never be forced into doing activities for which they are not ready. This is not to say that children do not need a little urging at times, but the teacher will need to know the children in order to decide if urging is needed. Accidents can happen at any time, but they are more likely to occur when children are pressured into doing activities for which they may be not quite ready.

Explore

Different ways of crossing a balance beam.

Discover

Children learn about their own level of ability in crossing the beam and changing direction.

Fig. 7-13
Climbing in different ways.

Implementation

The teacher should encourage children to try the following:

- *Find different ways to cross the beam.*
- *Go forward, backward, and sideways.*
- *Step over obstacles, such as milk cartons, placed on the beam.*
- *Step through a hoop or under a bar while crossing.*
- *Walk on balance beams placed at different heights.*
- *Walk on a sloping balance beam.*
- *Explore*

Different activities in which the weight is supported on the hands.

Discover

Children learn about their own limitations in supporting body weight on the hands and arms.

Implementation

The teacher should encourage children to try the following:

- Move in different ways on the hands and feet (involves direction, level, pathway, speed, and force).
- Jump the feet around (bringing them down softly), while keeping the hands on the floor.
- Place the hands on a bench and jump the feet over. (The teacher may ask how slowly this can be performed or how high the hips and feet can be lifted.)
- Leap frog over a low box.

- Transfer weight from hand to hand to foot to foot.
- Perform cartwheels.
- Make "bridge" shapes on three or four supports. Bridges may be long, high, or wide, or made with a partner.

Non-locomotor skills

The skills to be explored and developed in this section are balancing, rocking, curling, stretching, twisting, hanging, swinging, and supporting weight on the hands.

Explore: Balance

Activities to try would include:

- Balancing on different body parts used singly or in combination.
- Being in and out of balance (over-balance).
- Balancing on a partner's shape.
- Making different body shapes while balancing.

Discover

The nature of balance, and the difference between balance and stability. Children learn the effect of a change in body shape on balance and ways to balance on a partner.

Implementation

Children may try the following:

- Find body parts on which to balance.
- Balance on one, two, or three supports.

Fig. 7-14
A balance on two parts.

- Change body shape while maintaining balance.
- Develop a sequence of balance shapes.
- Roll out of a balance.
- Balance, roll.
- Balance and roll into another balancing position.
- Build a sequence of run, jump, roll, and balance.
- Find ways to balance on a partner's shape (partner can be kneeling, standing, or lying down).

The children should share their ideas with the class.

Explore: Curl, stretch, twist

As discussed in a previous section, these movements help in developing the flexibility of the joints, including the spine, and the strength of the abdominal muscles, back extensors, and the arm and shoulder girdle.

Discover

Children learn ways in which to develop and maintain flexibility and strength through curling, stretching, and twisting.

Implementation

The teacher may ask children how to stretch the muscles and joints. The class can discuss slow stretching movements and suggest ways of doing them. Some resistance is necessary to develop strength,

Fig. 7-15 *A three-point balance.*

so it would probably be beneficial to have children perform sit-ups (curling up with knees bent. Children may explore:

- Ways to curl up and stretch out from different starting positions (back, side, seat, kneeling). Stretching may be performed in different directions and utilizing different body supports.
- Sequences of three or more curls and stretches that show directional and speed changes.
- Back bends. The teacher may try to get all to do a back bend, which may be developed more easily from the bridging position.
- Letting different body parts lead the stretches.
- Adding twisting movements. Children can keep the feet fixed and let the top half of the body twist. This may be performed standing or lying down.
- Ways to twist the body.
- Development of a curl, stretch, and twist sequence.

It is a good idea to mix formal exercises with those of a more exploratory or informal nature. Children should develop a simple stretching routine for themselves.

Explore

Hanging and swinging on apparatus.

Discover

Different ways to hang on a bar and swing.

Implementation

Children may try the following:

- Explore ways to hang from a bar that may be waist high, shoulder high, or at full stretch height (with a mat underneath), using different body parts.
- Swing while hanging.

Manipulative Skills

This section primarily is concerned with activities that use balls and bats.

Explore

Different kinds of ball skills, including throwing, catching, rolling, kicking, and bouncing, moving a ball with different body parts, passing to a partner, and playing simple games utilizing a ball.

Discover

Different ways to throw, catch, and kick a ball. They learn how to manipulate a ball using different body parts and ways to pass to a partner. They may play simple ball games in small groups.

Implementation

Children need to have access to balls of all different sizes and textures, including footballs and occasionally balloons. The teacher must ensure that plenty of time is available for practice, which is

Fig. 7-16 *Knee hang.*

necessary for development of manipulative skills. Eye and hand coordination is improving at this level and children enjoy playing with balls. The teacher should remember that the children can throw a small ball the size of a tennis ball more easily with one hand than they can a larger one; however, they can catch a 6- to 10-inch playball more easily than a smaller one. The teacher should encourage children to keep an eye on the ball rather than turn the head away when catching.

Suggested task sequence.

The following is an activity sequence that may be used successfully.

- Find ways to move a ball on the floor by using different body parts (such as the hands or feet). Children should keep the ball close to their body (This utilizes the factors of direction, speed, and space, that is, staying away from other children). Each child must have a ball.
- Bounce and catch using two hands (utilizes different levels). Bounce close to the feet and far away from the feet.
- Roll the ball, chase it, and catch it. Children should try to get ahead of the ball and catch it as it comes to them.
- Roll or throw a ball against a wall and catch the rebound. Children should throw in different ways so that the ball

Fig. 7-17 *Catching a large ball.*

bounces on the floor before hitting the wall. The ball can bounce once before children catch it.

- Sit facing a partner, and try different ways to send the ball to the partner. (The distance separating partners can be varied.).
- Try to keep a balloon up in the air by hitting it with different body parts. The balloon may be hit over a net.
- Bounce a ball with one hand on different levels, while standing in place, while moving around, and while on different body supports, *e.g.*, kneeling, sitting, or lying down.
- Move the ball with the feet only. Children may use different parts of the feet, find different ways to stop the ball, or change speed and direction.
- Pass the ball to a partner while standing in place. After children succeed with this task they may try it with one partner moving, then with both moving.
- Throw the ball up gently and catch it softly. The teacher may direct the children's attention to what helps in catching a ball softly (reaching out to meet the ball and moving the hands with it). Children should think about the relationship of catching to landing softly.

Fig. 7-18 *It's hard to miss!*

- Throw a tennis ball hard against a wall, concentrating on developing the correct throwing pattern. (Transferring weight from back to front foot, turning sideways, pulling the arm back, leading the throw with the elbow.
- Throw at targets on the wall. The teacher should stress following through toward the target.
- Bowl or roll balls at targets or milk cartons. The distance of the target may be varied.
- Pass a ball within groups of three. The distance between children can vary and the groups may stand in place then try moving. Passes can be made following a specific order, then can be made to anyone. Two children may pass the ball and the third will try to intercept it.
- Try to pass the ball through a partner's legs using only the feet. Partners stand three or four yards apart. The teacher may ask with which part of the foot it is best to contact the ball, and what helps to give direction to the ball.
- Kick a ball against a wall and try to keep it going.
- Move a ball around obstacles using the feet.
- Play "Steal a ball." Half the class will have a ball, the others try to gain possession. The ball may be bounced or moved with the feet.
- Throw and catch a Frisbee, football, or deck tennis ring.

Passing should be developed first in a one-on-one situation, and then in two-on-one, two-on-two, two-on-three, and three-on-three situations. Each group will try to keep possession of the ball. This also can be tried using only the feet. Ball activities can be tried occasionally in small circle formations, although this is not an ideal arrangement for children because they cannot handle the ball as frequently as when they work on their own or with a partner. Teacher-class formations, *i.e.,* where a group of children pass a ball back and forth to the teacher, are not recommended. There should be no excuse for not having enough balls available!

Ball games.

Children can work in pairs or in small groups to invent games of their own. They can use hoops, milk cartons, a wall, nets, paddle bats, scoops, different kinds of balls, hockey sticks, or other items of equipment in association with the balls. Children need to have a space available and some idea as to how to start their games. The games can involve scoring points, or be collaborative or cooperative in nature. More specific games are described in the chapter on activities for third and fourth graders. Fleece balls and beanbags may be useful for children having difficulties with ball skills.

Explore: Striking Skills

Discover

Children learn different ways to hit a ball by using the hand or

Fig. 7-19 *Keep it up!*

a paddle bat. They may hit back and forth to a partner over a low net or against a wall. They also may keep a ball up in the air by using a paddle bat or hit a plastic puck or foam ball with a plastic hockey stick. Using a "whiffle bat, they may hit a ball off a tee or a pitched ball. They may volley a balloon or a light plastic or vinyl ball up in the air or over a net.

The teacher can develop these or additional tasks from the preceding suggestions.

Explore: Large apparatus The vaulting horse, parallel bars, and horizontal turning bar will be considered here.

Discover

Different ways to use the apparatus.

Implementation

Vaulting horse or box.

Children may try the following:

- Different ways to get on and off the equipment.
- Using the hands to support body weight in getting over the horse or box.
- Getting on, pausing, jumping off, landing, and rolling.
- Jumping off and making a shape in the air.

Parallel Bars

Children may try the following:

- Different ways to mount the bars, move along one or both bars, and dismount.
- Mount from the ends or middle of the bar, either inside or outside the bars.
- Move along the top of the bars underneath them.
- Different ways to hang, turn around, and swing on the bars.

Horizontal Bar (adjustable in height)

Children may try the following:

- Different ways to pull up on the bar, move along it or around it, or hang on the bar, using different hand grips.

Dance and Rhythms (Suggested program for Grades 1–3)

(Before implementing this program the teacher should review the activities suggested for kindergartners.)

The program should incorporate the following components:

1. Movement of body parts, both individually and in combination.
2. Locomotor activities.
3. Non-locomotor activities.
4. Manipulative activities.
5. Development of combined sequences for individual, partner, and group work.
6. Creation of dances.

As children move through the first and second grades and into third grade they are becoming more coordinated in their movement responses to tasks and challenges. They show enhanced body awareness and can develop movement sequences as they learn to combine different skills. Partner and group work improves. They demonstrate more interest in repeating activities and in expanding their ideas. At this stage children also can begin to discuss what they are doing in terms of a simple analysis and understanding of what, where, and how the body is moving.

Rhythmic development improves as children learn to coordinate their movements with a rhythmic beat. They can learn about natural rhythms, such as those of the heart and lungs, that usually are quite regular. Children can easily understand the rhythmic nature of walking and running.

Children may work on combinations of effort factors after they have experienced movements that individually utilize the factors of time, weight, and space. Each factor will have two components:

Time—Fast (sudden).
Slow (sustained).
Weight—Heavy (firm touch).
Light (fine touch).
Space—Direct.
Indirect.

The factors can be employed two at a time to produce combinations such as:

- Sudden–firm or sudden–fine.
- Sustained–firm or sustained–fine.
- Direct–sudden or indirect–sustained.

One factor may remain constant while the second factor is changed, or as illustrated above, contrasting pairs of actions can be used.

Explore and discover

Moving body parts in different ways.

What—Head, shoulders, arms, elbows, hands and fingers, legs, knees, ankles, and feet.

Keywords: Where—Direction, level, pathway. How—Sudden, sustained.

Heavy (firm), light (fine).

Direct, indirect.

Rhythmically.

Individual parts.

Combinations.

Alone, with a partner, in a group.

Relationship.

Implementation

The teacher should present an initial task and monitor the different responses of the children. The key words then can be interjected appropriately to encourage further exploration of the movements.

Examples

"Explore all the places your hands can move in the space around you. Try this from a lying, sitting, and standing position. Move your hands slowly and smoothly (quickly and jerkily).

"Now move your hands close to the body. Try moving them farther away."

"Repeat these movements using your feet."

"Try moving your hands and feet separately, then together."

"Contrast sudden–direct movements with sustained–indirect movements."

"Try movements using other effort combinations."

"Move different body parts to the beat of a drum."

"Develop a sequence of movements using different body parts to the beat of the drum." (Suitable music may be used also.)

"Move your various body parts according to these action words: shiver, shake, smooth, jerky."

"Develop a series of gestures using your hands and arms."

Fig. 7-20 *Providing the beat.*

"Try to communicate with a partner by using your hands and arms."

"Find some ways to tap or clap rhythmically by using your hands and feet. Clap with your partner in different ways."

"Develop a sequence of clapping with your partner. Try this to the music."

"See if you can tap hands and feet at the same time."

"Clap only on the accented beat."

"Can you clap the rhythm of the sound of your own name?"

"Clap out the rhythm of a nursery rhyme."

"Move your body parts to write your name in space. How big can you write your name? How small?"

"What other shapes can you describe in space? (Children may make circles, triangles, spirals, etc.)

Explore and discover

Different kinds of locomotor activities.

What: Walk, run, hop, skip, leap, jump, gallop, slide, or other responses which children make.

How and Where: *Directions*—forward, sideways, backward.

Pathways.

Effort—time, weight, space, flow.

Implementation

Examples

"Explore ways to move on the feet."

"Develop movement sequences that combine walking, running, hopping, skipping, jumping and stepping." (Children may develop their own sequences which should include changes of direction, speed, pathway, weight, etc.)

"Work out a sequence to these rhythmic phrases (or music)."

"Repeat and refine your sequences."

The children should share their ideas, and one half of the class may observe while the other half demonstrates their responses.

"Try walking, running, and skipping to the drum beat." (Other percussion instruments may be used.)

"See if you can walk twice as fast as the beat."

"Can you walk half as fast as the beat?" (Children should move on every second beat.)

"How does the drum tell you to move?" (The teacher may try different phrases.)

"How else can you move to this rhythm?"

"Walk around and clap in time with the beat."

"Develop a sequence of locomotor movements that includes clapping."

"Find some different ways to clap with a partner as you move around."

The children may combine locomotor activities with the movement of different body parts, for example, hop–skip–stop (freeze) arm movement–run. Children can accentuate the movement of different body parts, for instance, the knees, elbows, hands, arms, and head, while they are moving.

Children also may try the following:

- Follow the Leader. This is played in groups of two or three. The teacher can suggest to children the use of various actions, directions, levels, ways of moving on the feet and other body parts, pathways, speeds, and force.
- Combining different kinds of effort with locomotor movements. Children may utilize two components at a time. For example, they may contrast sudden and fine movements with sustained or heavy (and fine) movements.
- Adding the flow factor. Children may try moving in controlled rather than in a more free-flowing manner. This use of flow can evolve from the work with the other effort qualities. Music that suggests fairly free movements can be contrasted with that which suggests more controlled movements.

Explore and discover

Different kinds of non-locomotor activities.

What: Curl, stretch, twist, turn.

Keywords: Use effort factors.

Direction, pathway, level, speed.

Relationship.

Shapes.

Supports.

Implementation

Examples

"Find some ways to curl and stretch, that is, open and close different body parts. Now try your whole body. Try this by starting on different supports."

"Stretch into a symmetrical or asymmetrical shape."

"Let different body parts lead you into a stretch or stretched shape. Repeat this and make different shapes."

"Explore the different possibilities of effort and shape. Use sudden and sustained and firm and fine combinations. For example, move from a curled position into a stretching shape by using a direct and sudden movement. Try this again but use a direct and sustained movement."

"Make a sequence of three different ways to open and close or rise and fall."

"Curl and stretch into a shape on different body supports."

"Try some of the tasks we have just completed to this music."

"Mirror your partner's movements. Stay in place but work on changes of level, direction, and speed."

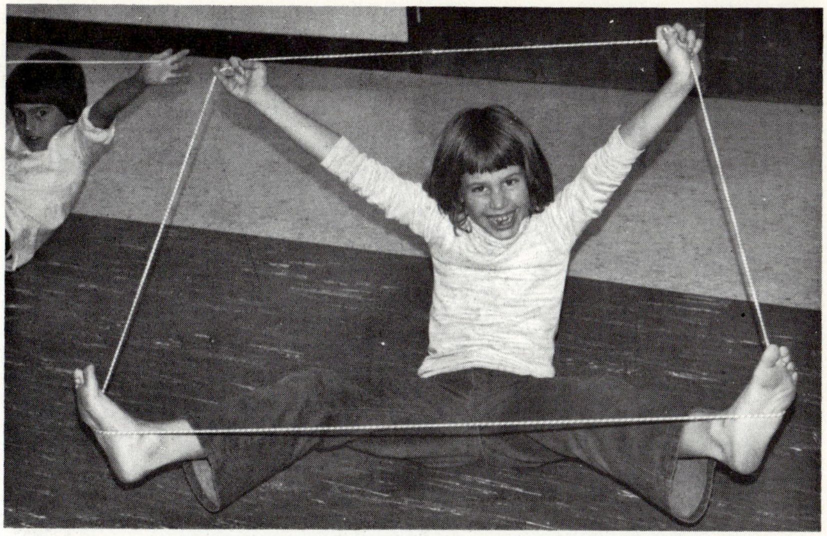

Fig. 7-21 *Using a stretch rope.*

"Explore different kinds of twisting movements while keeping your feet fixed in place."

"Explore twisting movements while you sit or lie down."

"Combine curling, stretching, and twisting in different ways."

Explore and discover

Manipulative activities.

What: The use of balls, jump ropes, hoops, rhythm sticks, ribbons on sticks, poi-poi balls.

Implementation

The teacher can distribute balls, jump ropes, and other "props" to the children in order to stimulate different kinds of movement.

Examples

"Move the ball in two hands in a swinging movement. Increase the size of the swing until you make full circles with the ball. Try this at different speeds."

"Try to bounce a ball rhythmically. What happens when you bounce the ball close to the floor? What happens when it is bounced farther away from the floor?"

"Bounce the ball in place. Now bounce it moving around and in time to music."

"Create different kinds of movements with the ball."

"Using your rhythm (Lummi) sticks, develop ways to tap in response to a drum beat (or music)."

"Tap the sticks on the floor. Tap them together. Tap them with a partner." (Children may use different levels and relationships, and heavy or light tapping.)

"Make up a routine with the sticks. Now do this with a partner."

Children can wave long ribbons tied to a short piece of stick, crepe paper streamers, or poi-poi balls (small foam balls which are fastened to about 18 inches of string) to describe patterns in the air. This necessitates using different levels, directions, and speeds. Jumping rope to music while standing in place or moving about is also of value. Children may try to create different kinds of foot patterns.

It is important that the teacher allow children to share their ideas and routines.

Combined movements—creating dance

A dance simply can be an expressive, creative way of moving. There does not need to be music or rhythm for dance to be possible. A more sophisticated dance composition requires an introduction, a middle, and a conclusion. In the primary grades children may begin to dance by putting together various movement combinations in short sequences. These sequences may involve such concepts as running lightly followed by a series of skipping movements and twisting jumps, or stepping turns followed by a series of leaps that change to stretches on different body parts. The sequences certainly will entail some degree of spontaneity on the part of the child and will help indicate his or her awareness of the movement factors.

Explore and discover

Different ways of combining locomotor, non-locomotor, and manipulative activities and the use of stimuli for developing expressive movement.

Implementation

Examples

"Combine walking, running, stepping, turning, hopping, and skipping with rising and falling, opening and closing, and spinning, in different ways."

"Try to match a partner's movement sequence."

"Let a movement of the arm or leg lead into a locomotor movement. Repeat this and add a pause while maintaining body shape."

The teacher may obtain variety in a sequence by varying the kind of effort used. For example, if a sequence was performed at a fairly slow speed and in a straight pathway, it may be repeated with a change of speed and pathway. Key words suggested in the earlier sections of this chapter may be employed to stimulate children. Shape and gesture can be added to the movements. Children gradually can begin to work with a partner or in a small group.

Rhythm.

The teacher can present rhythmic phrases and patterns to stimulate the children's movement or the children can develop their own rhythms with a drum or tambourine. Carefully chosen music also can stimulate movement.

Other stimuli.

Bearing in mind what was stated earlier about the use of imagery in developing movement, the teacher can help the children develop ways to move by offering them suggestions drawn from the following categories:

Machinery. This category can help elicit large, rhythmic movements suggestive of different kinds of machinery at work. Such movements might entail a regular or irregular rhythm, or they might have very strong directional patterns as well as utilizing different levels. Children can pretend to be a machine with a partner or group.

Occupational Activities. These activities can be built around the idea of pretending to be someone. The children can mime occupational activities. The teacher should encourage children to suggest occupations that are within their own range of experience. Additional ideas can also be derived from sports, cartoons, or television characters.

Stories and poems. Children can be invited to bring a story or poem to class that might lend itself to the creation of a dance or to story telling through movement. Emotions can be portrayed through movement, and generally children are more comfortable with positive, happy feelings. This category will provide children with the opportunity to imagine that they are moving on different kinds of surfaces, such as in deep snow, through thick mud, on hot sand, on glue, on gum, and so forth.

Action words. Children can make a list of words that indicate or suggest a certain kind of movement. A dictionary or a copy of *Roget's Thesaurus* will provide many words that can be used, such as slide, slither, glide, roll, dodge, step, gallop, swoop, and hurry. Words can be combined to produce sequences of movement.

Nature. Wind and rain, the snow, leaves, and seeds can provide a rich source of movement ideas while children can interpret in their own way. The teacher should function as a facilitator by asking questions, providing cues, encouraging quality, and offering appropriate feedback when it is needed. Children need to think about how it feels to be out in a gale, why things in nature move, and what forces are at work as things move.

Additional comments

Having presented activities for kindergarten and first and second graders, it seems appropriate at this point in the text to discuss the relationship of a more traditional program to a movement education curriculum. It is hoped that as teachers use this text they will give some thought to the purpose of the activities which children perform. The developmental aspects of exercise and activity cannot be ignored. Children need to develop strong healthy bodies and be physically fit as well as to learn useful physical skills. These skills generally will enable children to participate in the games and other physical activities which are part of our society. Creative and expressive movement must also play a significant role in the total education of the child. The program should involve children cognitively and affectively through a process that encourages thinking and caring about what they are doing. The teacher will be involved in the child's development by preparing and planning to teach a viable program that assists the child's acquisition of the needed skills.

If teachers learn how to develop a program that utilizes input from the children, and if they understand the educational implications of utilizing material that is based on children's needs, interests, and abilities, then real teaching can begin. Teachers will not need to rely on second-hand, ready-made lesson plans. All too frequently, the typical physical education lesson merely has consisted of several unrelated activities put together in some kind of a sequence that usually entailed a few calisthenics, a bit of tumbling, a game, or possibly a relay race. The idea was to get through these few activities, with very little real consideration given to the needs of individual children. Often the work was developed around units in gymnastics, softball, basketball, volleyball, and track and field, with most of the time spent in playing rather than in learning basic skills.

It is easy to be critical of other approaches, and in all fairness it must be stated that even under a traditional approach, particularly if the teacher recognized children's individual differences, the children could learn skills; however such a program usually was deficient in the cognitive and affective domains. If the "traditional" teacher was also an authoritarian, little happened in the way of creativity and self-direction.

Most teachers, however, function in a variety of ways. At times there is a need for a teacher to be authoritarian and direct, while at other times children can be given choices and a share in deciding what, when, and how they learn. Sometimes conflicts will arise between the different approaches. For example, a teacher who has become accustomed to teaching formal gymnastics may find it difficult to avoid demonstrating the program's activities, even if the concept of gymnastics as presented in this book is used. Gymnastics provide an excellent method for physical development as flexibility, balance, coordination, strength, agility, and self-confidence are improved by the activities of this sport. Such skills as cartwheels, round-offs, and back handsprings usually are taught in a way that entails a predetermined series of progressions. The activities themselves constitute a sport or activity in their own right. But it must be remembered that not all children will be interested in gymnastics, just as all children will not be interested in football or basketball.

In movement education, children learn to manage their bodies in situations that might loosely be called gymnastic. (This approach is often referred to as "educational gymnastics.") Children learn to balance on different body parts, to roll, and to transfer their weight in different ways. Specific stunts generally are not a program goal, except as they arise as responses to tasks. Children may, of course, learn "Olympic gymnastics" through clubs and recreational classes outside of school in the same way that they may participate in Little League and in other agency-sponsored activities.

Children occasionally may find physical education programs dull and boring when compared to other outside activity offerings. However, if the school can provide a good background in the basic skills, body management, and body awareness, and if it can expose children to a wide variety of activities that include such sports as bicycling, skateboarding, aquatics, ice skating, roller skating, and possibly the opportunity for outdoor education, then the activities pursued outside of school should serve as a complement to the movement education program.

It also will be necessary for children to begin to develop sound attitudes and values about competition, and about their relationships with others, and to acquire a sensitivity to other children who have different abilities and skill levels. The best thing that could happen to children is that they live fully as children and not need always to participate in or learn those kinds of activities that many adults feel they should learn. Children will only really learn the things they want to learn, and for most children movement skills are a high priority.

Sample lesson plans for first and second grade children

I. Running and dodging and the child's relationship with or awareness of others.

1. *Introduction.*

   Using all the space, children run anywhere but stay as far away from others as possible. Repeat the activity several times, each time making the space a little smaller until it is almost a quarter of the original size. Children should avoid contact. They should change speed and direction as necessary.

2. *Lesson Focus.*

   a. *Explore.*

   Running at different speeds and in different directions.
   Staying close to someone (marking or guarding).
   Keeping far away from others (dodging).

   Discover.

   Possibilities of moving quickly in a crowded space and in a more open space. How to get away when being chased. How to stay close to person who is moving quickly.

3. *Application.*
   - Find different ways to run around canes or milk cartons scattered randomly across the space.
   - At walking speed, stay close to a partner who dodges around the canes.
   - Repeat above task at a slow running speed.

- Follow the leader. Children play in groups of four, maintaining awareness of other groups. Children run around the obstacles. All children are given a chance to be a leader.
- Children run across the space by taking the straightest path. Task is performed again but this time children weave around the space.
- Practice running with a change of pace. Accelerate and decelerate.
- Use change of pace and of direction to escape from a partner who will try to catch the other child. Play "Capture the Flag." (See p. 227.)

Allow time for teams to discuss strategies of offense and defense.

II. *Rolling and Balancing.*

1. *Introduction.*

Children walk around the space. On a signal to "freeze," children stop in a balance on one body part.

Children repeat activity while running, with balance at high and low levels.

Children run, freeze in balance, roll out of balance and return to feet. Repeat.

2. *Lesson Focus.*

a. *Explore.*

Different ways to combine rolling and balancing.

Discover

Some possible ways to combine rolling and balancing.

3. *Application*

- Explore different ways of rolling from a crouch position. Try different directions. Ask children which way is easiest, and why.

Discuss and share ideas.

- Make a sequence of three rolls, each in a different section
- Balance on one foot and find some ways to roll from that position. (Hands can be used to help.)
- Roll from a bridge shape. Children practice until task can be performed smoothly. (Discuss which surfaces of the body are the best to roll on. If falling, which would be a good way to roll?)
- Use task cards. Set up stations. Basic tasks to be developed include:

—Roll with a curl and stretch.

—Balance into a roll.

—Walk, lower body into roll.

—Roll over partner's body stretched out on mat.

—Rock and balance or hold position at end of rock. Roll back.

—Develop a sequence of running, jumping, rolling, and balancing.

Study Guide

To better understand kindergarten children, read the description of five year olds in Chapter 3, and use the references cited in Chapters 3 and 6 for additional sources to consult in studying this age group.

Department of Elementary–Kindergarten–Nursery Education. *Kindergarten Education.* Washington, D.C.: National Education Association, 1968.
This source provides an overview of the child in kindergarten.

Elkind, David. *Child Development and Education.* New York: Oxford University Press, 1976.
This useful reference deals with the work of Piaget and looks at principles of learning and their classroom application.

For material pertaining to first and second grade children the reader is urged to examine Chapter 3 and these references listed in that chapter that deal with children of this age group.

Opie, Iona., and Opie, Peter. *Children's Games in Street and Playground.* Oxford: Clarendon Press, 1969.
Hardisty, Michael J. *Education Through the Games Experience.* Bellingham, Washington: Educational Designs and Consultants, 1972.

The texts also provide additional ideas for teaching children of this age.

Seminar Questions and Activities

1. Study a five year old. Make a survey of the child's ability level in hopping, skipping, balancing, throwing, and catching. Compare your findings with any available normative data.
2. Describe some simple games that would be suitable for kindergarten children. Teach these games to a group of kindergartners and describe the results.
3. Outline a movement curriculum for kindergarten. Indicate the amount of time you would spend on each area you list.
4. Ask a five year old how he or she would perform a certain movement or skill. Comment on their description.
5. Survey a first or second grade class and try to find out something about the children's needs and interests in physical activity. What can you discover about their attitudes?

8 the program for the third and fourth grades

A gradual change in the patterns of children's play becomes apparent as children go through the third and fourth grade. The period is one of transition as the children's thinking evolves from the "I—me" stage to that of the "We—us." Children are becoming ready and willing to cooperate with each other and to play in larger groups. In playing games, however, it is still desirable to use the smallest number of children that will make the activity possible.

There is still a need for children to continue work on the basic skills. Opportunities to refine those skills already acquired should be provided as well as time for working toward mastery of new skills. Children will have questions about their bodies and the way they function, hence the teacher can introduce additional ideas about exercise, health, fitness, and posture.

The program for Grades 3 and 4 is organized around basic locomotor, non-locomotor, and manipulative activities. Physical fitness testing can be discussed and ideas concerning games introduced.

Knowledge and Understanding

The teacher can introduce related information to children of this age level at appropriate points in the program. The teacher may introduce simple physiological concepts through questions such as "What happens to our bodies when we exercise?" (We get warm, we perspire, we get out of breath, our heart beats faster.) Often children will say they lose weight (probably because they have heard some discussion about this at home!). The teacher can show children how to feel their pulse at the side of the windpipe, or on the thumb side of the wrist. They can count pulse beats for 10 seconds and then multiply that number by 6 to discover their heart rate. A useful analogy for the teacher to make is to compare the working of the internal combustion engine to that of the human body. Just like the body, the car engine gets warm when it works, needs fuel and air, has a cooling system, and needs regular maintenance!

Children need to have some idea of basic anatomy and physiology. Topics such as the following can be discussed and worked on in class.

What happens to our bodies when we exercise?
How do we lose weight?
How do muscles work?
Why do we get tired when we exercise a lot?
What is a muscle cramp?
How do our joints work?
How can I make my muscles stronger?
Is a warm up necessary?
What is a balanced diet?
Why is it hard to balance?

Obesity must be discussed sensitively, especially if there are any overweight children in the class. Posture can be examined from the point of view of what is "correct" mechanically and physiologically efficient.

Other concepts such as balance, center of gravity, and applying and receiving force can be dealt with at the proper time. (See AAHPER's *Knowledge and Understanding*, 1973.) The teacher can use bulletin boards, wall charts, and posters to provide information to children on many of the topics covered in class.

Since many children will now be getting more involved in sports and games and will begin feeling the pressures exerted by parents and sponsoring agencies, the attitudes of the children and the teacher toward competition will need careful development. Children need to be able to accept other children who may have less skill and ability. Not everyone can be a winner in the competitive sense, yet if children are doing their best the teacher can arrange things so that the slogan "Every child a winner" has real meaning. Children should understand their own strengths and weaknesses and not have an exaggerated sense of how good they are. Sometimes the adult's expectations of a child's performance in sports are set very high, and the fun of the sport lost for the child in the often intense struggle to be first or best. (Additional readings about competition are suggested in the study guide at the end of this chapter.)

Physical Fitness Testing

The question of whether to administer physical fitness tests was discussed in Chapter 2. It is up to the individual teacher to decide if these tests will be used (unless required by the school or school district), beginning at the fourth grade. Movement programs develop muscular strength and endurance, agility, coordination, and flexibility, and place increasing demands on the heart and circulation. Physical fitness testing can provide some feedback to the teacher and child about the status of some of these factors. If the teacher can secure help in conducting the test by using aides, parents, or older students, if the tests are well organized, and if the results can be used, then testing may be worthwhile. (A Health Related Youth Fitness Test is being published in 1980 by AAHPERD).

The Program for Third and Fourth Grade

If children have participated in a movement education program since kindergarten or first grade, the teacher will find that some skills will only need a brief review before moving the class on to other concepts and challenges. If the teacher is introducing movement education to third and fourth grade children for the first time, more time may be needed on certain activities. (Ideas for reviewing skills can be taken from the program for first and second grades.)

Suggested activities.

Locomotor movements.

- Walking.
- Running.
- Hopping.
- Jumping and landing.
- Other movements on feet and other supports.
- Rolling.

Non-locomotor movements.

- Balance.
- Exercises for the spine: curling, stretching, rocking, twisting.
- Climbing, hanging, swinging.
- Supporting weight on the hands.

Manipulative activities.

Ball skills: throwing, catching, bouncing, kicking, volleying, striking.

Introducing games.

Rhythms and dance.

Program development in this area has been included in Chapters 7 and 9. Teachers also can use the activities suggested for use with children in the primary and intermediate grades.

The teacher can develop individual lessons by choosing an activity or theme and gathering ideas from the sections on "Implementation" to provide a lesson focus and appropriate applications. The teacher should always apply the analysis and selection process to all tasks. The tasks which follow are given as examples and are not intended to represent a special sequence of tasks that is to be performed as listed. Teachers can re-word the tasks or formulate their own. Sufficient time should be allocated for practice, especially for slower learners.

Locomotor movements.

Explore and discover: Walking. Correct motor pattern. Different ways of walking. Differences between walking and running.

Implementation

Using the movement factors and other variables, children change direction, pathway, speed, and size of step. They may try walking on different parts of the feet.

The teacher can ask such questions as: "When does walking become running?"

How do people walk in a race?" (The teacher may obtain pictures or enlist the aid of a local enthusiast to demonstrate.)"

"How long does it take to walk a mile?" (The teacher may change this to miles per hour.)

"How long would it take to walk across the United States or to walk to Washington from here?"

Teachers should discuss the use of suitable footwear for walking and running. Bare feet can be satisfactory indoors, but for outdoors, shoes usually are essential.

Explore and discover: Running. Different kinds of running. Short distances at a fairly quick pace, longer distances at a slower pace. What is jogging?

Implementation

Children explore running by using the variables of direction, pathway, change of speed, and contrast (heavy and light running). The teacher may ask "How do we run fast?" (Body leans forward, knees are picked up high, arm action is good.) For longer distances the teacher can discuss the importance of a good stride, a more upright body position, and carrying the arms lower. The proper heel and toe action can be discussed. Children may start by walking alternating with running and gradually decrease the walking.

Jogging is a fairly relaxed and easy heel and toe action that is designed to improve the heart rate without straining it. Joggers should be able to talk while jogging.

Children can practice running around obstacles, dodging and swerving, accelerating, and slowing down. The teacher can ask children what the best way is (for third and fourth graders) to start as opposed to a standing start. Active running and chasing games can be used.

To develop interest in running the following ideas might be tried:

Encourage children to jog a little each day and record on a map or chart the distance traveled. It helps if the school playground has distances marked out upon it. A map could record cumulative miles between two cities for a "run to Washington!"

- Place pictures of runners on a bulletin board.
- Investigate the marathon. Where did the name come from?
- Compare a man's speed to that of a horse, greyhound, and cheetah.
- Investigate the world's record for the 100-yard dash. Could a person run this fast for a mile? Why not?.
- Research who the first person was to run a mile in under four minutes. Where and when was this done?

Explore and discover: Hopping. Ways to hop on one foot. Combine hopping with other skills.

Implementation

Hopping mainly is used in conjunction with other locomotor skills, such as skipping, which is a combination of step–hop. Dances such as the polka use a hop. Hopping on one foot often is used as a test for children who have poor motor coordination or balance. Hop scotch is popular in some areas. Children can apply the variables of direction, speed, force, pathway, and size of step to their hopping. The teacher may have children explore the number of hops they need to cross the gym. Children can combine hopping into a sequence of hop, step, jump, or step, jump, hop. The children should be warned not to land too hard on their heels in hopping.

Skipping and galloping should be reviewed occasionally, and it is useful to have children skip or gallop to an uneven beat or to suitable music. The side-slide is in fact a sideways gallop which is often used in folk dances.

Explore and discover: Jumping and landing. Jumping in and out of, over, down from, and on and off a variety of objects. Standing long jump, running high jump, vertical jump. Jumping combined with other activities.

Implementation.

The teacher should review the activities suggested for first and second graders. Tasks can be formulated to develop jumping and landing skills. Children will need more challenges and can create many for themselves. Sometimes jumping is referred to as part of a category of movement called "flight," which refers to what the body is doing in the air between take-off and landing. Different body parts can initiate and lead the body into flight. The body can make different shapes in flight, and even change its shape as it goes through the air, and take-off and landing can occur on different body supports.

Basic review

As a review, the teacher may have children perform the following:

- Jump over lines on the floor or obstacles such as carpet squares, milk cartons, or cardboard cartons.
- Demonstrate a soft landing and their understanding of the principle of absorbing force.
- Demonstrate application and sequences of the five basic jumps. Jump the widening creek in different ways. Jump over different body shapes made by a partner. Practice jumping by using three or four people, two to make shapes and the other two to find different ways to jump over the shapes.
- Jump in and out of hoops held at different heights. Jump over wands resting on boxes, cones, or stacked milk cartons set at appropriate heights.
- Jump down from different heights.
- Jump off the agility ramp, land and roll in different ways.
- Run over a series of low hurdles.
- Attempt the standing long jump for distance.
- Perform a vertical jump off two feet. The teacher can use chalk to mark the height of the jump.
- Perform a running long jump into sand pit with a take-off from a board or from behind a scratch line.

The high jump

Children can explore different ways to jump over a bar which initially is placed 12 to 18 inches from the floor.

Examples

"Run and jump over the bar. Find out which foot you prefer for take-off."

"How high do you think you can jump this way?"

"Instead of running straight at the bar, is there a different way to jump?"

"If you tried running at an angle to the bar, which leg would go over first? Why?"

"Develop the 'scissors' style of jumping in which the leg closest to the bar goes over first."

Fig. 8-1 *Using the agility ramps.*

Fig. 8-2 *Low hurdles.*

The teacher might explain the scissors jump in this way:

"For a left foot take-off approach from the right side (as you face the bar), swing the inside leg up and over. This style is very inefficient as the top half of the body stays upright in clearing the bar. Start again by hopping over the bar (taking off and landing on the same foot). Try from the side now with the take-off foot next to the bar. That is, with a left foot take-off, approach from the left side, as you face the bar. Hop over with a turn through 90 degrees to the left, reach down with the hands to the mat or landing pad, and land on one foot and two hands. The jump becomes a roll over the bar."

Some children may automatically do a "straddle" jump, that is, they take off from the foot nearest to the bar but throw the outside leg over and land on the opposite foot. The "western" roll described above requires taking off and landing on the same foot. The bar gradually can be raised in height as children are successful and become comfortable with either style. The high jump should only be made into a sand pit or thick foam pads.

Discuss the world and Olympic high jump and long jump records. Hold the bar at record height and measure out the distance of the world record long jump.

Fig. 8-3 *Some help with the backward roll.*

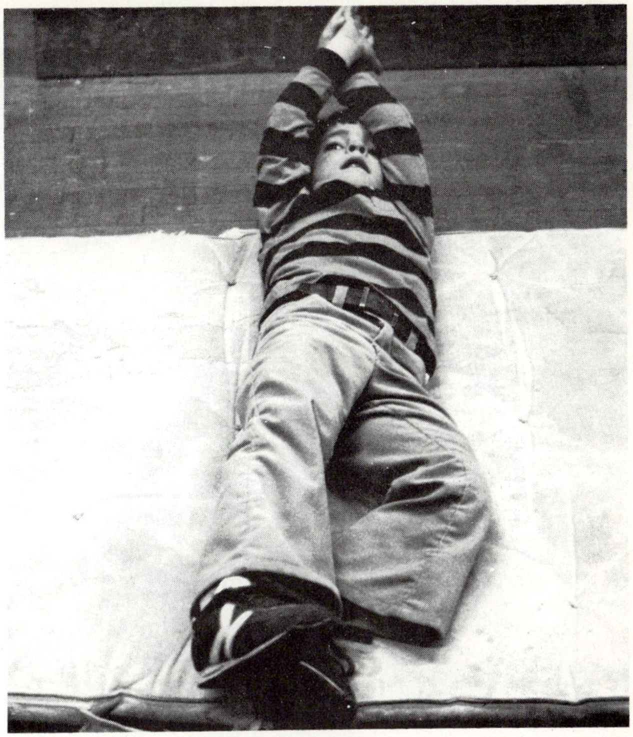

Fig. 8-4 *Log roll.*

Rolling

Review the basic rolls (forward, backward, sideways, and log rolls). Children may then perform the following:

- Children may do a front roll from a high bridge shape on four supports, lowering themselves onto their shoulders and tucking the head. They may roll to their feet and roll and jump. Children may join together different kinds of rolls.
- Roll with a partner.
- Reach and roll, dive and roll.
- From a standing position, children slowly lower themselves to the floor and go into some kind of a roll. They should think about touching the floor and making the contact smooth.
- Walk and lower into a roll, slowly run and lower into a roll, recover on the feet.
- Run, jump, roll, and balance.
- Balance and roll, taking the weight on the hands.
- Roll very slowly, roll quickly.

Other locomotor movements

Children can be encouraged to explore other ways of moving on different body supports and at different levels, using the movement factors to obtain variety in creative and original ways.

Fig. 8-5 *Going into a roll.*

Examples

"Show me some ways to move with your body really close to the floor."

"Try those movements at different speeds.

"How else could you change these movements?"

"Find some ways to move in which part of your body is sliding on the floor."

"Join together to make a sequence using three different ways of sliding. Practice this sequence until it works very smoothly."

"Find some different ways to move, keeping your feet together. Which would be the fastest way to move like this? Which way would use the least energy?"

Non-locomotor movements

Explore and discover: Balance. Review the work for Grades 1 and 2. This unit can include balancing on different body parts, on a partner, and on apparatus; developing a sequence of balances alone or with a partner or a movement sequence on the balance beam.

Implementation

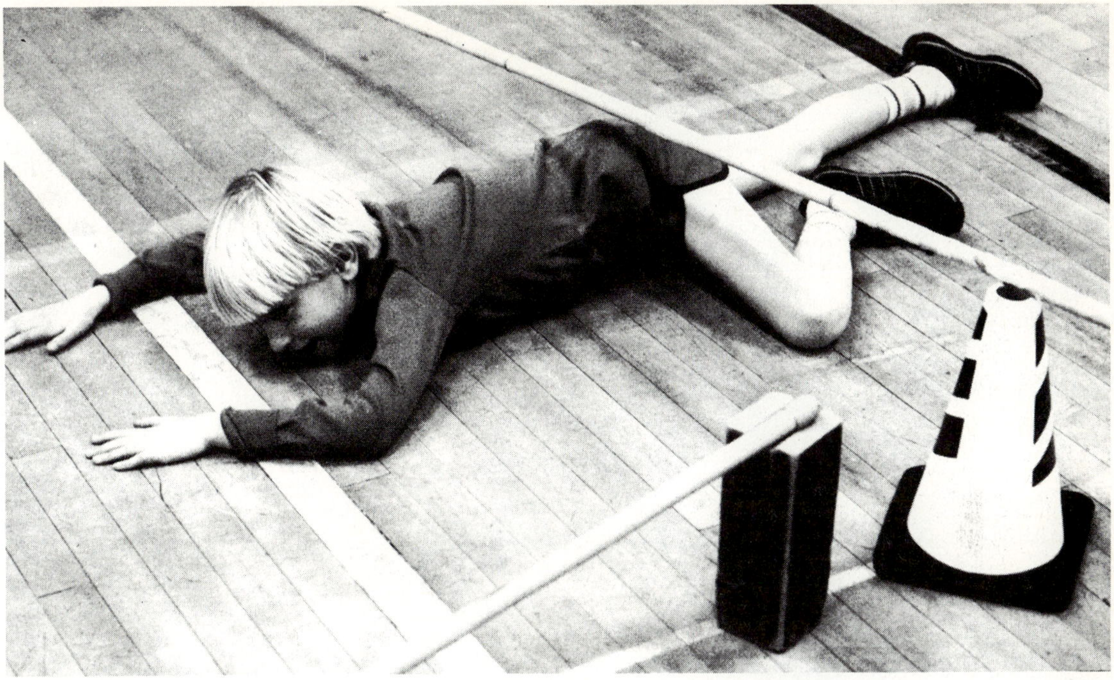

Fig. 8-6 *Sliding/crawling under a bar.*

Examples

Contrast balances with stable positions. Find all the different parts of the body on which you can balance." (Children should share ideas and the teacher can suggest that sequences be developed.)

"Find some different ways to balance on two, three, and four body parts. How many different ways can you find to balance on two hands?" (See Chapter 8, page 206, for a review of supporting weight on the hands.)

One way to clarify the difference between a balanced and a stable position is that a person who is in balance is easy to push over, whereas a person who is in a really stable position is very hard to displace. Stable shapes have a wide base, while balance positions usually have a small base. The teacher may use the analogy of a pyramid: on its apex a pyramid is completely unstable, but it is very stable on its base. (Refer to the discussion on balance on pages 97–99.)

"Make some stable positions on three and four body supports. Now try some very unstable positions on three and four supports."

"From any balance position go into a roll. Roll back into a balance." (Children can share their ideas as their movements are analyzed, then practice to refine them.)

Fig. 8-7 *A partner balance.*

"Develop some ways of balancing on your partner. Build a sequence of balances with your partner." (Again children may share their ideas and members of the class may try those ideas they like.)

"From different bridge shapes made on two, three, or four supports, roll out and back into another bridge shape or balance position."

Dynamic balance skills

Balance beam

Children may explore different ways to cross the beam, including forward, backward, and sideways. They may hop across the beam or try to skip. The children may bounce a ball as they cross the beam, or try to pass the ball to a partner coming across from the opposite side of the beam. Obstacles such as boxes, sticks, or hoops can be placed on the beam for children to step out, under, or through. The beam can be crossed by using four supports, *e.g.* the hands and feet. Balance and rocking boards can be used. Children can develop a sequence on the beam that shows a way to get on (mount), a way to cross, and a way to get off (dismount). The beam should be placed at about waist height.

Fig. 8-8 *A variety of balance challenges.*

Explore and discover: Exercises for the spine. Flexibility and strengthening work. Bending, stretching, twisting, and rocking.

Implementation

The teacher can encourage exploration by presenting tasks based on chosen themes. The themes can be developed by using cues (sub-themes), usually in the form of questions, which help the student to clarify what he or she is doing. The teacher will determine what to do next based on the initial responses of the children to the task. As the teacher analyzes the responses, and depending on whether the teacher is working toward a predetermined goal or is leaving things more open, he or she will be able to provide information to the student as to whether to repeat a certain movement, change it in some way, add to it, or combine it with a different movement in a sequence. Movement responses occasionally may be inappropriate for the resolution of the task and if so may be discarded. The teacher then will suggest in a very positive way that the child try again. This, in fact, would entail a redirection of effort rather than telling the child that the movement response is wrong. The art of teaching in this instance requires a blend of knowing how to analyze what children are doing, how to intervene, how to encourage children, how to redirect or accept a response, how and when to share ideas, and how to think on one's feet.

Teachers must focus their attention on the process involved in developing the movement responses of children. Similar tasks can be presented to any grade level, but the children's responses will vary. In exploring curling, stretching, and twisting tasks, children will utilize the experiences they acquired in Grades 1 and 2. Thus, although it may seem that the tasks are repetitious, the responses of the children certainly will be different. Of course, some responses will be predictable but many will be new and original. This is the exciting thing about this teaching concept: It is the children who take the teacher through the work and contribute to its development. The teacher's role is that of facilitator, shaper, and guider of the learning process.

Explore and discover: Curling and stretching.

Children can perform the following activities:

- Stretch from different starting positions (from the feet, seat, back, side, knees, or shoulders).
- Stretch into different shapes and onto different supports.
- Stretch in different directions, and with different speeds.
- Develop sequences of curling and stretching.

Relaxation can be introduced as a contrast to stretching.

Examples

"Let the stretch go out of your body. Now bring it back into your arms and legs.

"How could I tell if your muscles are relaxed?"

"Show me some ways to move in which you curl and stretch as you go."

Fig. 8-9 *Curling backwards.*

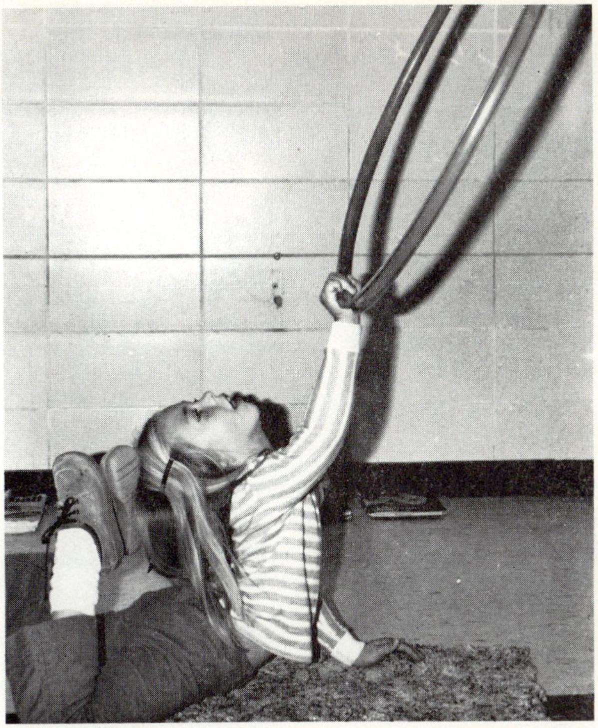

Fig. 8-10 *Curling on a different body support.*

"Lay face downward. Now see how far you can bend your body sideways."

Twisting.

Children may:

- Experiment with different twisting movements.
- Try to twist in different positions (standing up, lying down, from different stretches).
- Do the twisting movements very slowly.
- Try some twisting movements while sitting down (standing up), bending at the middle.
- Devise some formal calisthenic-type twisting exercises.

Rocking

Children may:

- Rock on different supports or body parts.
- Rock in different directions and at different speeds.
- Rock with the body curled up or stretched out.
- Rock to an end position and hold, then rock back a different way.

Climb, hang, swing

Using the available apparatus, including ropes, bars, ladders, geodomes, climbing frames, parallel bars, cargo nets, and peg boards, children may experiment with:

Fig. 8-11 *Twisting through a hoop.*

- Ways to climb a rope, or two ropes. Various foot grips can be tried.
- Using two ropes to hang upside down ("Skin the Cat").
- Swinging on a rope, landing and rolling.
- Different ways to get around, move along, or hang from a horizontal bar. Children can move along the bar using their hands only, or their hands and feet. The bar can be placed at waist, shoulder, head, or full stretch height.
- Combining different pieces of equipment to make small obstacle courses for children to go through in different ways.

Supporting weight on the hands

Children need plenty of experience to help in developing this area, including the use of gymnastic movements.

- Children may do a head stand, hand stand, cartwheel, round-off, or walkover.
- Different ways to move on the hands and feet can be explored.

Keywords

Face down, face up, moving at different speeds, in different directions, at different levels, in different pathways. From both feet to both hands and back to feet. Alternating hands and feet. (Using these keywords and variables, the teacher can encourage children to:

- Curl and stretch as they move.

Fig. 8-12 *"Skin the Cat."*

- Explore movements of the feet while keeping the hands shoulder-width apart on the floor. (Fingers point forward.) The children may move the feet separately or together, hold the hips high, take the feet as high as possible, and bring them down softly. The body can be curled or stretched.
- Get over a bench or vaulting horse by placing weight on the hands alone. Children may jump the feet over a rope or low bar by supporting their weight on their hands.
- Ways to balance on hands.
- A crouch or elbow balance, walking on the hands or a handstand (against a wall or with a partner for support). It is important with a handstand to have the head back and shoulders over the hands in order to kick up.

Manipulative movements

(Review ball skills and activities suggested for the first and second grades.) Eye and hand coordination improves in third- and fourth-grade children, and they can generally throw and catch quite well. The skills learned can be more readily applied in games.

Explore and discover: Ball skills. Different ways to pass a ball, throw and catch, kick, hit, bounce, and volley.

Fig. 8-13 *Getting over a bench.*

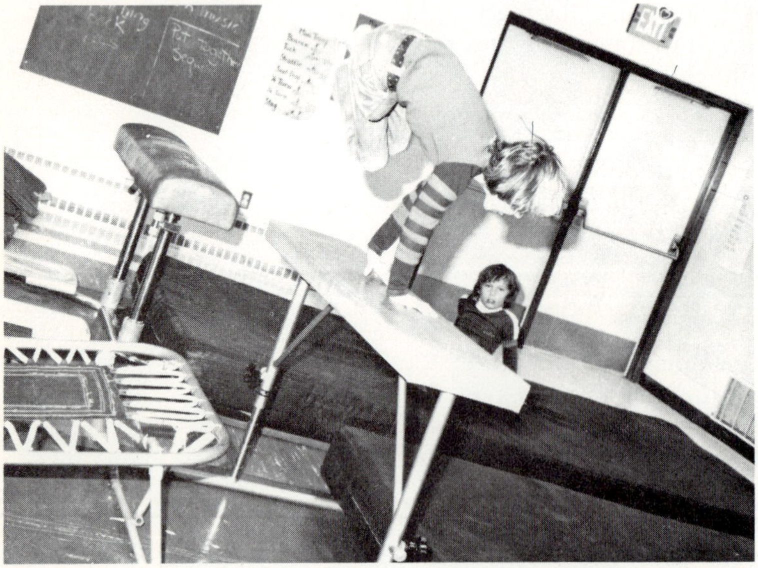

Fig. 8-14 *Over a vaulting horse.*

Implementation

The children can explore:

- Bouncing and catching by using two hands.
- Bouncing with one hand, at different levels, and near to or far away from the body.

Fig. 8-15 *Really "feeling" the bounce.*

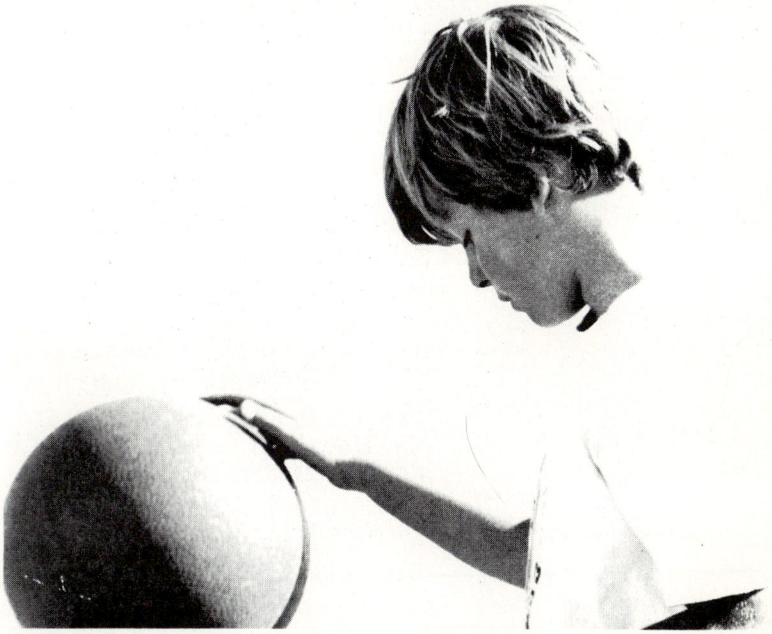

- Changing body support while bouncing at different levels and near to or far away from the body.
- Moving around while bouncing, changing direction, pathway, and speed, and maintaining awareness of others.
- Moving the ball around using the feet only and keeping the ball close.
- Using all the variables, including stopping and starting.
- Finding the best part of the foot to use to control the ball and the amount of force needed.
- Moving the ball (dribbling) around obstacles such as cones or milk cartons.
- Playing "steal a ball." Children try to get the ball away from a partner who is using either the hands or feet to control the ball.
- Passing to a partner

Children can explore different ways to pass the ball to a partner by using either the hands or feet. Teachers should remember to include the use of footballs for this task.

Examples

"Find a partner and get a ball. Show me some ways to pass the ball at different levels to your partner. Use two hands and make the pass easy for your partner to catch."

"Pass the ball at about chest height. How can you get more force into your pass? Does it help to step forward as you pass? What else might help you to pass faster?" (The answer the teacher seeks is use of the fingers, a wrist flick, and following through)

Variable.

Passing can be performed by applying these variables: overhead pass, passing with a bounce, a roll, one-hand pass, two-hand pass, passing in place and while moving around.

Examples

"Get in groups of three and pass the ball around the group. Keep changing the way you pass. Let one person move around."

"Find some ways to move and pass the ball while the group assumes different shapes, such as a triangle, or a straight line."

"See if two people can keep the ball away from a third person. How many passes can you make before your passes are interrupted?"

"How can you keep the ball away from the other person? What can the passer or receiver do?"

"Try a little game now—two-on-two passing." "Let's see which pair can make 10 complete passes."

The teacher can further develop passing by using two-on-three and three-on-three arrangements. (One group or team will need to be identified in some way.) Children also can try some of the above ideas using only the feet.

Examples

"Try to throw a tennis ball really hard against the wall. What things help you to get a lot of force in the throw?" (Children should discover that this would involve taking a sideways position, stepping forward on the opposite foot, rotating the body, transferring weight from the back to the front foot, and following through.)

"Who can catch a ball really softly?"

"'See if you can catch a ball sitting down. Can you stand up and catch it?"

"Move around and keep a ball up in the air. Use any part of your body above the waist to keep it up." Frisbees, deck tennis rings, or balls of different sizes can be used to vary these tasks.

Explore and discover: Throw or volley over a net. The net can be placed at waist, shoulder, head, or full reach height.

Fig. 8-16 *Catching sitting down.*

Implementation

Nets, a crossbar, stretch elastic rope, or long wands can be used. At first children should simply throw and catch light vinyl balls, then they may try hitting balloons over. The teacher should supply at least one ball or balloon for every two children. Children can explore ways to use the hands to volley a ball against a wall and how to deal with a low ball if it cannot be caught. They may try a simple volleyball serve.

Other ideas for working with balls include:

- Throwing and catching in different ways (using a wall for rebounding).
- Simple activities performed in a circle by four to six children. These may entail:

—Passing around or across the circle.

—One person standing in the center to try to intercept the ball as it is passed by the other players.

—Circle players passing the ball back and forth to the center player, who stands in place. Circle players may walk or run around clockwise or counter-clockwise, passing as they go. Different kinds of passes may be tried.

—Center player attempting to pass the ball out through the

Fig. 8-17 *Getting it over the net.*

Fig. 8-18 *Keeping a ball up against a wall.*

legs of the circle players. Circle players keep their feet apart.

—All players standing in the circle, with player having the ball passing to someone, then taking the place of the receiver, who will then pass to someone else, etc. (Watching the ball, following through, releasing the ball, and transferring weight should be emphasized.

—Having groups invent their own circle ball games or activities.

Explore and discover: Striking skills. This involves hitting a ball with the hand, paddle racket, bat, or hockey stick.

Implementation

Children may try the following:

- Hit an "All" ball against a wall with the hand.
- Use both sides of the hand to hit a ball while standing sideways.
- Hit a ball back and forth to a partner, letting the ball bounce before hitting it.
- Practice watching the ball and following through.
- Improvise a low net and rally over it.
- Use paddles for the above task.

Fig. 8-19 *Using a paddle.*

- Invent some rules, including ways to score points, for a net racket game.
- Use a paddle to keep a fleece ball or a balloon up in the air. Children also may try using a badminton bird, Whiffle ball, All ball, or tennis ball.
- Use a badminton bird in a net game.

Fig. 8-20 *Cooperative support.*

- Hit the ball against a wall by alternating with a partner.
- Hit a Whiffle ball off a batting tee. Children should discover the best way to stand, swing, follow through, and hold the bat.

The teacher should discuss these problems in order to derive from the children acceptable and functional responses which can be repeated and practiced. Children then can try to bat a slowly pitched ball or a ball on a batting tee. Groups of three or four can practice batting and fielding. "Rounders" is a good game for introducing children to the idea of running bases and fielding (see page 257). Hockey sticks can be used similarly in order for children to learn to manipulate a puck or ball. Simple passing games that include scoring can be tried.

Lifting

The teacher should discuss the correct way to lift a fairly heavy object, that is, keeping the back straight and letting the legs do the lifting. The teacher may ask why it is incorrect to bend over and keep the legs straight while lifting heavy objects.

Fig. 8-21 *A good way to lift.*

Pushing and pulling

This area explores different ways to push or pull a partner.

General comments. The teacher can plan lessons by using an introduction, working through the skills suggested, and applying these skills to games, dance, and other activities. Third- and fourth-grade children can learn to work on their own by using task cards and learning centers (see Chapter 10). Individual differences in ability and interests will become more apparent by this stage, and programs should take this into account. The children's skills are not yet too specialized, and it is important that they develop a broad base in a wide variety of movement skills and activities.

Attitudes toward movement and learning will be developing slowly as children participate in the activities and interact with their teacher and peers.

Fig. 8-22 *One way to pull.*

Getting into games After the children have learned to pass, throw, catch, and kick fairly well, they are ready to play some simple team games that involve scoring. Instead of reading a list of rules and procedures to the children, the teacher can suggest that they play a game which requires four players on each team, with the children learning how to play the game by asking questions. The teacher will be familiar with the structure of the game and will be able to answer the children's questions. Typical questions which the children may ask might include "Can you run with the ball?" "How do you score?" "Can you tackle?" "How can we pass the ball?" From time to time the teacher may ask if the children know enough about the rules to play, since some essential questions never seem to be asked. The last question to be asked is how the game starts, and children usually do not ask about boundaries, the procedure after a score, or where they should stand at the start of the game. This system works well in getting children to think about the structure of a game and the need for rules. Some suggestions for games suitable for the third and fourth grades are:

Fig. 8-23 A different way to pull.

1. Children score by throwing (passing) the ball to a teammate who is standing on a mat at the opposite end of the gym. After the catch is made the catcher bounces the ball back into play and leaves the mat. The person who made the score proceeds to the mat to become the new catcher. The ball may be passed anywhere, but passes to the catcher must be made from behind a line drawn across the gym about five or six yards from the end line. The game can be started with a jump ball. (The teacher may discuss fair ways to start a game.) The rules are not absolute and can be modified to improve the game.
2. Other ways in which children may score could include
   - Bouncing the ball into a hoop placed in the middle of a circle having a six foot radius.
   - Knocking over a milk carton placed in the middle of a large circle.
   - Keeping the ball on the floor, children play ball with their hands and serve it by hitting it between two chairs or cones placed to form a goal.
3. Once children understand these types of games they can develop their own versions of them to create completely new games. Instead of a ball, children may use a quoit or deck

tennis ring. Teams will need to wear colored pinnies or be identified in some other simple way. Games can be played across the width of the gym with teams consisting of up to six players. (Methods of organizing a class with more than 30 children is discussed in the next chapter.)

Whether children in Grades 3 and 4 should play basketball, volleyball, soccer, flag and touch football, or softball is a question that needs to be discussed. Most of these games were designed for adults, yet they often are imposed on young children, and rarely is the equipment scaled to the size of the youngsters. Children may derive more fun and enjoyment from participating in games such as those described above. Certainly children can play and enjoy modified versions of the major games, but teams should be kept small so that children do not lose interest while waiting for a chance to play ball. For example, soccer can be played with five or six players on a team and use scaled down goals and a reduced playing area. Volleyball games frequently are conducted in school and with up to 15 children on each side of the net, but there are better methods of organization than this! In volleyball, children should play over a net that is placed at about reach height for most children, and balls of light weight should be used. In basketball, the hoops should be lower than the regulation 10 feet and balls should be smaller and lighter. Both games can be played with three children to a side.

Most games can be modified to make them more appropriate to children's developmental levels, although the teacher should bear in mind that "lead-up" games are games in their own right.

Planning lessons

The learning process for this age group is essentially that discussed previously, *i.e.*, explore, discover, analyze, select, and repeat. Lessons will be organized around the basic skills and their applications and will utilize a format consisting of an introduction, a lesson focus, and application.

Of course, the teacher can combine formal and more direct teaching with a more informal method, and a thematic approach with a more structured approach. It is difficult to be a purist in terms of solely utilizing a single approach to teaching. Children need to experience different approaches to learning, and teachers need to be free to teach in the way they feel to be consistent and appropriate to the needs of children and compatible with their own beliefs, values, and personality.

It is also a concern of this text to help teachers integrate movement education with a more traditional kind of program. Implementing a program of movement education does not mean that some of the older and more traditional games and activities should not be taught anymore. Many of these activities are part of our heritage, and many provide excellent opportunities to apply and learn basic skills as well as to have fun and confront a challenge.

STARTING A LESSON

The introductory part of a lesson generally should be related to that which follows, but occasionally a teacher must gauge the mood of a class and provide a different introduction than that which originally was planned. Children need variety and vigorous exercise, and a good introduction can capture their interest and set the tone for the rest of the period. Some suggestions for alternative ways to start a lesson rather than by introducing a theme are given below:

1. Moving to a drum beat or to music. Children can respond to a beat in various ways, that is, by walking, running or jogging or by free movement, such as hopping, swinging, skipping or sliding. These movements can be utilized in such activities as:
    - Follow the leader. The leader determines the movement and the rest follow. (For small groups of three to five children.)
    - Circles. One child stands in the center of the circle and performs a movement in time with the beat. The other children copy the movement (For five or six children.).
    - Calisthenics. Children develop their own calisthenics to music. (For individual or group work.)
    - Bounce a ball or jump rope to music.

    (The teacher should use the keywords of direction, pathway, level and speed.)
2. Chasing and tag games. These are suggested for use only after children have practiced moving in different directions at different speeds and have acquired the ability to be aware of and move in relation to others.
    - Children can invent different kinds of chasing games.
    - The teacher may need to discuss with children how to catch or tag, the boundaries for the game, and how the catcher will be identified. (Elimination games are not used.)

      The following games are suggested:

    —Chinese wall. In this game, the class must cross two parallel lines which are drawn about three feet apart through the center of the gym. The catchers stay on the wall, and anyone caught on the wall remains to help catch the others.

    —Shipwreck. The class lines up along the center of the gym. On the teacher's command to "man the lifeboats" or "man the quarterdeck," the children run to either side wall. Other commands that may be made are to "freeze," hit the deck" (everyone drops down on the floor), and "man overboard" (everyone lies on his or her back with the feet in the air). Teachers can vary or repeat the commands to see if the children move before they think or think before they move!

—Fox and Geese. Groups of five or six children form a line and hold each other around the waist. One child stays out in front (the fox) and tries to tag the last child in line (the "tail" of the "goose").

—Bumper cars. The children stand in pairs facing each other and place their hands on their partner's shoulders. One child steers the other backward while trying to avoid collisions with other "cars."

—Tail tag. All the children tuck a "tail" into their belt or pants, and four or five chasers try to get a tail.

3. Free practice. Children are given time to practice using a ball, jump rope, hoop, or other equipment. They can practice movements they enjoy and are good at, those they need to improve upon, or those suggested by the teacher. This procedure should be introduced gradually so that children become accustomed to freedom with responsibility.
4. Vigorous activity. Children may play short games or other activities that involve vigorous movement and perhaps resistance work as well. Such activities might include:
   - Tug-of-war. (For partners.).
   - Pushing a partner.
   - "Call out." Someone calls out "run," and the class runs. Other calls might be to hop, skip, crawl, jog, walk, etc.
   - Poison. In groups of four or five, children join hands around a small chalk circle or hoop, with the objective of pulling or pushing the others to make them step into the circle or hoop.

   Partner combatives could be used, such as:

—Chinese boxing. Children face a partner and, using an alternate wrist grasp, try to touch the partner on the head.

—Sitting back to back. With elbows interlocked, children try to tip their partner over sideways. (Backs are together and the feet are spread apart.)

—Shake hands. Partners try to turn each other's hand over.

—Children face a partner and interlock the fingers of both hands with the partner and try to force the partner to his or her knees.

—Sawing wood. Children face a partner, interlocking fingers with him or her by curling the fingers inside his or hers. Each places the left foot forward and begins a vigorous "sawing" motion.

—Pushing. Facing a partner, each child places both hands on the partner's shoulders. Both bend forward and attempt to push the partner across the gym.

Some relay races which are fun and involve continuous participation include:

Fig. 8-24 "Chinese" boxing.

—Racing tunnel ball: Children form teams of four or five, with a leader who has a ball. The ball is sent through the legs (the tunnel) and the last person catches it and runs out in front to a line or mark about 10 to 15 yards away. The rest of the team remains in order, but runs to stand behind this person. The process then is repeated, with the ball going back to the last person, who catches it and runs out. This goes on until the original leader is in front again.

—Zig-zag relay. About six children form a line. The last person in the line runs forward, zig-zagging in between the other team members. As each child is passed by the runner, each follows him or her, going all the way through the team. After going through the entire team, the first runner (the last person in line) runs back to where he or she started from and everyone goes around that person and zig-zags back into place.

5. Exercises. The teacher or a student may lead exercises which are chosen for specific purposes. The exercises should be performed with good form and effort, and should mainly involve stretching and flexibility work.

Naturally, there will be many other activities that the teacher may want to utilize. On cold days or when there is no indoor space available children will need to be kept on the move with activities that are relevant and constructive and not just a form of "baby sitting."

SAMPLE LESSON PLANS

Three lessons are provided that utilize the theme, "Getting into team games."
Grade level: 4. Length of lesson: 30 minutes. Number of children participating: 30.

Lesson One

1. *Introduction:* Two children share a ball.
   Task: Find some different ways to pass the ball to a partner by using the hands.
   Keywords: Distance apart, level, force, in place, moving around.
2. *Lesson Focus*
   Explore and discover: Different ways of passing a ball while working in groups of three.
   "Make a triangle shape with three people. Stay in place and pass the ball around the group in order."
   "Repeat this activity but pass in any order."
   "Make the pass easy for the others to catch."
   "Now repeat this activity but everyone moves around."
   "Try moving close together. Now move farther apart."
   "Make different patterns as you pass." (Children can make straight lines, weave about, stay in the triangle pattern, etc.)
3. *Application*
   The teacher can suggest that the children play a game in their groups of three.
   Examples
   "See if two players can pass the ball to each other. The third person is to try to intercept the passes." (The teacher should stress that no personal contact is allowed.)
   "How many consecutive passes can the two players make without the ball being intercepted?" (Each child in the group takes a turn at intercepting.)
   After a few minutes the teacher should discuss and analyze the possible strategies involved in the game, such as what the passer or receiver can do to avoid having the ball intercepted or what strategy the intercepter should employ. After this discussion the class can practice again. At the end of the period the class may discuss any games in which a two-on-one situation may occur.

Lesson Two

1. *Introduction: Review:* Team passing involving two on one. The class is in groups of three.
2. *Lesson Focus*
   Explore and discover: Development of team passing in larger

groups including two-on-two, two-on-three, and three-on-three situations. (Colored pinnies should be used for each group of three.) The teacher should gradually build up the size of the group. The class can discuss the implications of even-sized teams and odd-sized teams, and the fact that larger teams should always have an advantage in maintaining possession of the ball.

In implementing this lesson, the teacher can impose certain limitations, such as speed (players must walk for part of time) and level (the ball must stay below head height when passing, or the player holding the ball, or in possession of it, can take only two steps).

3. *Application*

The class can discuss playing strategies involving goups in a three-on-three situation. Such strategies might include situations in which their team has possession and those in which the other team has possession of the ball. The class can compete to determine which group of three can complete the highest number of consecutive passes.

Lesson Three

1. *Introduction: Review:* Three-on-three passing. Four-on-four passing may also be tried.
2. *Lesson Focus*

Explore and discover: By asking questions, the class will try to learn the rules and scoring system for a simple team game involving passing. For example, the teacher wants to initiate a game involving three-on-three passing, with points made by knocking over a milk carton placed inside the basketball free throw circle at each end of the space. One player can stand inside the circle to guard the carton.

The children will need to be guided along as play develops. Questions may arise as to whether dribbling is allowed, what the boundaries are, or what happens after a carton is hit, etc.?

3. *Application*

The teacher can divide the class into small groups for playing games that utilize the skills developed in the lessons. The teacher will observe and officiate the games. Any problems or ideas which the class has that pertain to offense and defense may be discussed. The class also may develop similar games with different scoring methods.

Bibliography

American Alliance for Health, Physical Education, and Recreation. *AAHPER Youth Fitness Test Manual.* Washington, D.C.: AAHPER, 1976.

______. *Knowledge and Understanding in Physical Education.* Washington, D.C.: AAHPER, 1973.

Study Guide

The reader is urged to look at Chapters 2 and 3 of this text for information on the growth and development of children in this age group.

These sources are recommended for additional reading on growth and development.

Albinson, J. G., and Andrew, G. M., eds. *The Child in Sport and Physical Activity.* Vol. 3. Baltimore: University Park Press, 1976.

Rarick, G. Lawrence. *Physical Activity: Human Growth and Development.* New York: Academic Press, 1973.

The role of games becomes increasingly important as children move through school, and the teacher might want to examine these sources for some different ideas about games teaching.

Riley, Marie. "Games and Humanism," *In Journal of Physical Education and Recreation.* February 1975.

Riley, Marie, ed. "Games Teaching." *In Journal of Physical Education and Recreation.* September 1977.

Morris, G. S. Don. *How to Change the Games Children Play.* Minneapolis, Burgess, 1976.

Mauldon, E., and Redfern, H. B. *Games Teaching.* London: Macdonald and Evans, 1969.

Fluegelman, Andrew, ed. *The New Games Book.* Garden City, New York: The Headlands Press, Inc., 1976.

All of the books or articles listed above will provide a very good picture of the trends in games and games teaching. The ideas are based largely on a movement education approach, with the exception of the Morris and Fluegelman texts. The ideas presented by Morris suggest that if games are analyzed, many can be changed or modified to make new games or ones which are significantly altered. Games should be examined by the teacher before being played by children in order to determine their purpose. *The New Games Book* is different from the more usual kinds of games book. "Play hard, play fair, nobody hurt" are the bywords of these games, which are designed to be competitive but yet in many cases cooperative. Games for two people, for a dozen, two dozen, or even more are included, and many of the games are in fact not new but resurrected games that have been around for a long time, simply because children enjoy them.

Seminar Questions and Activities

1. Develop a series of task cards that children could work through on their own and that will encourage the development of ball skills or balance.
2. Develop a list of simple physiological concepts that are important in exercise. Describe how you would present them to third and fourth grade children.

9 the program for the fifth and sixth grades

As children move into and through the fifth and sixth grades, the broad skill foundations developed earlier can be consolidated, refined, and employed through participation in a wide range of games, sports, gymnastics, expressive movement, and dance. It is likely that some children will still need to work on the basics described in previous chapters.

Children at this stage of development in the intermediate grades are becoming more responsible, are capable of working for longer periods of time on tasks, cooperate more readily in team play, and have greater endurance and strength. Some girls may be taller and heavier than boys since they mature faster. Children of these ages tend to have a keen sense of fair play, but frequently argue about rules and the makeup of teams. In addition, children are now more capable of self-evaluation, and are better able to understand concepts and express more interest in learning about exercise and the body. They can understand some of the mechanical principles of movement and will practice longer if they are being successful.

The program still must provide challenge without overdoing competition. Some children will begin to participate in agency-sponsored sports outside of school, while others will participate in activities such as ballet, gymnastics, soccer, Little League, "Young

America" sports, ice skating, and swimming, or in many other programs.

As the teacher gets to know the children better, he or she can share with the children decisions concerning how and what the children learn and the program content. Simple inventories can be completed by children and the teacher may interview them to determine their needs, interests, abilities, and preferred learning styles. This information can help the teacher diagnose and prescribe a more individualized program.

Suggested Program Outline

1. Basic skills and their implementation
   Locomotor
   Walk, run, hop, skip, roll, jump, other.
   Non-locomotor
   Climb, hang, swing.
   Curl, stretch, twist. Activities to develop flexibility and strength.
   Circuit training.
   Balance.
   Supporting weight on the hands.
   Manipulative Skills
   Throw, catch.
   Kick.
   Bounce.
   Hit, strike.
   Lift, carry, pull, push.
2. Small group and other team games.
3. Organizing for large classes.
4. Miscellaneous enrichment activities.
   Using a cage ball, parachute, roller skating, skate boards, scooters, group problem solving.
5. The "new games."
6. Large gymnastic apparatus.
7. Dance and rhythms.

BASIC SKILLS

Locomotor

If a teacher is using the methods of movement education for the first time, it is suggested that the students be introduced gradually to guided discovery and problem solving. If the children have always been told exactly what to do and given little chance to make choices, explore, or experiment, the teacher can choose activities that will assist them in adjusting to a different approach.

Explore and discover: Walking. Correct pattern—heel to toe, arm swing from the shoulder in opposition to the foot, head up. Feet pointing forward.

Implementation

By this stage students should be walking correctly. They may explore walking using the following variables:

- Keeping away from others and using all the available space.
- Walking close to other people without actually touching them.
- Walk while utilizing a change of direction (speed and/or pathway), force, or size of step, stopping and starting, or walking around obstacles. (The teacher may decrease the amount of space available.)
- Walking to a drum beat or to music.

Students now can learn to combine the different variables without the need for too many cues by the teacher. It should be expected that the children can adjust their movements to a particular situation. They can walk and demonstrate changes of speed, direction, and relationship to others, as the situation demands. Walking should be combined with other locomotor skills.

Explore and discover: Running. Children discover their own limitations in terms of how fast they can run over short distances, and their endurance over longer distances. Changes of speed—accelerating, decelerating, starting. Changes of direction—suddenly, slowly. Correct style for different kinds of running, lightness. Relationship to others—near to, far away from.

Implementation

Running is a very important skill to master. Students will need to be able to dodge and swerve in games, or change speed in football, soccer, or basketball. Some children may be able to run quite fast, while others may prefer to run longer distances. There also will be some children who do not like running at all; however, most children seem to enjoy running and chasing games, several of which were described in Chapter 8.

The teacher can implement the following running games and activities.

- Capture the flag. This is an excellent running and chasing game, and children can discover the game format by asking questions. The game is played with two teams having up to 10 players on each side. The playing area should be fairly large and divided in half by a chalk line or by cones. Each team has an object (the "flag" which may be a ball, beanbag, old sneaker, or small flag) which it must prevent the other team from capturing. The object is placed toward the back part of each team's territory. Once a player crosses the halfway line he or she may be tagged, and if caught must go to a "jail" located some yards behind the halfway line. Players can be released from jail if one of their own team members gets to them without being tagged. The flags may not be guarded too closely. Teams should wear identifying colors and the rules can be modified as necessary. The sides are changed after the flags have been captured.

- Basketball dribble tag. Three of four players dribble balls and try to tag the rest. If tagged, a player must carry on the dribble and try to tag someone else. (See the chasing and tag games described in Chapter 8, pages 219–220.)
- The 30-, 40-, and 50-yard dash.
  —How to start: This is an excellent opportunity for children to try problem solving!

  Examples

  "How can we find the best way to start in a race? Let's try a standing start first."

  "How shall we place our feet? Let's practice. If you have found a good way, show it to me."

  "Have you seen anyone start a track race another way? Who would like to show us?"

  "Where do runners put their hands and feet? Why are they placed like that? In which direction are we trying to move fast?"

The teacher can experiment with the students and come to some agreement on the positions of the hands and feet. There may not be a single standard position that will be best for all children. Starting blocks might be obtained or improvised, and the students may experiment with different foot positions and try to decide at what angle the knees should be bent for maximum push in the crouch start.

Fig. 9-1 *How shall we start?*

Arm action can be discussed and also running "through" the finishing tape. Children gradually can build up to running the 50-yard dash and perhaps even the 75-yard dash.

• Running longer distances. Children gradually can build endurance for running distance by alternating walking with running. They should start by going about 500 yards and increasing the distance each time. The running distance increases as the walking distance decreases until children are running the entire distance. There should be no suggestion of racing in the early stages. After the teacher becomes familiar with the children's abilities, he or she may time the children's speed over 600 yards, but children should still have the option to run or walk if they wish. Alternatively, the children can be encouraged to see how far they can go in eight or nine minutes. Different ideas for encouraging children to run or jog were given in the previous chapter.

Running should be fun and enjoyable. When the children ask if they can keep going or do another lap the teacher knows that the motivation and enjoyment is there. Children should be encouraged to jog every day, and maps charting progress can be used to record cumulative miles. A "Run to Washington" or to another distant location, such as the state's capital, can provide an interesting challenge.

Marking out distances in some permanent fashion somewhere on the school grounds can be of value. Shorter distances, such as 30, 40, 50, and 75 yards, as well as longer distances should be measured out. Finally, if the teacher can jog along with the children, so much the better. Different styles of running can be discussed and videotapes used to illustrate the differences between running the dash and longer distances.

Explore and discover: Jumping and landing. Jumping over things, down from, on to and off, across. Standing and running long jump, high jump. Children explore own limitations and preferences in jumping.

Implementation

Students should be given many opportunities for jumping experiences and practice. Through tasks and challenges, the teacher can provide a variety of different activities for jumping. Analysis and selection of activities to repeat and refine should be based largely on individual abilities and interest.

Trampolining

A word of caution must be given to teachers who may consider using a trampoline in a movement program. There is currently some controversy about the place of the trampoline in physical education programs, and some school districts have discontinued the use of trampolines altogether. The main reason for discontinuing its use is that children have received serious injuries including severe neck and back injuries, on trampolines. In many other programs, teachers have eliminated somersaults and increased supervision.

Another problem with trampolines is that only one child can perform at a time, and the children do not get many turns during a single period or lesson. However, Godfrey and Kephart (1969) recommend the trampoline for children with perceptual motor problems, and certain activities which can be performed on a trampoline do help children to orient themselves in space as well as affording good exercise even if only for a short time. Teachers must closely supervise children on trampolines, and this means that the rest of the class must be able to engage in other activities largely on their own. The teacher will have to decide whether the advantages of trampoline activities outweigh the disadvantages and problems presented by safety and supervision considerations.

A position paper on the use of trampolines may be obtained from AAHPERD. The four basic bounces—knee drop, seat drop, front and back drop—can be taught in conjunction with simple twists and combinations.

Examples

"In a group of three, set up equipment (boxes and wands of various sizes) so that you can jump over it at different heights. Explore different kinds of jumps, for instance, two to two, hop over, run and jump, sideways jumps, and backward jumps. Try to make soft landings."

"Set up the equipment in such a way that you can do a series of jumps, one after the other."

"Run up the agility ramp and jump off in different ways. Do a roll when you land and finish on your feet."

"See how far you can jump with a standing long jump. Use a mat to land on. A good distance is your own height plus about a foot. Can your arms help you to jump farther?"

"When you land, try to pitch forward rather than back on your seat."

"Let's try a running long jump. Does the run help you to jump farther than if you just did a standing jump?"

"Remember, it's a single foot take-off. Do you know from which foot you prefer to take-off?"

"What things might help us to get a longer jump?" (Children should suggest running faster, jumping higher, shooting the feet out on landing, and moving the body in the air.)

"If we take off from a board, how can we be sure we can hit the board every time we run up?" (A sand pit should always be used for this kind of jumping.)

The running high jump can be performed in three ways including the western roll, the straddle jump, and the Fossbury "flop."

Fig. 9-2 *Shapes in the air.*

Fig. 9-3 *Standing long jump.*

(All high jumps usually are performed using a thick foam pad or mat which is about 18 to 24 inches thick.) The roll and the straddle were described in Chapter 8. The Fossbury flop utilizes an outside foot take-off, a fairly straight approach, and a curve to the right (for a right foot take-off) as the bar is approached. The inside knee is thrust up and the arms lead over the bar, with the back to the bar.

The teacher should avoid a situation in which the entire class lines up to await a turn to jump. Other stations should be used so that everyone is kept active. Not every child will enjoy high jumping, so the teacher can decide in conjunction with the children how far high jumping will proceed.

Examples

"See how high you can jump vertically." (Using a piece of chalk, the teacher can first make a mark on the wall at the child's full stretch height. A second line is made to mark the child's at the top of a jump.

"Find some obstacles or equipment from which you can jump down. Land on a mat. How softly can you land?" (Equipment can be arranged so that it is at about knee, waist, shoulder, and head height.)

Fig. 9-4 *Vertical jump.*

Fig. 9-5 *Catching a pass.*

"Jump to head a soccer ball or to catch a ball in the air. Jump to shoot a basket. Jump to spike a volleyball. In which activities does it help to jump? What kind of a jump is best?" (Groups of three or four children can try this task.)

"Set up three or four low hurdles which are about 18 to 24 inches high at regular intervals. Practice "running" over the hurdles until you can do it smoothly." (A good distance for the intervals between hurdles is the average length of a student's running stride. The height of the hurdles can be raised gradually, and the number increased to five or six.)

"Running over the hurdles may appear to you like a series of high jumps. Look at some pictures or films of hurdlers and see how they do it." (Hurdlers change the rear leg clearance of the hurdle in order to stay as low as possible. This activity would be ideal for a learning center, as discussed in Chapter 10.)

"Develop different sequences involving jumping. Use changes of direction, different jumps, and an immediate rebound." (This may be done with or without apparatus.)

"Develop sequences involving jumping, rolling, balancing, hopping, leaping, and supporting your weight on your hands."

Fig. 9-6 *Asymmetrical shapes in the air.*

Explore and discover: Other locomotor skills, including hopping, skipping, and galloping. Different ways of moving on the hands and feet and on other body parts. Different ways of moving on the feet other than walking or running. Develop sequences and/or patterns of different kinds of locomotor skills.

Implementation

Examples

"Find ways to move with your body close to the floor. Explore these movements using different speeds and going in different directions. Use your hands or feet to provide the moving force."

"Play "Follow the Leader" in groups of five. The leader will determine the pattern or movement to follow, which should involve different ways to move on the feet." (The teacher may beat a drum or play music for this activity.)

"Make circles of six people. Develop a sequence that uses a side-slide, skip, step-hop, walk, and run." (Appropriate music can be played.)

"Explore moving on your hands and feet by using all the variables."

Children also can learn the steps to folk or square dances and explore the different uses of locomotor skills as they are applied to various sports. (More ideas pertaining to applying skills to dance, expressive movement, and rhythms will be provided later in this chapter.)

Non-locomotor skills

Explore and discover: Climb, hang, and swing. Climbing and swinging on ropes. Use climbing apparatus for climbing and hanging. Different ways to hang from, get around, travel along, pull up to, and swing on the horizontal bar.

Implementation

The difficulties inherent in challenging older children soon become apparent unless the school can provide the appropriate equipment. At least four climbing ropes should be available, and

Fig. 9-7 *Using a peg climber.*

a cargo net, peg climber, and adjustable horizontal bar or two or three chinning bars of different heights are useful. Outside on the playground larger pieces of equipment may be used that are suitable for climbing, hanging, and swinging.

Examples

"See if you can swing on the rope by holding on with only your hands. How can you make a bigger swing?"

"Experiment with a foot grip on a climbing rope. What is the least number of pulls you need to reach the top?" (The teacher should not allow students to slide down the rope as the friction may burn their hands.)

"Find a way to swing while holding on to two ropes."

"Try to skin the cat while holding on to two ropes."

"Find ways to hang upside down on one or two ropes."

"Hang on the horizontal bar with your feet off the ground. Can you pull up to the bar? Try this with your hands grasped over (under) the bar. In which way is it easier to pull up on or chin the bar? Why?"

Fig. 9-8 *Another way to climb.*

Fig. 9-9 *Chinning the bar.*

"Find ways to move along the bar by using only your hands. Try this by using your hands and feet."

"How many pull-ups or chin-ups can you do?"

Children should be able to climb a rope by the end of the sixth grade. Most children usually are weak in the arms and shoulders because they lack the opportunity to participate in activities which develop the shoulder girdle. Children should be encouraged to try those tasks in which their weight is off the ground and supported by their arms and hands. Children also can try a flexed arm hang rather than pull-ups. No special skills are required here; these tasks simply present the opportunity to increase strength and respond to challenges.

Explore and discover: Balance. Static and dynamic. On different body parts used singly or in sequence. Different body shapes while balancing. Counterbalance with a partner. Balancing on or with a partner. Balancing on apparatus. Balancing, overbalancing, recovering.

Implementation

More challenging equipment for balance is necessary for fifth and sixth graders. A beam should be obtained that is at least waist high. The balance beam bench is a versatile piece of equipment that can be inclined or placed at different heights.

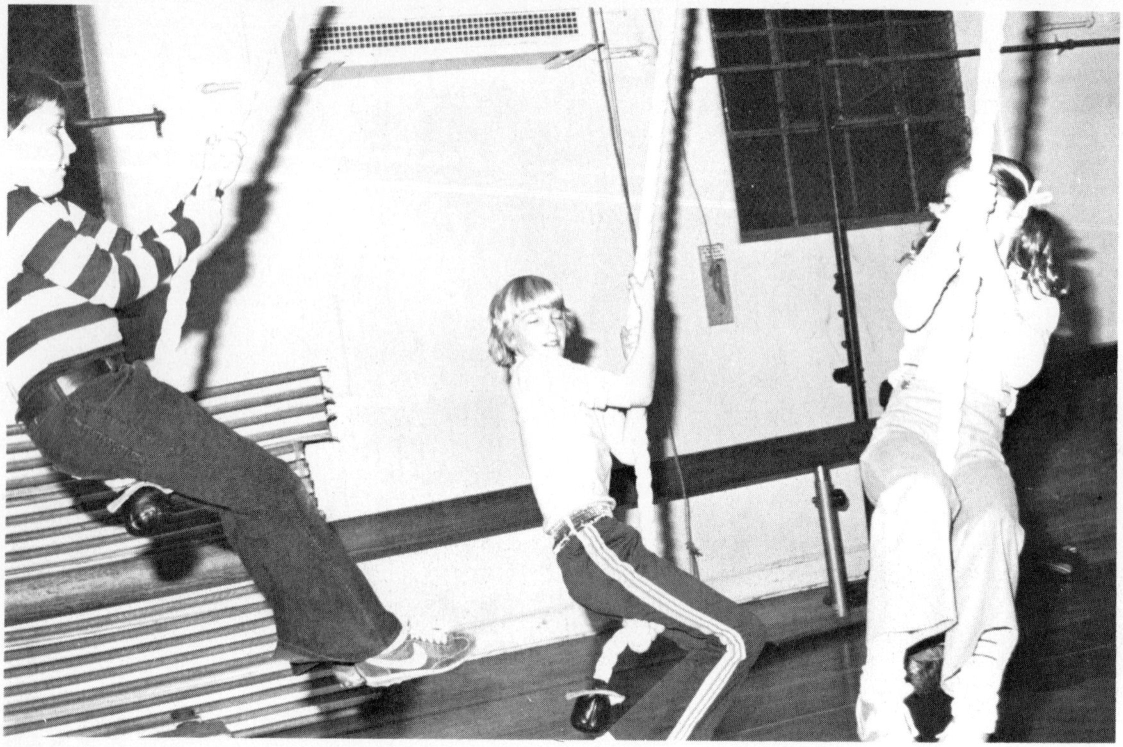

Fig. 9-10 *Swing on the ropes.*

Examples

"Develop a sequence of six different balances on the floor. Repeat the sequence until you can do it smoothly."

"From a standing position, see how far you can lean in any direction before you fall over. Experiment with different foot positions."

"Stand with your back to a wall, and your heels touching the wall. Now try to pick up a beanbag placed on the floor just in front of your toes. Why is this difficult?"

"While holding on to a partner, see how far apart you can lean before you both overbalance. We call this process counterbalance. Find different ways to counterbalance."

"Find a way to mount a balance beam, move across it, and dismount. Practice this routine until you feel you are ready to show it to others."

"Find ways to balance on any two parts of your body. Try this with your body curled and then with it stretched out. How many ways required you to be on your hands? Why is it so easy to balance on our feet, and so much harder to balance on our hands?"

Fig. 9-11 *Counter balance.*

"Try walking across the balance beam with your arms stretched out sideways. Now try with your arms at your sides. Next, hold a long bamboo pole in the middle at about waist height. Which way gave you the best control over your balance? Why?"

Answers to some of the questions posed above could be discussed in small groups or by the entire class. Students might even write down their answers.

Balance beam benches could be arranged as shown in the illustrations to provide different challenges (see page 150).

Explore and discover: Exercises and movements to develop flexibility in the joints.

Implementation

Students should understand the importance of stretching muscles before strenuous exercise. Stretching movements should be done slowly, with a little extra stretch at the end of the full range of movement. Vigorous, rapid stretches should be avoided. Exercises should focus on the shoulder joint, the spine, hip joint, and ankle. A blend of formal and informal exercises or movements is recommended.

Fig. 9-12 *A different way.*

Examples

"See if you can touch your toes easily when you are standing up. Now sit down with your legs straight out in front of you and try to touch your toes again. Which way was easiest? Why? Which muscles need stretching to make toe touching easier?" (The answer the teacher is seeking is the hamstrings.)

"Let's try some hamstring stretchers."

"Try some movements that put the arms through a full range of movement. Try these movements in different directions."

"Who can make the biggest circle with his or her nose?"

"Find five different ways to curl and stretch. Use different starting positions, directions, and speeds."

"How flexible is your hip joint? Try some exercises to improve flexibility in this joint. Which activities need a loose hip joint?"

"Find out all you can about yoga." (Yoga can be discussed with the class.)

"How high can you swing your leg up in front of you? This would be important for what skill?" (Punting and kicking are possible answers.)

Explore and discover. Activities for developing strength. How do muscles get stronger? How will we know if they are getting stronger? Which muscles must be strong and why? What kinds of exercises and activities will make muscles stronger?

Implementation

Increased muscle strength is produced by overload, that is, for any particular exercise the number of repetitions must be increased. Generally, the students will be working with their own body weight providing the load or effort. For example, simply doing 10 push-ups every day will not increase muscle strength; one must either do more than 10 push-ups or decrease the time it takes to do the 10 push-ups.

CIRCUIT TRAINING

Circuit training involves a series of exercises which students perform one after the other as they move around the gym. A series of exercises or activities is known as a circuit, and the exercises are chosen for a specific or general effect on the body. Students can move through the circuit at their own rate.

As an example, suppose six exercise "stations" are placed around the gym as follows:

1. Sit-ups.
2. Push-ups.
3. Vertical jump.
4. Squat jumps.
5. Chins.
6. Bench stepping.

A chart would be made for each exercise. For example:

Sit-ups

Red	15
Blue	11
Black	8
Green	5

This chart shows that at the sit-up station the student would do the number of repetitions indicated by the green number, that is, five sit-ups. When the student proceeded to the next exercise (push-ups), he or she would perform the number of push-ups indicated on the card by the green number. Children should be encouraged to go through the circuit three times (laps). At the end of three laps a student would have completed 15 push-ups. The idea here is that it is better for the child to do 5 push-ups three separate times than to do 15 all at once. It should be pointed out that the order of activities is such that different muscle groups or parts of the body are alternately exercised. Two strenuous arm exercises performed one after the other would be too much specific exercise.

Students are assigned to each station in groups of approximately the same size. They then perform the exercises, with each proceeding at his or her own rate. A target time of about 10 minutes can be set, and if a student completes three circuits of a particular color level, he or she will proceed to the following level the next time the circuit is worked through. The students must realize that the circuit is not a race against others but competition against oneself and the exercises must be done properly. Individuals may keep their own records if it is so desired.

Circuits can contain numerous activities and can be designed to produce various results. Other activities which could be included in a circuit are suggested below:

- Jumping rope.
- Shuttle run.
- Rope climb or swing.
- Stepping up and down on a bench.
- Jumping Jacks or other calisthenics.
- Running through hoops or tires.
- Partner combatives.
- Shooting baskets.
- Volleying or throwing a ball against a wall.
- Dribbling a ball around obstacles.
- Passing a ball to a partner a certain number of times.
- Climbing a cargo net or peg board.

Students could design their own circuit in consultation with the teacher, maintain their own records, and possibly go through the circuit at times other than during class periods.

General strengthening of muscles results from climbing and hanging activities, including pull-ups and chin-ups. Supporting the body weight on the hands and feet, such as in bridging, and jumping, gymnastics, rocking, partner combatives, push-ups, and vigorous running activities all contribute to have a general strengthening effect.

Children can enjoy isometric exercise by using a jump rope folded into quarters. They grasp the rope in two hands and attempt to pull it apart. A six-second count is used for each concentrated pull. The children can find different places and levels at which to pull, such as overhead, behind the back, out in front of the body, sitting, or lying down.

Manipulative skills

Ball skills should be reviewed. These were discussed in the previous chapter. Children in the fifth and sixth grades usually can throw and catch well and are ready to apply their skills in a variety of game situations.

Fig. 9-13 *Isometrics.*

Explore and discover: Throwing, catching, kicking, volleying, striking, bouncing.

SMALL BALL SKILLS (TENNIS AND SOFTBALL SIZE BALLS.)

The children can throw and catch against a wall. They may practice throwing hard and throwing at targets by using the correct overarm throwing pattern. The distance from the wall can be varied.

Example

"What helps us to throw hard?" (Children should respond that transferring weight from the back to the front foot, rotating the trunk, snapping the wrist, and following through are of help.)

Children may throw at targets on the floor, such as milk cartons or cones.

Example

"How else can you throw?"

Outside, children may throw for distance. They may utilize a standing position and a run.

Examples

"Can you throw farther if you use a run? How can we get into a good throwing position from a run without losing momentum?" (The teacher should explain that it helps to get into a sideways position, with the weight back.)

"Throw and catch with a partner, or field balls which are thrown or rolled to you by your partner." (Children should use different levels and speeds and vary the distance between them.)

"See if you can hit an All ball against the wall and keep a rally going. Try to hit the ball directly off the wall sometimes, and sometimes let it bounce on the floor first." (Children may vary the distance from the wall and the force of the hit. This task may be repeated with a paddle bat.)

Fig. 9-14 *Keep it going—using a wall.*

"With a partner, try to keep a ball or badminton bird in play over a net." (The net should be at waist height if a ball is used, and at chin height if a badminton bird is used.)

The teacher can suggest that children use both sides of the paddle (forehand and backhand) and discuss whether standing sideways helps in hitting. The teacher also may discuss the need for rules, a system of scoring points, and court boundaries. The students can develop their own rules, with the teacher advising and helping if necessary. If rackets are available the children can try to play badminton. "Shorty" tennis rackets could be used to hit a ball against a wall or over a net.

Fig. 9-15 *Keep it up.*

Examples

"Throw and catch a ball by yourself. See if you can find some things to do while the ball is in the air. For instance, throw the ball from a sitting position or while lying down and stand up as you catch it. Try this by reversing the movement."

"Try to juggle two tennis balls, then three. What is the process you must use? Try to juggle two balls in one hand."

"With a partner, try to keep a ball going against the wall by using your hands, paddles, or scoops."

LARGE BALL SKILLS (BALLS SIX INCHES IN DIAMETER AND LARGER.)

Examples

"Get a ball and show me some different ways to move it around. What are some of the things we can change or do?" (Reminders for cues or for additional questions: direction,

Fig. 9-16 Throw from lying down.

level, speed, parts of the body moving the ball, relationship to others, dribbling, bouncing, keeping ball in the air.)

"Find some ways in which you and your partner can pass the ball to each other. Use different levels and vary the distance apart. Stand in place, move around, use your hands, and use your feet." (Children may pass a football as well.)

"Pass a ball against the wall by using two hands and try to hit different targets. What helps you to hit the target? How hard or how quickly can you do this?"

"Using only your feet, try to kick the ball and hit the targets on the wall. Try to knock some milk cartons over."

"Which part of your foot provides the best control in contacting the ball? Where should you be looking as you kick the ball? At the target or at the ball?"

"Pass a ball to a partner by using your feet. The partner should find some ways to control or trap the ball."

The class should share ideas on ball control and passing, and analyze and select the functional ways that seem to be effective. The teacher should ensure that everyone participates in the discussion. The tasks should be repeated as children need plenty of

Fig. 9-17
Scoops in action.

Fig. 9-18 *Dribble on different supports.*

Fig. 9-19 *Kick over a carton.*

Fig. 9-20 *Pass to a partner.*

time for practice and to consolidate their skills. Slower learners will need more time than those who learn rapidly.

Examples

"Try to keep a ball up in the air by batting it up using an open, flat hand or a fist. Don't catch it." (A light vinyl ball should be used for this.)

Fig. 9-21 *Keep it up.*

"See if you can volley the ball against a wall. Hit it high on the wall. Is it better to use one hand or both hands to hit the ball?"

"How can you raise the ball up if it gets quite low?" (The children's responses hopefully will demonstrate bending low in order to get both hands under the ball—digging—and bumping it up again.)

The teacher can discuss the way in which the hands might be held together to hit the ball. A net placed at about stretch height for an average-sized student can be utilized.

Fig. 9-22 *Over the net—using groups of four.*

Examples

"Find ways to keep the ball going over the net without catching it. Try this with a partner, and then in a group of four. The ball can be hit twice on your side of the net by different people. Make up some rules and play a game."

"Get in groups of three. Develop ways to pass to each other by using your hands or feet. Stand in place, then try moving around."

"Play 'Keep Away' or 'Two on One.' In these games, two people try to pass as many times as they can before the ball is intercepted by the third person."

The teacher gradually can increase the size of the groups. Four children can play two-on-two, five can play two-on-three, and so on up to about four-on-four or five-on-five. This activity also can be played using the feet as in soccer. Passing in groups then can lead to different games using scoring and rules.

The teacher can set up batting tees which the students will use in groups of three. One child hits the ball off the tee while the others field the ball. This mainly is a batting practice.

Examples

"Where should you stand in relation to the tee?"

"In which directions can you make the ball go?"

"How should you hold and swing the bat in order to hit the ball?"

Fig. 9-23 *Beginning "keep away."*

Fig. 9-24 *Which way will the ball go?*

"Should you stand still while hitting or step out?"

"Have a partner pitch a slow underarm ball for you to hit with the bat. Make sure nobody is standing near you when you try this. Is this harder or easier than hitting off the tee? What is the best position to be in when you are waiting for the ball? Why?"

Students also can practice with plastic hockey sticks and learn to manipulate a tennis or sponge ball or puck.

Examples

"Practice passing to a partner by using your hockey stick."

"See if you can shoot the puck between two milk cartons which are about three feet apart."

"Play Keep Away in threes. Use hockey sticks and a puck."

"What is a good way to stop the puck when it comes to you? Can you pass to your partner when you both are moving about?"

SMALL GROUP AND OTHER TEAM GAMES

As children learn the basic skills required for sports and games they can start to apply the skills in games of their own making or in recognized games such as soccer, volleyball, basketball, flag football, or softball. Whatever the game, the main considerations

Fig. 9-25 *Getting into hockey.*

are that it is suitable to the developmental level of the children, that there is maximum participation and enjoyment, and that emphasis is placed not so much on winning but on doing one's best. Children should play on teams in which their ability counts. Games become a legitimate part of the movement program after most of the necessary skills have been mastered. Many traditional programs were not too much concerned about skill development because it was thought that children would develop them by playing. This probably was true for a few children, but many others lost interest completely because of a lack of success and enjoyment.

The skills that have been discussed throughout this text were approached through a method that provided an understanding of why things are done in a certain way. Through guided discovery, teachers can provide suitable cues and questions to direct skill development. Self-discovery takes a little longer than simply being told what to do or what to expect, and occasionally, when time is short, teachers may be tempted to demonstrate more. Being patient and waiting for things to happen can be frustrating at times,

Fig. 9-26 *Small team soccer.*

Fig. 9-27 Volley ball serve.

but it is very rewarding to see students develop understanding and come to terms with their own limitations and abilities in acquiring skill.

In developing games, it is well to remember that all games originally were invented by someone. Some of the games we play were developed comparatively recently while others have a longer history. Some games are a combination of other games; for example, speedball is a combination of soccer, basketball, and football. Children may wish to try combining the skills of different games to create a new and original game.

Team size should still be small. To have 11 players on a soccer team means that some players probably will touch the ball only once or twice during a game! Modified soccer, with only 5 or 6 on a team, would be much better and more appropriate in the elementary school. Similarly, the rules of an activity can be modified in order to improve the game. Children have a sense of fair play, but they may cheat if the pressures placed on winning are too great, so they may need the teacher's assistance and understanding in order to abide by the rules.

Games for small teams were discussed in Chapter 8. These games usually are very popular with fifth and sixth graders; however, the children may be starting to play the standard team sports at this time. The following suggestions may prove useful in guiding children at this stage.

Volleyball

Children should practice the skills needed to keeping a ball up in the air, and can practice volleying a ball while sitting down, either with a partner or in a small group. The teacher should encourage children to discover the best way to serve (guided discovery) and provide plenty of practice time for skill mastery. One or two tries is just not enough.

Children can play over a net placed at about stretch height. One ball to every two to four children is a good ratio. The teacher gradually can introduce the set-up and spike, and discuss strategy and blocking. The server may be allowed to stand closer to the net if it is necessary. Teams having more than eight or nine players should be avoided.

Fig. 9-28 *Now try this way.*

Soccer

By now children have learned how to move a ball about by using their feet, so other specialized skills are required, such as shooting at the goal. The teacher may ask which part of the foot should be used to produce a hard low drive (the instep, or the area where the laces of the shoe are), and where the non-kicking foot should be placed in relation to the ball for a low or a high kick (beside the ball for a low kick, behind it for a higher kick, with follow-through determining the path of the ball). If a ball goes out of bounds, it may be returned to play by a "throw in," a two-handed, over-the-head throw. Teachers can compromise on rules for coed soccer.

The goalkeeper will need to practice fielding the ball, or deflecting it away from the goal, and can practice at first by having someone throw balls to him or her. Later, the goalkeeper can practice by having someone kick the balls to him or her. Simple ideas about defense and offense can be discussed as the need arises in play.

Students should practice using both feet to manipulate the ball, although some will prefer to use one foot. Different ways to trap and control the ball should be practiced as well as tackling. If boys alone are in the group they can shoulder charge, but if it is coed play, no personal contact should be made.

Soccer essentially is a passing game in which the ball is played close to the ground. Students should intensively practice small

Fig. 9-29
Trying a shot at goal.

group passing and keep-away activities. Teams should be readily identifiable.

Heading is a skill that is peculiar to soccer. The teacher may ask students which part of the head is best to use, and may advise them to try to keep the eyes open as the ball contacts the head. This skill can be learned by having partners toss a light ball onto each other's head. Players "nod" the head in the direction the ball should go, and should practice heading in different directions as well as jumping to head a ball.

Basketball

Like soccer, basketball is a running, passing game. If teachers have directed students through the ball skill work described earlier, the students will be familiar with different ways to pass a ball while moving and in playing Keep Away. Other skills which they will need will be shooting, rebounding, guarding, and shooting free throws. Simple offensive and defensive strategies will be necessary.

The baskets should be less than 10 feet high for use in elementary schools. (Ideally, baskets should be adjustable in height.)

Examples

"Find ways to shoot a basket from a stationary position. How high do you need to send the ball? What pathway does a ball take in the air? Where is the highest point of the flight? Where should you be looking when you are shooting? Try some one-handed (two-handed) shots. Can you jump and shoot? Does the ball need to touch the backboard before it goes through the hoop?" (The teacher will need to discuss these questions.)

"Can you run toward the basket while dribbling the ball and take a shot?" (This is a lay-up shot, which is usually performed with one hand from under the basket.)

"Find a way that works for you in shooting from the free-throw line."

"How would you shoot if someone were trying to block your shot? Have someone try to block a shot and see what you can do to avoid having the ball blocked."

"Work out the best places for your players to stand at a center tip-off. What are you going to try to do?"

"Develop some scoring plays. Should all players try to score? What about defense?" (The teacher can help students resolve these questions by talking about player-to-player and zone defense. The rules as modified for elementary school children can be mentioned.)

Softball

Rounders is a good game for children to try before playing softball. The bases in Rounders are four-foot poles which are placed at a distance similar to that of softball bases. A short piece of wood 12 to 18 inches long and 1 inch in diameter is used as a bat. The pitcher uses an underarm pitch which should arrive between the batter's knees and shoulder. After a fair hit the batter runs the bases, carrying the bat along and attempting to touch each base with the bat before the fielder or baseman touches it with the ball. The game is played in a manner similar to softball, and teams can have about eight or nine players to a side. Here again, the rules can be modified to improve the game. Occasionally children playing softball come in to bat, take three swings, miss each one, and that is P.E. for the day! There is a lot of standing around, and the game tends to be dominated by a few highly skilled players. However, the game must provide fun, enjoyment, and activity for all players. The teacher must devise ways to allow more participation within the time allocated for play, such as by keeping the team size small. All children will need a lot of batting practice in order for them to derive any enjoyment from the game.

Children can practice fielding, batting, and running bases in groups of three. Remember, a bat and a hard softball are dangerous weapons if not used carefully. Children should never stand close to anyone who is batting, and bats should never be thrown!

Children must learn to concentrate and follow the play. Gloves should be provided for base players and a catcher's mask and glove (mitt) for the catcher.

Flag Football

It is probably better for elementary school children to play flag rather than touch football so that there will be little doubt about who was touched! Children will have already practiced throwing and catching a football, so a new skill, such as the punt, may be introduced.

Examples

"Hold the ball in both hands and find a way to release it so that you can punt it with your foot. Which part of the foot is best? How do you direct the kick? Is there any follow through?"

"Try a punt from a stationary position. Then try it with a run."

The class can play simple games involving the forward pass, the punt, the center pass. A junior size football or Nerf football should be used.

Floor Hockey

For this game, a suitable indoor floor space is needed. The rules can be discussed and goals of official size constructed. Children should understand the need for safety and controlling flying sticks. Before playing the game, children should receive plenty of practice in passing, receiving, shooting, and goalkeeping. Simple offensive and defensive concepts can be discussed as the need arises.

Teachers interested in pursuing team games in greater depth can obtain the official rules and additional ideas about playing from the sources listed at the end of the chapter.

ORGANIZING FOR LARGE CLASSES

One of the factors that led to the evolution of the "traditional" method of organizing and teaching physical education, which included relay races, mass exercises, and games utilizing large numbers of players on each team, was the problem of dealing with large classes. However, the physical education teacher should not have to instruct a class that is larger than the normal size unless assistance is provided. Quite often classes are doubled up for physical education so that up to 70 children participate at once, even in schools which supposedly are dedicated to providing individualized instruction! During those periods of the year when it is impossible to teach physical education outside because of bad weather, and when there is only one teaching station inside, it may be necessary to double up classes in order for students to receive even three periods of physical education each week. Some schools nave a gym and a cafeteria, thus affording two teaching stations for part of the day. School planners should consider this problem when designing buildings.

If large classes are unavoidable, the teacher may find the suggestions listed below to be of help in coping with the problem.

- If there are two teachers, one teacher can serve as the lead teacher and the other can provide support for specified periods. Using guided discovery methods, one teacher can present the initial tasks, with both teachers providing feedback, cues, and sub-tasks to individual children, small groups, or the entire class. Of course, there must be enough equipment available so that all children can be involved in the activity. This method will work as well with 70 children as it does for 30. However, the larger the group, the more difficult it will be to provide individual feedback. This situation is far from being ideal.
- The group can be divided into smaller groups, with each teacher working with about half the groups. Each group can work at a station or learning center. (See Chapter 10.)
- The space can be divided and each teacher can work separately. This arrangement usually is not very satisfactory.
- If at all possible, one class can be sent outside while the other stays in. In good weather both classes can be taught separately outside.
- Some children can work on contracts, at stations, and at learning centers, while others can work directly under a teacher's supervision. Teacher's aides, high school students, and occasionally parents may be available to help.

- The working space may be arranged as indicated below:
—For a class of 50, 10 to 12 stations can be utilized for gymnastics, ball skills, games skills, or apparatus, depending upon the equipment available.
—Half the class may use the open floor space while the other half works at stations or at learning centers. The groups can switch areas halfway through the period or at the next class meeting.
—The gym can be divided in half, with games played on both halves or on one half, while the other is used for skills or for drill stations.

MISCELLANEOUS ENRICHMENT ACTIVITIES

Parachute

A parachute provides a novel way of getting exercise, and children enjoy its variety of uses. Parachutes, which are used without the lines attached, can be obtained in various sizes.

Children may try the following activities with the parachute:

- Arranged evenly around the edge of the parachute, children hold on to it and walk around in a clockwise direction. They change direction and jog, skip, or side-slide. Older children enjoy running as fast as they can without letting go.
- Tug-of-war. Children can pull in different ways, including

Fig. 9-30 *Making waves with a parachute.*

standing up, sitting down, using two hands, using one hand, and facing outward.

- Making waves. Holding the parachute with both hands at about waist height, the children shake it vigorously up and down.

—"Pop" the beanbags. Children toss beanbags up and down in the parachute while making waves.

- Making a dome or mushroom. Children hold the parachute close to the floor, then with a lifting motion, they raise both hands above the head so that the parachute rises. If the group takes a few steps in toward the center, the parachute will fill and make a high dome.

—After the parachute has made a dome the children can run underneath it, or trade places according to a system. (The teacher should be sure that in the excitement the children do not run into each other!)

—The dome can be lowered and the children can kneel on the edge to trap the air inside a "mountain." The children can flatten the mountain by using their hands and body.

—The parachute can be pulled down so that everyone is sitting on the edge of the parachute inside the dome. (In order to get inside, children reverse the grip and face outward, pulling the parachute down and sitting on its edge.)

—Pull the dome down and have everyone lie with the head inside the dome. This can be reversed so that everyone's head is outside the dome.

- Children may try to invent some circle dances to music while holding on to the parachute.

The children can invent other ways to use the parachute.

A parachute is something of a gimmick and should be used as such, although there is a temptation to use it once a week from kindergarten on or to use it as the "carrot" that will make children do their exercises!

Cage ball

A cage ball can be used for a variety of activities.

- "Keep it up." Groups of six or eight children get under the ball and try to keep it up in the air by tapping it gently. Groups can compete to set a record time.
- "Crab soccer."
- Game using a net with the cage ball.
- With the group arranged in a circle, square, or in two lines that face inward, attempts are made to throw or kick the ball over the heads of children on the other side.
- The class is divided into two groups, with the cage ball in the center of the gym. By throwing smaller balls, each team tries to maneuver the cage ball to the other end of the gym. Players must stay on their own half of the gym.

Roller skating Some school districts invest in roller skates and purchase enough to enable an entire class to skate at once. The skates are shared among different schools, with each retaining the skates for two or three weeks at a time. Skates tend to lift up the polished or sealed surface of tile floors and can create a lot of dust, but roller skating is an excellent activity for all grade levels.

Skateboards The gym could be made available for skateboarders at certain times, or suitable playground space could be set aside for skate boarding for certain periods of the day.

Fig. 9-31 *Under the bar on skates.*

Gym scooters Scooters are popular with children and provide good exercise and a challenge. The edges of the scooters should be covered with carpet or rubber edging. Scooters can be dangerous if fingers get trapped between two colliding scooters, and children should be cautioned to prevent long hair from being caught in the wheels.

The children can find different ways to move on the scooters by using different body supports and changing direction and speed. Relays can be tried using scooters; the "shuttle" type of relay works particularly well. For a shuttle relay, each team places half of its members on the opposite side of the gym. A player makes

Fig. 9-32 *Scooter ride.*

one trip across and gives the scooter to a player on the other side. This player then returns on the scooter and so on.

Group Problem Solving

Students are divided into groups, given a task, and told how to set up equipment for the task. Usually the tasks are such that they involve some group discussion and initiative. The groups can work on various problems, then rotate stations to try other tasks.

Example

"Find the quickest way to get a plastic glass or bucket of water over a cargo net." (Children's attempts can be timed.)

Two scratch lines or benches can be used to define a space on either side of a climbing rope. The distance should be such that it is impossible to reach the rope without stepping into the marked space. The object is for the group to get a bucket of water as well as all group members across the space. The teacher can devise rules about not touching the scratch line or benches or the space in between. The bucket can be full of "dynamite" etc.

A net can be suspended across the center of a balance beam which is about 30 inches or more off the ground. The group must start on top of the beam and get to the other side without going over the net, which clears the beam by only three or four inches.

The children can see how many can balance on a solidly built, low stool.

(Other ideas for group problem-solving activities are given at the end of the chapter.)

THE "NEW" GAMES

The "New" games movement, which started in California in 1973, sought to provide alternatives to traditional sports, and those games which were developed spread rapidly throughout the world. The motto of the new games movement is "play hard, play fair, nobody hurt," and although the games involve competition, the objective is not so much who wins, but that everyone is a winner who plays hard and does his or her best. Some of the games were old, some well known, and others more obscure. If necessary, the original rules were changed or modified to make the game more enjoyable and creative. Many of the games demanded cooperation and collaboration, for instance, earth ball (a large cage ball which has a map of the world painted on it) can be played by a large group. The object of this game is to push, lift, carry, or roll the ball past the opposing team's goal.

Other games devised by the movement require little or no equipment, although such simple objects as parachutes, Frisbees, and balls are used in many of the games. Games are designed for 2, for 12, or for larger groups of people. For more information see *The New Games Book,* edited by A. Fluegelman (1976). Teachers who are interested in learning more about games should see *Children's Games in Street and Playground,* by the Opies (1969). Another interesting book is *How to Change the Games Children Play,* by Morris (1976). Other references are provided in the study guide at the end of the chapter.

LARGE GYMNASTIC APPARATUS

Parallel bars, vaulting horse or box, mini-tramp
Explore and discover: Different ways to use the apparatus.

Specific stunts or skills are not discussed as such in this text. Children who are interested in pursuing gymnastics can learn more about the sport through gymnastic programs offered after school or in community programs.

The early books on gymnastics (see Munrow, 1955) indicate that people once, in fact, did leap over their horses—if they would stand still long enough—and created a variety of different stunts they could perform in leaping. Eventually someone made a wooden horse giving rise to the art of vaulting.

Children should be encouraged to explore the possible ways of getting on, off, and over the apparatus, under the teacher's guidance. Safety considerations are very important. As they learn basic skills, children discover how to land and roll safely in jumping down from various heights. If children attempt only those activities which they feel capable of doing, or if they seek help or advice when they need it, they should be able to use the equipment safely and bring no harm to themselves or to others.

Parallel bars

Examples

"Find ways to get on (mount) the bars. First use one bar, then use both bars. Make sure there is a mat underneath."

"Once you are on the bars, find ways to turn around on the bars, or move along the bars, either on top of them or below them."

"Find ways to get off (dismount) the bars."

"Try these tasks with uneven bars." (This can be done if the bars are adjustable.)

"Try moving along the bars by supporting your weight on your hands or on your hands and feet. Try other body parts."

"Find ways to hang from the bars."

"Find several ways to mount the bars, move along or around them, and dismount. Practice your sequence until you can do it smoothly. Try to obtain a good starting and finishing position."

Vaulting horse

Examples

"Practice getting on the horse in different ways. Try jumping off on two feet by placing the hands on the horse and then bringing the feet up. Jump off and make different shapes in the air. Roll after landing."

"Find different ways to get over the horse, taking all the weight on the hands. How can your feet clear the horse?" (The feet can clear the horse between the hands or to one side of the hands.)

"Try the horse 'longwise.' Find ways to get on and off. Try a roll along the top."

Mini-tramp

The mini-tramp should never be used without supervision and flips or somersaults should not be performed on it. (See current recommendations from AAHPERD regarding use of the mini-tramp and trampoline.)

Examples

"With the mini-tramp sloping toward you, carefully step on it and try a few easy bounces. Lean forward and jump off. Remember to do this in your sneakers and not in your socks!"

"Walk up to the mini-tramp. Step off on one foot and land on two feet on the bed. Jump off. Let the bed give you enough lift to take you off. The more you depress the bed the higher it will push you."

"Jump off and make different shapes in the air. Land and roll."

"Put the mini-tramp next to a vaulting horse, with the tramp sloping away from the horse. Jump down from the horse onto the tramp. This will thrust you away from the horse. Try and keep the body fairly upright."

"Try to twist in the air as you leave the tramp. Try a half twist and a full twist. Keep the body upright."

DANCE AND RHYTHMS (THE PROGRAM FOR THE INTERMEDIATE GRADES.)

Program outline

1. Review activities suggested for the primary grades.
2. Body awareness—moving body parts separately and in combination.
3. Locomotor activities.
4. Non-locomotor activities.
5. Manipulative activities.
6. Ideas for developing rhythmic activities.
7. Developing sequences for dance.
8. A look at folk, square, and contemporary dance forms.

Boys and girls in the intermediate grades are ready for more sophisticated and challenging dance and rhythms concepts. They can work together in groups and can develop longer sequences that require better control and understanding of effort factors. Rhythmic development can be facilitated at any stage of the program by using percussion instruments or music.

Effort qualities can be examined individually, or two or three at a time. Elsewhere in this text, in the section devoted to the program for primary grades, effort qualities were employed two at a time. If effort factors are now explored three at a time, eight combinations are possible:

	Time	*Weight*	*Space*	*Name*
A	*Sudden*	*Firm*	*Direct*	*Punch*
B	*Sudden*	*Firm*	*Indirect*	*Slash*
C	*Sudden*	*Fine*	*Direct*	*Dab*
D	*Sudden*	*Fine*	*Indirect*	*Flick*
E	*Sustained*	*Firm*	*Indirect*	*Wring*
F	*Sustained*	*Firm*	*Indirect*	*Wring*
G	*Sustained*	*Fine*	*Direct*	*Glide*
H	*Sustained*	*Fine*	*Indirect*	*Float*

Laban referred to these combinations as the eight basic effort actions. The four pairs of effort actions which are opposites are linked as AH, BG, CF, and DE. Other patterns are fairly obvious, such as the pairs of factors which have two factors in common and a third which is different. The names given to the eight basic factors are listed above. Teachers can study the combinations carefully and work out the various possibilities. Ideas for using the effort factors, either singly, in pairs, or three at a time, are described in the material which follows.

Explore and discover: Moving body parts separately or in combination.

What?—Have children list the parts that can move (head, arms and shoulders, hands and fingers, legs and feet, etc.).

Keywords—If the children have been working in movement education for some time, let them try to list the where and how variables. Wall charts may be used to illustrate some basic ideas.

Where—Directions (forward, sideways, backward), pathways, levels.

How—Using effort qualities taken one, two, or three at a time. Moving rhythmically, using gesture, using props, using shape.

Alone, with a partner, in a group. Relationship.

Implementation

The teacher should present different tasks, then observe the varied responses of children and select those which are appropriate for repetition and refinement.

Examples

"Find ways to move different body parts, as suggested by the keywords."

"Make sudden movements with the hand or arm. Now try some slower, sustained movements."

"Make these movements direct (straight) or indirect."

"Try the same thing using both arms."

"Try making different body shapes by using the arms and legs."

"Make a sequence of different shapes. Change shapes suddenly, then slowly."

"Make a sequence of shapes by using sudden and direct and sustained and indirect movements."

"Mirror a partner's arm and hand movements."

"Use your arms and hands to work through the eight basic effort actions."

"Add the fourth movement factor of flow to your movements. Illustrate in movement the difference between 'bound' and 'free' flow."

"Try contrasting with a partner's movements or gestures. For example, if your partner moves quickly, you move slowly. Try firm or fine and direct and indirect movements. Add directions and levels, and contrasting or complementary shapes."

The above suggestions could be performed with a musical accompaniment. Sequences should be repeated and refined, and the children allowed to share their ideas.

Explore and discover: Different ways of moving on the feet and on other body parts. Sequences.

What?—Walk, step, run, hop, leap, jump, skip, slide, gallop, other movements.

Keywords—Same as for previous activity.

Implementation

Examples

"Explore ways to move on the feet. Show changes of direction, pathway, speed, and force."

"Develop a sequence using the basic locomotor movements." (This can be tried to music or with percussion instruments.)

"Play Follow the Leader. Get in groups of three or four. Your group should move in different formations, such as a line, a triangle, or side by side."

"Find ways to move that do not involve walking or running. Make a sequence of these movements."

The teacher can arrange children in four groups of about five or six children. A group will work from each corner of the space. The groups can try different ways to cross to another corner, with all group members performing the same kind of movement, travel alternately, or pass through or meet other groups. Children can try moving to different kinds of rhythmic phrasing which accents different beats. For example, children may follow a pattern of .—.—.—, or —..—..—..., or ——..——..——.., where the symbol . represents a regular beat and the — represents an accented beat.

Working in small groups, children can develop their own rhythms by using a drum or tambourine and explore note values to which they can move. Locomotor movements can be combined with movements of different body parts and shapes. Children may contrast sudden and firm locomotor movements with those which are sustained and fine.

In circles of six, children can create different kinds of movement patterns. Using 4–4 or 8–8 patterns, children can circle left, circle right, move in or out, and so forth. Simple circle dances can be created and the teacher should allow time for ideas to develop. Each group can show its dance.

Explore and discover: Non-locomotor activities.

What?—Bending, stretching, twisting, spinning, shapes, gestures.

Implementation

Children may try different ways of stretching and curling (rising and falling, opening and closing). For instance, they may rise with a slow turn or spin, make a shape, and spin down quickly. They may develop a contrasting sequence with a partner that involves opening and closing the body, turning and spinning, and changing level. They may work on some rhythmic twisting and turning that alternate with periods of stillness in a shape.

Examples

"Keeping one foot fixed, reach out with different sized steps on the other foot. Use direction and heavy and light combinations. Let the arms make different kinds of shapes as the foot steps or pivots."

"Create a movement 'dialogue' with a partner. Keep one foot fixed. You may advance and retreat, strike or cover-up, and so on."

"Combine non-locomotor movements with locomotor activities."

Explore and discover: Manipulative activities.

Use balls, beanbags, jump ropes, rhythm sticks, poi-poi balls, ribbon sticks, crepe paper streamers, paddle bats.

What?—Bouncing, tossing, catching, tapping, swinging, manipulating.

Implementation

These are mainly rhythmic activities (although rhythm or music is not always essential). Children may bounce a ball, jump rope, toss and catch a ball, swing a hoop, or pass a ball to a partner to the accompaniment of a drum beat or music. They may develop a sequence of movements using a piece of small apparatus, and match or mirror a partner's movements.

Examples

"Use different floor and/or air patterns in a sequence."

"Show firm and fine actions."

"Using ribbon sticks or crepe paper streamers, contrast indirect and fine movements with those which are direct and firm. Use plenty of free movements."

"Let your arms, head, or whole body bounce or swing. Use different levels, directions, speeds, and range of movement."

"Using rhythm sticks, develop a sequence while sitting in a circle with four or five other people. Work out a sequence to a particular piece of music."

Ideas for rhythmic activities

While sitting down, children can try clapping or tapping to music or percussion instruments. They may develop a sequence using various levels and move their hands together or alternately. They also may move individual body parts, either singly or in combination.

Relationships

Children clap their hands near to the body, far away from the body, above it, or behind it. They also may try:

- *Combining clapping* and *tapping* with the hands and feet.
- Moving to different rhythms and rhythmic phrasing.
- *Mirroring or matching* rhythmic actions with those of a partner.

- *Imitating machinery* with a partner or in a small group. Children use various levels, speeds, and firm or fine movements, rotating, turning, and spinning.
- Copying occupational activities and rhythms.
- *Adapting ideas* from *sports* and *recreational* activities.
- Tinikling (Phillipine stick dance). For this dance, two children hold two long bamboo poles. (The ends of the poles should rest on pieces of wood to keep them off the floor.) The stick holders hold the poles about 18 inches apart and establish a rhythm by tapping the sticks together twice. The rhythm is tap-tap-together, tap–tap–together, but it could also be 4–4 time, with two taps together and two apart. When the sticks are apart a dancer steps in between them for two counts, then steps out when the sticks are brought together. Various patterns of steps and rhythms can be developed. This presents an excellent problem-solving situation.
- Using puppets. The rhythmic, staccato movements of puppets may provide the children with ideas.
- Responding to the rhythm of words, phrases, rhymes, and jingles.

Developing sequences for dance

Dance can develop through the stimuli provided by:

- Music. The impressions and feelings elicited by listening to music can provide the framework for a dance. Children can be introduced to music that ranges from classical to contemporary. The children should listen to the piece carefully several times and the teacher can discuss some of the ideas which the children have suggested. The music may be such that children can categorize its different phrases or segments. It may suggest different moods, actions, or activities, or the children may be able to create a story to fit the music. Different ideas may develop, so the children may interpret the music in different ways to create a dance or a kind of dance-drama. This could be done individually or by a group.

  The movement teacher can cooperate with the school's music teacher for this segment of the program. (Additional suggestions regarding music are made at the end of this chapter.)
- The movement framework of what, where, and how. This framework can provide cues that will assist in the development of expressive movement.
- Poems, stories, historical events, mythological themes, and the occurrences of everyday life. All these sources can provide material for dance. Children can discuss whether a poem or story, for example, requires certain kinds of characters or activities. It may be possible to divide the story into smaller components or segments. The line dividing dance and drama is not very clear.

Essentially, dance is nonverbal, with ideas communicated by movement. Gestures and facial expression are important aspects of expressive movement. Mime may also be included as part of a dance program. Sounds may be added.

- Action words. Sequences can be developed from action words suggested by the children.
- The world of nature. The teacher may pose questions such as the following to start children thinking about the movements of nature.

  Examples

  "What things move in the world around us that we can feel?" (Children can respond by mentioning such things as wind, rain, and snow.)

  "How do these things affect human movement when we are out in them?"

  "Different surfaces and media affect our movement. What things cause resistance to movement?"

  "Make pathways in snow or sand or mud."

  "Other things in nature move, such as leaves, snowflakes, seeds, and raindrops when they fall or blow in the wind."
- Miscellaneous sources. Children can obtain movement ideas from:

—Puppets. (Controlled by strings, puppets make jerky movements and move in different ways.)
—Toys.
—Robots, mechanical people.
—Ghosts, witches.
—Characters from television. (The Muppets, Sesame street, and so on.)
—Animals.
—Machinery.
—Emotions.
—Human interaction, such as meeting and greeting, parting. This activity can employ partner and group work.
—Clowns.
—Fireworks.
—Sports and games.
—Combat.
—Occupational activities.
—Transportation.

FOLK AND SQUARE DANCE

Quite often in different countries or in other societies adults originated dances and children learned these dances as part of their culture. The steps of the dances usually were variations or combinations of walking, running, hopping, skipping or other locomotor movements. The dances were performed with a partner or in a larger group, and circle formations were frequently used.

Folk dances can be taught to children in the intermediate grades. The steps are learned first, then the entire dance is taught using the whole–part–whole method. However, if the steps and patterns are complicated and require a long time to learn, children may not find dancing very enjoyable or immediately satisfying. They may not spontaneously respond under these conditions and may need to be drilled into learning dances.

Children can more readily create their own dances modeled after folk dance. Music can provide the ideas for development of all kinds of dance patterns and small groups of children can create different circle or partner dances. The teacher initially may provide the children with cues and movement ideas, such as counting four beats and changing direction or pattern. This kind of development can follow directly from other work in locomotor activities.

Relationships between sexes, in terms of dancing together, are generally less inhibited in the elementary school, although sex antagonisms can develop. Getting boys and girls to hold hands usually can be managed if dance is an accepted part of a movement program. If the teacher joins in occasionally he or she will help to create the proper atmosphere.

The same philosophy and similar concepts can be applied to square dancing. Set patterns and movements, along with the terminology necessary to describe the particular patterns of square dance, can be learned. Children also can create their own style of square dancing after an introduction to this type of dancing.

CONTEMPORARY DANCE

Children enjoy trying out styles of dance that are currently popular, such as disco dancing. Different steps and patterns can be created to the appropriate music. Such dancing can be developed individually or with a partner, although it should not be forced in any way but allowed to develop spontaneously.

Developing quality in movement

As was discussed earlier, having children explore tasks which lead them to discover activities they can do produces a quantity of movement, some of which may not be of very high quality. As the teacher monitors and observes the movement responses of children, he or she may ask "Are they responding to the set task?" "How well are they responding?" and "How can the responses be improved?"

There are some points that need to be discussed here, such as how do we decide what is quality of movement and how do we recognize it? Is quality determined the same way for creative movement as it is for functional movements or skills? To the child, the movement may feel good and be satisfying, yet look terrible to the teacher. In highly skilled performance, quality can be recognized in that the movement looks effortless, graceful, and efficient. In competitive gymnastics, judges award points for quality and creativity, with aesthetics coming into the picture as well. In creative movement, all of these aspects of quality can be present, that is, the movement looks graceful, smooth, efficient, effortless, and generally is aesthetically pleasing to watch.

In the learning sequence discussed earlier, the child is encouraged to explore and experiment within the framework of a task. His or her discoveries or responses to the task then must be analyzed from several different standpoints and the child provided with information or feedback about his or her response. This feedback may take the form of additional cues or sub-tasks, or may be provided more directly. Analysis is critical in terms of helping the child recognize what should be repeated or practiced as the skill or activity is developed and learned. The teacher cannot keep on saying "Good, now find another way," because this does not provide children with the information they need to fully develop their movement responses. As the teacher observes children's movement, he or she must comment and provide cues or questions in order to supply the child with the information he or she needs concerning the responses. Generally, the teacher should accept responses in a positive way, even though some responses may be inappropriate. If the response is inappropriate, the teacher must redirect the movement toward the desired goal. If the response is appropriate, the teacher can draw the child's attention to certain aspects of the movement that may need to be changed, repeated, or refined.

Utilizing the effort qualities may provide one guide to the teacher. How is the child using the movement factors of speed, force, flow, and pathway? How is the movement being performed in relation to direction and level? What is the relationship of body parts to each other, or the relationship of the individual to apparatus or to other people? Such questions will aid the teacher in evaluating a response. The teacher may make comments to children such as:

"Is that the way you meant to finish that roll? Try it again and see if you can make it smoother this time."

"Should that toe be pointed?"

"Where are your hands going to meet the floor? Fairly close to your feet or farther away?"

"That was good, but next time try a softer landing."

"Did you really mean to do that as fast as you did? Try putting your hands down more slowly next time."

"How can we help David to do a smoother roll?"
"Which part of your body could help you to throw harder?"
"That was a good sequence; now do it again and make the connecting movements fit together a little better. Let me see it again after you have practiced."

"Practice makes perfect" is a popular slogan, but everything depends on what you are practicing! This slogan should be changed to "correct practice makes perfect." Of course, this applies to the student who is striving to perfect a single model of a skilled performance. The teacher of movement education has to make many decisions during a lesson about what the student will practice, and there may be no single model of performance to be achieved. The children's increasing body awareness will, of itself, provide a degree of intrinsic feedback which will help students to monitor their own feelings about the quality of their movements. Developing quality in movement is an ongoing process that demands a continuous and determined effort on the part of the teacher.

Planning lessons for the fifth and sixth grade

Planning the total program is discussed in Chapter 10, together with a look at learning centers, contracts, and "open" gym. This chapter concludes with six examples of lessons for this age group. Some teachers have found that it is better to schedule two class periods a week of 45 to 50 minutes rather than three periods of 30 minutes.

SAMPLE LESSON PLANS

I. (This lesson is one of a series concerned with developing basketball skills.) The objectives are:

1. To improve the student's ability to dribble a ball while utilizing changes of speed and direction.
2. To improve the student's skill in passing a ball in place, while on the move, and against opposition.

   Equipment: Enough balls for each student to have one. (Balls other than basketballs may be used.)

   Introduction

   As students enter the gym they pick up a ball and practice dribbling, showing changes of speed and direction as well as an awareness of other students who are also dribbling. (Teacher monitors students and provides feedback, praise, and additional cues to individuals.)

   Explore and discover:

1. Dribbling with change of speed and direction.
2. Development: Add stopping and starting, stress accelerating

with control of the ball.

3. Ways to protect the ball or evade a challenger. Six to eight children put their balls away. The rest of the group dribbles the balls, those without a ball try to get one. (The teacher should stress that there is to be no personal contact.)
4. Find ways to pass to a partner, with both players moving. Vary distance apart, speed, and direction.

(This part of the lesson can take about five minutes, although the teacher can decide whether to continue longer.)

Providing opportunities to practice dribbling and passing.

Lesson focus

For this task, children are divided into six groups and each group is assigned to a different station. (Groups can be formed according to the teacher's opinion of how well children will function together. Children having lower skill ability should be placed in a group in which their ability counts. If there is a wide range in abilities, the teacher might want to develop special tasks for these children.)

Group tasks

1. Children face a partner in the middle of the gym. One player has a ball and tries to dribble across the gym to the opposite wall. Activity is repeated with partners alternating possession of the ball.
2. Team passing, three-on-three. Children on a team try to make as many passes as possible before the ball is intercepted. The teacher can discuss strategy or the mechanics of passing plays, moving into the open space, etc.
3. Circle Keep Away. Each player goes in the middle of a circle for about a minute and attempts to intercept the ball. The ball must be below head height as it is passed.
4. Three players find ways to dribble and pass while traveling down the court. The players change speed and direction.
5. Running circle catch. A player stands in the center of a circle and feeds the ball back and forth to players running on the perimeter of the circle. Players change direction, speed, and type of passes.
6. Players dribble in toward the basket and shoot. Opposition tries to prevent a score. This is essentially a one-on-one situation.

Groups should change activity every five or six minutes. The teacher can spend the entire class time on this part of the lesson, or may utilize only three or four activity changes.

Application

The class can play two games of five-pass basketball. (This will take 15 minutes or so.) Teams can consist of five or six players, and players can rotate in or be substituted every 3 minutes. Each team must make five passes before trying a shot. The game can be played at walking speed for a few minutes. The teacher can use the games to discuss the use of space and positional play for better passing. If a large number of children are inactive, only one game should be played and the rest of the time allocated for station work.

If the group tasks are going well and students appear to be involved and making progress, the teacher does not have to abbreviate this part of the lesson in order to play the game, which can be tried another time. Lesson plans are meant to guide the teacher through the curriculum and do not have to be rigidly followed if circumstances indicate a change. Teachers should be flexible enough to know when to continue with certain learning experiences and when to change them. As teachers move more and more toward individualization, rigid structures and plans will give way to more flexible methods of organization. Teachers also will need to find simple, but easily understood ways of writing out a lesson.

II. (Lesson is part of the basic skill sequence.) Theme: Moving on the feet and utilizing changes of speed and direction.

Explore and discover: Running with changes of speed and direction.

Introduction

1. Students demonstrate free running with directional and speed changes.

Tasks

1. From a sitting position, children slowly get up and start moving. They gradually increase speed until they are going as fast as possible (for a short time). Children gradually slow down and return to complete stillness on the floor. (Students do this independently, *i.e.*, they do not all need to finish simultaneously.)
2. Children find an efficient way to completely reverse direction. (The teacher should look at the responses and discuss the use of feet, body, etc.) This can be performed at different speeds.
3. Children try to beat a partner across the gym, starting from a line and running across to touch another line with the foot, then returning.
4. Someone times children for a shuttle run consisting of four trips over a 30-foot distance. The feet must touch the lines as the children turn. Children try to beat their own record.
5. Children try to elude a partner by running, changing speed and direction. The partner will try to tag the runner.
6. The teacher sets up six to eight cones or tires and times the children as they run in zig-zag fashion through the cones to the end and return.

7. Children find an effective way to reverse direction while dribbling a soccer ball or a basketball. This should be practiced until it can be done easily.

The teacher can organize the tasks as station activities or class activities. The period can conclude with a game that applies some of the skills practiced.

Application

Play a chasing game.

III. (Lesson is part of the basic skill sequence.) Theme: Rhythmic jumping, jumping with a rebound. Equipment: A jump rope for each child, boxes, wands, or canes. Benches.

Introduction

Children have free practice with jump ropes.

Example

"Let me see who can skip rope." (Teacher indicates that children should try skipping rope in place and encourages different ways of skipping rope while in place or while moving.) Children try different foot patterns.

Explore and discover: Tasks involving jumping with a rebound, jumping continuously, sequences.

Tasks

1. Children work in pairs, with one partner making a shape on the floor. The other partner develops a series of continuous jumps to go around and over the shape. Partners should change places frequently. Children should concentrate on taking off immediately after landing and utilizing different kinds of jumps (on one foot, on two feet, twisting, etc.).
2. Children work in threes, with two making shapes while the third jumps, as in task 1.
3. Two or three jump ropes are arranged on the floor so that spaces are created for jumping in and out of or over.
4. With a partner, children find ways to swing or turn around a rope so that it is parallel to the floor. One person turns the rope while the other jumps over it.
5. Equipment (boxes and wands) is set up so that children can jump and easily rebound again over another object. Children should try to develop five or more continuous jumps, varying the way the jumps are made.
6. Children attempt to cross the gym in the fewest hops or leaps. They may try to beat their own record.
7. Children jump on and off a low bench continuously and rhythmically.
8. With two or three others, children alternate turning a long rope and jumping over it. They may try "going in" as the rope is turned toward them, then as the rope is turned away from them.

Application

Several long ropes can be arranged so that children may work on developing simple routines involving jumping the long rope.

Children may get tired from too much jumping. The teacher might decide to intersperse jumping activities with those that give the children a rest.

IV. *Explore and discover:* Using movement words to create different sequences.

Introduction

Working in their own space, children are asked to move their feet across the space to the beat of a drum. The teacher feeds in cues or picks up ideas from the children, and can suggest changes of direction, effort, size of step, and foot patterns. The teacher may vary the tempo of the rhythm. Children can share their ideas and time can be provided to allow children to observe each other.

Lesson focus

Using movement words to develop movement sequences.

Examples

"Who can tell me some words that describe movement?" (The teacher may write the words suggested by the children on a blackboard or a large sheet of paper. Children may suggest such words as spin, shiver, slide, or freeze.)

"I want you to choose any two words, join them together, and make a movement sequence." (For example, spin and freeze, slide and spin, shiver and freeze, etc.)

"Try this again, but reverse the order of the words."

As activity proceeds the teacher can move around to offer encouragement to individual students, praise good ideas, and provide cues as needed.

Example

"You have all had some interesting ideas. Now see if you can add a third word and make a new sequence. Remember to explore your sequence at different levels or use different shapes or body supports."

After some practice, and after the children have had time to develop their sequences, they can demonstrate their sequences to one another. (This can be accomplished by allowing half the class to perform at a time.)

Application

Children may add a fourth word and try to put the whole sequence together in different ways. They may make different shapes, freeze, or spin on different body parts. Again, the children can demonstrate their sequences after refining them. If time permits, the children could work with a partner to develop a sequence based on the same words.

V. *Explore and discover:* The creation of a movement sequence suggested by a piece of music.

Introduction

Children should sit down and listen to a piece of music, for instance, the first part of Grieg's "In the Hall of the Mountain King." The early part of the work may be repeated again so that children acquire a feeling for the music.

Example

"What does the music suggest to you? Can you think of some ways that you could move to the music?"

The teacher can discuss some of their ideas and suggestions with the children. The music may make children think of ghosts, giants, elephants, or hunters; or it may suggest movements to them, such as heavy and direct, light, angular, spiky, or twirling.

After the discussion, the children can find a space to work out a beginning for the early part of the piece. The teacher can assist and work with individuals, while at the same time restarting the music frequently. This might be a good time to introduce ideas about effort qualities such as slashing, pressing, and possibly punching.

Lesson focus

Children should listen to the way the music builds to a climax and discuss their ideas for the middle part of the dance as well as a possible ending. The children may see possibilities for working with a partner or in opposing groups that come into conflict.

Application

The teacher can select different ideas for the entire class to utilize. The dance could represent a series of mock battles, with whirling, slashing, and punching movements, that culminate in a series of vigorous leaps and a final collapse.

VI. *Explore and discover:* Moving rhythmically to music.

Introduction

The teacher can choose some music with a lively beat and ask the class to walk or jog to the beat. The teacher should stress that the children should show changes of direction while keeping as far away from others as possible. The teacher may then ask the children to find different ways of moving to the beat that do not involve walking or running. (The teacher can pick up ideas from the children and share them with the class.) As children move they may clap to the beat.

Lesson focus

Clapping and moving over the floor on the feet to rhythmic patterns.

Children continue to try different ways of moving, including hopping, skipping, and jumping in place. The teacher may have them sit down and clap to the rhythm using the first phrase of the music, stand and move to the second phrase, clap with a partner for the third, and so on. The children can develop ideas for moving different body parts as well. The teacher may suggest movements to do with a partner or in a small group.

Application

The children can build sequences of movements that are based on moving and clapping. They may work individually, with a partner, or in a small group. Patterns can be varied as the children work out their ideas, and the teacher may need to provide cues relating to direction, pathways, floor patterns, and recognizing the phrases in the music. Children may share ideas and observe each other.

Seminar Questions and Activities

1. Outline a movement program for fifth- and sixth-grade children. Give details to support the way in which you have allocated time to the different activity areas you propose. Choose either a thematic approach or a skill-sequence development. Include the following:
   - How to improve flexibility.
   - How to develop arm and shoulder muscle strength or abdominal muscle endurance.
   - Invent games for two, three, four or six players. Use:
     —Beanbags and boxes.
     —A ball and two hoops.
     —A ball and unobstructed wall space.
     —Gym scooters, a ball, and two milk cartons.
     —Develop several circle ball games.
2. Discuss the place and purpose of dance in the elementary school physical education program.
3. Survey the students who are at the fourth, fifth, or sixth grade level in a school to find out the amount and kind of participation by them in out-of-school recreational games and sports. Develop a simple table that will illustrate your results. Do the results have any implication for the school physical education program?
4. Develop a series of six or eight cards for circuit training. Try the program with a group of 5th or 6th grade children or other students in your class. Do you need to make any changes in the order of the stations or in the number of repetitions of each activity?
5. Examine the "games analysis" model as presented by Morris, then choose any game with which your class is familiar and have the group suggest modifications or ways to change the game. Use the games analysis grid to help you explore the possibilities of developing different approaches.
6. Quite often dance is a neglected part of a physical education program. Discuss the reasons for this and suggest ways in which dance can become a more valuable component of the program.
7. Briggs (1974) has suggested that, if there is to be real involvement and participation (p. 156), two factors are very important in educational dance: the facial expression and the inner attitude of the dancer. How might a teacher encourage children to develop such qualities in learning to dance?
8. Make a list of suitable music for use in a creative dance or rhythms program. For each piece of music, indicate several ideas that could be used

to encourage or stimulate children to develop creative dance.

9. Read *Beyond Balls and Bats* by Hellison (AAHPER, 1978). Are there any implications that can be drawn from this source that are relevant to the physical education teacher in the elementary school?
10. Discuss the desirability of including team sports in the elementary school physical education program. Could (or should) they be left out?
11. Look at the *New Games Book* and decide if the kinds of activities described in this book have a place in an elementary school physical education program.
12. Why should gymnastics be included in the physical education program?
13. How could the use of Laban's effort factors be applied in developing creative dance?
14. Develop three dance lessons that form a sequence and are based on a theme of your own choosing. Teach the lessons to a class. Comment on the way the lessons developed.

Bibliography

Fluegelman, A. *The New Games Book.* San Francisco: The Headlands Press, Inc., 1976.

Godfrey, B., and Kephart, N.C. *Movement Patterns and Motor Education.* New York: Appleton-Century-Crofts, 1969.

Opie, Iona, and Opie, Peter. *Children's Games in Street and Playground.* Oxford: The Clarendon Press, 1969.

Morris, G. S. Don. *How to Change the Games Children Play.* Minneapolis: Burgess Publishing Co., 1980.

Munrow, D. *Pure and Applied Gymnastics.* London: Edward Arnold (Publishers) Ltd., 1955.

Study Guide

Games

One of the most interesting trends in physical education has been the fresh look people have been taking at games. The reader should start by referring to:

Mauldon, E., and Redfern, H. B. *Games Teaching.* London: Macdonald and Evans, Ltd., 1969.

This book discusses the role of games in education, the complexity of games, and their developmental stages. An analysis and classification of games is presented along with suggestions for organizing and teaching games.

Lenel, R. M. *Games in the Primary School.* London: University of London Press, 1969.

In her book, Lenel applied Laban's principles to games, suggesting that the principles are appropriate to educational gymnastics and modern educational dance. The book indicates that children are capable of creating rules and inventing their own games. Lenel develops a program around the use of small apparatus such as beanbags and balls, chasing and dodging games, and progressions for such games as soccer and basketball. Themes are not utilized as the organizing focus.

Hardisty, M. J. *Education Through the Games Experience.* Bellingham, Washington: Educational Designs and Consultants, 1972.

Hardisty offers a different approach and suggests that the games program should be closely based on the child's psychological and physiological needs. Five basic actions, the components of most games, are identified: striking, dribbling, throwing, carrying, and collecting or stopping an object. Problem solving is utilized as the teaching technique and lessons are built around the five basic actions or combinations of them. Children also are encouraged to invent games on their own.

Stanley, S. *Physical Education: A Movement Orientation.* Toronto: McGraw-Hill, 1977.

Stanley looks at the teaching of games through the use of Laban's analysis of movement. He uses body awareness, space awareness, effort qualities, and relationships to examine participation and performance in games. Themes are used as ideas for structuring lessons and children are encouraged to invent their own games.

Morris, G. S. Don. *How to Change the Games Children Play.* 2nd ed. Minneapolis: Burgess, 1980) proposes a games analysis model which has six categories: players, equipment, movement pattern, organizational pattern, limitations, and purpose. The games analysis model can be used to assist in the process of student decision making with regard to the structure of a game, designing new games, and using a problem-solving approach to teaching games.

Riley, Marie, ed. "Games Teaching." *In* The Journal of Physical Education and Recreation, September 1977.

Contemporary views on games and games teaching are presented in this article.

Kruger, Hayes, and Kruger, Jane M. *Movement Education in Physical Education.* Dubuque, Iowa: Wm. C. Brown, Co., 1977.

Logsdon, Bette, *et al. Physical Education for Children: A Focus on the Teaching Process.* Philadelphia, Lea and Febiger, 1977.

Kirchner, Glenn, *et al. Introduction to Movement Education.* Dubuque, Iowa: Wm. C. Brown, Co. 1978.

Several other ways in which the teaching of games can be approached are presented in these references.

Docherty and Peake. "Creatrad." *In* The Journal of Health, Physical Education, and Recreation, April 1976.

This article presents an interesting idea for combining traditional approaches with those of movement education.

Rohnke, Karl. *Cowtails and Cobras.* Hamilton, Maryland. Project Adventure. 1977.

Rohnke describes group problem-solving experiences.

Competition

Competition for young children also is a topic that causes considerable discussion.

Thomas, Jerry R., ed. *Youth Sports Guide for Coaches and Parents.* Washington, D.C.: The Manufacturers Life Insurance Company and The National Association for Sport and Physical Education, 1977.

Martens, Rainer. "Kid Sports: A Den of Iniquity or a Land of Promise." *In Proceedings* of the 79th Annual Meeting of the National College Physical Education Association for Men, January 1976.

Albinson, J. G., and Andrew, G. M., eds. *Child in Sport and Physical Activity.* Baltimore: University Park Press, 1976.

"Echoes of Influence." AAHPER, 1977.

This collection of articles looks at competition.

Magill, R. A., ed. *Children in Sport: A Contemporary Anthology.* Human Kinetics, Champaign, Illinois, 1978.

This is another article dealing with competition.

"Educational Gymnastics." In JOPER, September 1978.

Recent ideas on educational gymnastics are discussed.

Dance and Rhythms

There are many excellent resources dealing with dance and rhythmic movement.

Lofthouse, Peter. *Dance.* London: Heinemann Educational Books, Ltd., 1970

This is an excellent handbook designed for the person who has little knowledge or intuition about how to begin a dance or movement program. This book leads the reader into teaching principles and techniques and then develops the first 7 of Laban's 16 original themes as specimen lessons. (The source used is Laban, R. *Modern Educational Dance.*)

Russell, J. *Creative Dance in the Primary School.* 1968.

Russell discusses the place of dance in the elementary school and then develops material for teaching. The topics she utilizes are body awareness, effort, space and shape, and relationships. Ideas for developing a curriculum in dance, together with suggestions for planning lessons, are clearly presented. (A more recent edition is: Russell, J. *Creative Movement and Dance for Children.* 2nd ed. London: Macdonald and Evans, 1975.)

Boorman, J. *Creative Dance in the First Three Grades.* New York: David McKay Company, Inc., 1969.

Boorman, J. *Creative Dance in Grades 4–6*. Ontario: Longmans Canada, Ltd., 1971.

In these two practical books, Boorman presents teaching progressions which provide great flexibility for the teacher as well as permit originality and creativity on the part of children. The first book deals with the primary grades and the second one looks at Grades 4 through 6.

Carroll, J., and Lofthouse, P. Creative Dance for Boys. London: MacDonald and Evans, 1969.

Carroll and Lofthouse have recognized the fact that many teachers have felt that teaching creative dance to boys in the intermediate grades and in junior high school was both difficult and unsuitable. However, the authors state that there is no difference between the movement experiences that are valuable for both boys and girls and suggest mixed classes. The book will provide ideas for teachers interested in the fuller development of dance in the elementary school.

Fleming, G. A., ed. *Children's Dance.* Washington, D.C.: American Association for Health, Physical Education, and Recreation, 1973. (See also the September 1979 issue of JOPER.)

This series of collected articles examines the philosophy of children's dance, dance programs, ethnic dance, professional preparation in dance, and resources for dance.

Briggs, M. M. *Movement Education: The Place of Movement in Physical Education.* London: Macdonald and Evans, 1974.

Two other excellent resources are:

Murray, Ruth L. *Dance: Elementary Education.* 3rd ed. New York: Harper and Row, 1975.

Winters, Shirley. *Creative Playtime Movement for Children of Elementary School Age.* Dubuque: Iowa. Wm. C. Brown 1975.

Rules of Games

AAHPERD. *Rules for Coeducational Activities and Sports.* Washington, D.C., AAHPERD, 1979.

10 developing the curriculum

Introduction

"If only I were organized," or "Next semester will be better" are sometimes the cries of teachers who have started the school year without preparing any firm written plans for the classes they are going to teach. Consequently, what usually happens is that they come up with exactly the program they used the year before—one that is easy to teach, easy to grade, and repeats similar activities across the different grade levels. Such a program usually is organized around blocks of activities: three weeks of soccer followed by four weeks of flag football, gymnastics, basketball, and so on. Experienced teachers often memorize most of the activity schedule and mechanically go through the same sequence year after year.

Many teachers openly admit to not preparing written lesson plans, or if they do write them down, it is the same plan for Grades 1 through 6. Occasionally teachers will indicate that they planned lessons for their first year of teaching and then gave up the idea! This sometimes is described as having had 20 years' experience, but it was the same year repeated 20 times! Of course, many teachers do work from a master plan for the school year, and take into account the age and developmental level of the children as they prepare their lessons.

In order to plan their lessons, teachers need to be informed of current developments in the field of physical education. Many teachers do not belong to a state or national physical education association. Keeping up to date on new ideas, curriculum trends, and position papers is a very good way to obtain material for teaching. Reading current professional journals, and attending workshops, clinics, conferences, and conventions can contribute to helping teachers establish goals and objectives. Formulating one's own philosophy of physical education cannot be done in isolation. Teachers should continually ask themselves why they are teaching, what they are teaching, and also how they are teaching. Having contact with other ideas and philosophies can help to either change one's own philosophy or strengthen existing beliefs and values. Teachers should always be able to justify what they are doing and, if necessary, defend the approach chosen.

Ready-made philosophical statements are not always easy to accept, and sometimes they are not even read. It is better for teachers to develop their own program goals and objectives. This may be done within a school district by a group of teachers, or at the state level by administrators and teachers. If everyone who is going to work with the established philosophies has a chance to participate in and contribute to their formulation, acceptance of the philosophies should follow. Even in situations in which there is a curriculum guide, teachers are not always obligated to follow it. The professional person probably should have some latitude in deciding the what, when, why, and how of his or her program, but there are good reasons for having a few common goals and objectives. Some teachers may decide to ignore certain parts of the curriculum, while others may always have their classes play games. Conveying knowledge and developing understanding may not be handled adequately, or children may not be exposed to very much dance or creative movement. All of these are possibilities, of course, even in a prepared curriculum; however, there is more likelihood of a curriculum being followed if a written guide is provided as well as frequent in-service programs aimed at helping teachers implement the curriculum and discuss problems concerning it.

Planning the program

Planning a program does take time, but it is well worth the effort. The author remembers being appointed to a new school and being asked by the principal to prepare the physical education curriculum for the entire school, and being given only three months in which to produce it!

Some guidelines for program planning are presented below.

1. Decide on broad goals for the program that are based on and

adapted to the local situation. This will mean learning about the community, the school, the catchment area for the school population, the types of children, and the educational goals of the school district. Other influences may be the teacher's own philosophy of education and his or her attitudes about learning, children, and the subject matter. Goals may be stated for the three areas of knowledge, skill, and attitude, as well as for the three developmental channels of physical, socioemotional, and intellectual growth.

2. Before proceeding any further, these goals should be compared to any goals established by the school, the school district, or the state, or to position paper statements published by AAHPERD.
3. Select the content areas for each grade level. (The text has suggested five content levels: pre-school, kindergarten, first and second grades, third and fourth grades, and fifth and sixth grades.) The whole program is essentially a continuum and teachers can select material and ideas for particular children from any level.
4. Decide approximately how much of the year will be spent in certain program areas. (Use rough percentages only.)
5. Try to establish a daily period for all classes before accepting anything less. Find out how long the periods will be.
6. A school year is approximately 180 days, or 36 weeks, which usually are divided into four quarters of 9 weeks each. Knowing this, it is easy to calculate approximately how many periods there are to work with. For example, a class meeting three times a week for a quarter would have 27 periods.
7. Think about having shorter periods in the primary grades and possibly fewer but longer periods in the intermediate grades. Sometimes more flexible schedules can be arranged, especially if the school utilizes an integrated day and bells do not ring every 20 minutes.
8. The teacher must decide on how the program is to be implemented, that is, the method(s) that will be used to facilitate learning on the part of the students.
9. Individual lessons can be developed from the master plan or yearly schedule for each level.
10. Materials must be designed to permit work with the entire class as a group, with pairs, small groups, or individuals, and with learning centers and contracts.
11. Find out what other assistance can be made available in terms of aides, cross-age tutoring, and parents.
12. Design and develop a systematic way to record the progress of each student.
13. Design and describe evaluative procedures for the student, teacher, and program.

DISCUSSION REGARDING PLANNING

Goals and objectives

Broad goals for a program were stated in Chapter 2; the teacher can use these goals to begin planning. Other frameworks are suggested in the study guide at the end of this chapter. It has been said, "Beware the person of the single book!" meaning that the teacher should not rely on a single source for all his or her information and ideas.

Generally, a goal is a broad statement of aim or purpose. Objectives are statements concerning the steps by which goals will be achieved, and quite often are stated in behavioral terms. This means thinking about the observable behaviors the children should exhibit after they have learned a task or activity. Mager (1962) has outlined the steps necessary to describe the desired end product: First describe the knowledge, skill, or attitude desired; then specify under what conditions the desired end product will be demonstrated; and finally, identify the criteria which describe an acceptable level of performance.

Only as many statements as are necessary to clearly describe the outcome should be utilized. Choosing an action verb to describe the desired behavior is not always easy, and phrases such as "to understand," or "to appreciate" or even "to learn" are inappropriate unless it can be stated how the students will demonstrate that they do understand or have learned the task presented to them. A good way to write objectives is to use the format "The student will be able to. . . ." Another format is to state "When the student can describe (identify, demonstrate, explain, show, write, etc.). . . ." Objectives do not need to be written for each and every skill that the teacher expects the children to learn or acquire, since this would make objectives too trivial and too numerous to even be considered.

Objectives can be written for a whole series of lessons as well as for individual lessons. Evaluation should be based in part on ascertaining if the children did, in fact, achieve the objectives presented to them.

Teachers can decide to what degree they are going to prepare objectives in behavioral terms, or, alternatively, in terms of performance only. The latter are easier to write, but are not as precise as behavioral statements. There is not much evidence to suggest that writing behavioral objectives significantly improves student learning. Objectives may help teachers to clarify what they are trying to do, but unless the benefits are fairly evident, teachers may have difficulty in getting motivated to spend the time and effort required to write them.

Recent studies reported by Yinger (1980) provide some indications that behavioral objectives do not form a central part of teacher planning. Teachers appear to be much more concerned with active content, activities, and materials.

THE COMMUNITY

In making decisions about the program, the teacher will want to learn something about the local community. This really means taking a look at the neighborhoods from which the children come. The teacher should get some feeling for the socioeconomic level of the local families, that is, whether it is an inner city, suburban, or rural community, since this can have an effect on the way children approach learning. If there are any local facilities that can be used for the movement program, such as parks, swimming pools, ice or roller rinks, the teacher can explore the possibilities of using them to enhance the program.

For a variety of reasons, children sometimes are bussed to school from another area. This may limit the amount of after-school activity for some children.

It also will be useful to find out what kind of support parents provide to the school, such as a strong PTA which might be prepared to work with the movement teacher to purchase equipment.

THE SCHOOL

The teacher should find out how the school functions in terms of overall organization. There are many organizational possibilities such as self-contained classrooms, open space (with children grouped in different ways), or a combination of self-contained classrooms and open space. Other methods of organization might include "continuous progress" or individually guided education (I.G.E.) Some schools operate on a year-round basis, with children in school for 14 weeks and out for 3. There are other plans as well, and teachers will have to adjust to systems such as rotating schedules, differentiated staffing, and team teaching. All of these procedures may have an effect upon the program and its development.

THE CHILDREN

One of the most important factors in program development is for the teacher to consider the needs, interests, and abilities of individual children. Simple questions can be presented to the children, either verbally or through checklists, in order to ascertain such things as the children's favorite activities, the activities they would like to learn more about, and the physical activities they participate in with their families or through agency-sponsored programs. It may be important to know which activities, if any, they dislike. (Attitude inventories are discussed in Chapter 11.)

Local or state curriculum guides These often are available for teachers to use. Some will be current, while others will be in need of revision. Many guides merely contain material for teaching and do not always provide statements of goals and objectives.

Content Content could be developed in several ways, depending on how the teacher wants to structure the program. One way is to:

- Describe activities on a grade-level basis.
- Outline, for each content area, a scope and sequence plan for kindergarten through sixth grade.
- Use themes to develop the work after defining content areas. There may be some division into activities for the primary and intermediate grades.

Time The teacher needs to decide how much time to spend on certain activities. Maintaining a balance may be difficult at first, but for each program level, decisions must be made about the percentage of time that will be allocated to basic locomotor, non-locomotor, and manipulative activities, and their applications to gymnastics, games and dance, and other activities. To assist in this task, the teacher can devise a chart that shows the percentage of time allocated to activities for the first year of the program. If necessary, these figures could then be modified at the end of the year. Goals and objectives also could be reviewed in the light of experience.

BASIC ACTIVITIES	GAMES	GYMNASTICS	DANCE	OTHER
Pre-school				
Kindergarten				
Grades 1,2				
Grades 3,4				
Grades 5,6				

Percentages then can be translated into actual numbers of periods for each area. A difficulty will be encountered when lessons actually do not consist of all basic skills or all gymnastics; however, the main thing is to ensure that a balance, with variety, is obtained.

There will be a gradual shift in emphasis from a heavy concentration on mastering the basics to application of the basics and development of more specific skills as the child progresses from kindergarten through sixth grade. There may not be an equal distribution of time to games, gymnastics, and dance, in the intermediate grades, with the dance area usually not being allocated as much time as the other two areas. Dance must have a fair share of program time.

In order for the teacher to obtain an overview of the total year's program, he or she should construct a chart that shows the activities that any particular grade level is involved in during a specific time period. A sample chart is shown below.

	WEEKS			
GRADE	1	2	3	4
Kindergarten	Basic skills	Basic skills		
Grades 1,2	Basic skills	Basic skills	Etc.	
Grades 3,4	Balls	Games		
Grades 5,6	Games	Games	Basic skills	Dance

From the teacher's point of view, offering a variety of activities during any day or week can provide a welcome change. In the actual scheduling of classes, the teacher will need to think about the use of space and equipment. If the classes are working in gymnastics and using a lot of apparatus, it would make sense not to make too many changes in activities, otherwise a great deal of time and effort would be spent in moving apparatus. Another point to be considered is the sequence of classes for physical education. The teacher might possibly schedule similar grades to follow each other rather than have a kindergarten class followed by a sixth grade, for example. Sometimes the younger children can be scheduled for the morning, and the older children for the afternoon.

Because physical education usually requires a specific indoor space, scheduling will often present problems if the teacher wants more flexibility. A teacher might teach 35 to 40 periods a week, and if each class has physical education three times each week, 14 classes in a two-round school would require 42 spaces for the seven grade levels from kindergarten through sixth grade. This is one of the reasons why classes sometimes have been combined in order to schedule all classes into the week. The alternative is to have another teacher and, hopefully, another teaching station. If, as Bloom (1976) has indicated, slower learners need a lot more time than faster learners to achieve mastery, then teachers have to find ways to either be more flexible in scheduling time or in arranging instruction so that the slower learners do not fall too far behind. Some schools are able to provide more flexible scheduling, especially if different types of pupil groupings are used.

In planning individual periods or lessons, it is useful to prepare another chart in order to plan (or record) the program in more detail. One way to do this is shown below.

KINDERGARTEN	**WEEK 1**			**WEEK 2**		
Activities	1	2	3	1	2	3
Locomotor	X	X				
Non-Locomotor		X			Etc.	
Ball skills			X			
Etc.						

The chart can list all the activities that the class will work through. Instead of citing fairly specific activities, themes could be listed. One chart will be needed for each grade level. Notations could be made on the chart during the year so that the chart becomes a record of progress as well as a class plan.

Lesson Planning

A method of planning a lesson was discussed in Chapter 5 (page 90). Plans can be formulated for the entire class, with similar tasks being performed by everyone under the guidance of a teacher. The outline suggested consisted of an introduction, lesson focus, and applications.

Lessons also can be planned around themes, as was discussed in Chapter 4. Used in a very broad sense, themes can be organizing ideas for a single lesson or for a series of lessons. Originally developed by Rudolf Laban as 16 basic movement themes, themes now often are modified to fit different approaches to teaching. A lesson begins with the main theme being stated, generally as a problem or task. Sub-themes then are utilized to develop the main task. Modifications have occurred as the original themes have been applied to gymnastics and games, and as they have been used with young children. Essentially, themes consist of ways of exploring what, where, and how the body can move, so that after considerable experience with the way the body moves in space with different kinds of effort, the individual is able to understand and appreciate how to move efficiently and in a functionally appropriate or expressive way, depending on the particular activity or situation. A list of ideas suitable for use as themes is presented.

1. An awareness of the ways in which the body can move in or through space, in different directions, at different speeds, changing shapes, at different levels, transferring weight, on different supports, using different amounts of force, and in the air (flight).
2. An awareness of the ways in which different parts of the body can move (the same factors as for item 1, above).
3. Exploring effort (combinations of space, weight, and time factors) See Chapter 7, page 179, and Chapter 9, page 266. Exploring effort and shape relationships.
4. Exploring balance.
5. Applying and receiving force.
6. Exploring relationships of body parts to each other and the relationship of the body to other people or objects.
7. Working with a partner or in a group.
8. Exploring flow, continuity, and control of movement.
9. Exploring different ways to move rhythmically.

Awareness, as referred to above, implies a conscious perception of the aspects of movement, what Ruth Foster calls a "knowing in my bones." Familiarity with the themes, and work with many different variations and combinations of them, helps children to acquire this awareness.

In both of the preceding methods of lesson organization, individual differences can be considered as the lesson progresses. The teacher can apply different levels of challenge in the sub-tasks or cues that are suggested to children. The difficult part is to conduct this kind of differentiated instruction for any length of time. There are a number of other ways a teacher can organize for teaching and learning. Children are quite capable of learning on their own, and they can also learn from each other. If a situation can be created in which some children learn on their own, the teacher then might serve more as a facilitator and a consultant, with more time available for slower learners and for individual children.

GUIDELINES FOR DEVELOPING TASK CARDS

Starting in the primary grades, children can be introduced to working in small groups. Different sized groups can be assigned to work at a variety of activities related to the content area of the lesson or series of lessons. Tasks for each station can be presented verbally at first, then written on task cards. (Usually there are a few children who can read and they can be dispersed among the groups.) Tasks can be stated directly, with a definite progression of skills, for such areas as gymnastics, ball skills, apparatus work, or simple activities using jump ropes, hoops, beanbags, jumping, or tumbling. Tasks also can be presented in written form by using questions instead of specific directions and themes to be explored. The sequence of tasks can guide discovery toward a specific goal, or may possibly be more open ended. The cards can be made out of strong paper and then laminated. They should be large enough to contain several questions or tasks and be easily legible.

Fig. 10-1 *Children using task cards.*

The cards can be developed in sequences for any kind of activity, and range from a very simple and easy level through more challenging and difficult tasks. They can be coded and classified for different grade levels.

Examples of Task Cards

Rolling Skill Level 1. No. 1.

1. With a partner or by yourself, and using the mat, find different ways to roll.
2. What kind of body shape is the best for nice smooth rolls? Can you make your body into this shape?
3. How many different ways of rolling have you discovered so far? Can you think of any other ways to roll? If you can't think of any more, look on the other side of this card. (The card will

contain ideas such as the use of different directions, curling up or stretching out, starting or finishing the roll, etc.)

4. Tuck a beanbag under your chin and see if you can roll forward and keep the beanbag in place the entire time. Were you able to stand up at the end of the roll?
5. Find some other places to carry the beanbag while you roll.
6. From a standing position, lower yourself slowly onto the floor. When you get down close to the floor, go into some kind of a roll. Try to make your roll smooth and safe. (Try to keep your head, elbows, and knees out of the way.)
7. Walk slowly toward the mat. As you get close to it, lower yourself down and roll on the mat. See if you can roll in different ways (forward, sideways, or backward) by turning and twisting.
8. Try the ideas presented in item 7, but run slowly, lower your body, and roll.

Note: Pictures or stick figures also may be used on the card.

Vaulting Box, Skill Level 3. No. 1.

1. Walk up to the vaulting horse or box and find a way to get on the top. Sit on the top and carefully get off. (There should be a mat for you to land on.) Now find different ways to get on the horse. Try taking off from both feet and putting both hands on the horse. Stand up on the top and jump off. Try to land softly on the mat.
2. Try to land on top of the horse on your knees or seat. As you jump off, explore ways to make different shapes in the air before you land.
3. Add some kind of a roll to your landing. Try to finish on your feet and under control.
4. Now try to get over the horse with only your hands touching it. Can you find some ways to get your feet over the horse? You may need to run up to the horse to get a little more spring.
5. Get on the horse, lay on the top, and find a way to come down hands first on the mat. Do this slowly at first. As your hands meet the mat, tuck your head under and roll.
6. Try approaching the horse from different sides or angles. Jump off with a twist and land facing backward.
7. Develop six different ways to get on, off, or over the horse. Show a clear starting and finishing position.

Jumping, Skill Level 1. No. 2.

1. Get a jump rope and make any kind of shape with it on the floor. Now find some different ways to jump over the shape, or jump in and out of it. Keep changing the shape of the rope. (Did you try different kinds of jumps, such as jumping sideways, on one foot, twisting, or making a shape in the air?)
2. Join your rope to a partner's and make a bigger shape or a dif-

ferent kind of shape to jump over. Can you both jump at the same time without getting in each other's way?

3. Stretch the rope out into a long length and find some different ways to jump over the rope from side to side as you move along the rope. Make up a sequence of six different ways to do this.
4. With two other people, arrange three ropes and three hoops on the floor and jump in and out or over them. Try jumping together, keeping as far away from each other as possible.
5. Have a partner shake or wiggle the rope from side to side while you jump over it. Try to jump as the rope is being shaken up and down.
6. As a change from jumping, lay the rope out again and see if you can "walk the tight rope." Balance walk along the rope in different ways.

Children can be assigned to the groups randomly or according to some other method. They can get any necessary equipment ready and help with putting it away at the end of the period. They can put away equipment they took out, or equipment from the last station at which they worked. Children can rotate to different stations every few minutes on the teacher's signal. The teacher should be sure the children know to which station they go next. Quite often the class may not rotate through all the stations in one lesson. The teacher will need to keep a record or have some way of remembering where each group finished. The teacher can move around the groups to observe the children's ideas and help by providing cues and feedback. Occasionally the groups can watch another group work and afterward share ideas. The teacher will need to analyze the various responses and suggest which ones should be further refined and practiced.

After some experience in working in groups at various stations, the children can be encouraged to move to other stations on their own. It might be suggested that they visit a certain number of stations and that there should not be more than four students at any one activity.

Stations can be used for any area of the program, such as basic skills, games, gymnastics, and dance. They can include activities or sequences for slower or faster learners.

In gymnastics, the stations could utilize different pieces of equipment requiring different skills and activities. For games, stations could be arranged to introduce new skills, for the practice of skills already learned, and possibly for having children invent and create games. For example, stations in basketball could be arranged for different shooting drills, for activities such as "give and go" or "keep away," for passing two-on-two, two-on-three, etc., and for dribbling practice. Some practice could involve opponents in order to make the practice more like the game situation.

In terms of greater sophistication or learner participation, the station activity can become a learning center in which students spend more time on tasks and do some self-evaluation.

GUIDELINES FOR DEVELOPING LEARNING CENTERS

The following outline will help the teacher to establish a learning center.

1. The first thing to do is to make a list of the specific activities to be included at the center.
2. Centers can be organized in such a way that initially only a few children work at the center, with the rest of the class working as a group with the teacher. The number of centers can be increased gradually.
3. After working with fairly simple task cards students should encounter no problems in working at learning centers. The teacher needs to be sure the students can handle their freedom and use their time well.
4. This item is related to item three, and this is the development of responsibility in students. Careful supervision is necessary and the teacher will need to provide plenty of positive reinforcement. If the centers are challenging, interesting, and related to students' needs and abilities, there should not be too many problems. Students also may be accustomed to using centers from their work in the classroom.
5. As different centers are developed and students become accustomed to working at them, they can be given some choice as to which centers they will work at. Choices should be monitored by the teacher so that students make their choices based on their interests and needs.
6. Students should be able to get out and put away any necessary equipment required for station work.
7. After students complete the work at a particular center, they should know what to do next.
8. There must be some method for students to record their progress as well as evaluate their performance at the learning center. Several methods are suggested below:
   - Checklists. As the students complete a task or series of tasks satisfactorily, they can be checked by the teacher or an aide.
   - Teaching. One way to find out if a student has learned or mastered a task is to have him or her teach it to someone else.
   - Self-evaluation. Students can be taught to evaluate their own performances. The teacher again can monitor this process at first. Tasks at the center can be programmed in the sense that mastery is necessary at each step before the student moves on to the next task.

Setting up a learning center

Instructions need to be developed for each center that will be complete in themselves. As snags become apparent the instructions can be modified.

TITLE. The title should indicate which aspect of the program is being utilized. If the center activities are part of a sequence, each center can be numbered and perhaps color coded to indicate the level and/or program area of that center.

OBJECTIVES. These need to be clearly stated, generally in behavioral terms. Statements such as "At the end of these tasks you should be able to . . .", or, "When you have finished the activities at this center you should be able to . . ." may be used. A description of the behaviors students will be expected to demonstrate then should follow.

DIAGNOSIS OR PRE-TEST. Before the student proceeds with the center activities, it may or may not be necessary to establish what the student knows or can already do in terms of skill.

STUDENT ACTIVITY AT THE CENTER.This refers to tasks, questions, practices, or instructions applicable to the center.

a. *Evaluation.* This means how the student can assess or evaluate successful progress. Statements such as "When you can demonstrate . . ." should be followed by some statement of acceptable criteria for completion of the task. The student then may ask the teacher to observe or check off the task on the card.

WHAT TO DO NEXT. Indications should be given to the student as to what to do next. If a particular center is part of a numbered sequence, the student can be told to obtain the next card or chart in the sequence.

The tasks and activities can be written on cards or typed on sheets. For long-term use, a strong card which can be laminated with a clear plastic cover is recommended. Centers can be designed so that individuals or small groups of children can work at them. If the center pertains to games, creating dances, or certain other activities, small groups of six or more can work together.

The activities at a learning center may also require that students look at diagrams, pictures, charts, or film loops or use videotape or other resource materials.

Examples of learning center activities

I. Gymnastics—Balance, Skill Level 3. No. 1.

Objective: At this center you will learn something about balance and stability. You will be able to demonstrate several ways to balance on different parts of the body, and should understand the meaning of being in a balanced or a stable position.

Equipment: One tumbling mat, a cardboard triangle, and a pyramid.

Phase 1.

1. Find a space in the gym for the mat that you will be working on.
2. Find some different surfaces or parts of your body that you can balance on. (One way to think about a balanced position is that if someone gave you a push you would very easily fall or roll over.)
   How many different balances have you found?
3. As you balance on different supports, try making different body shapes or try changing your shape without over-balancing. In what kind of shapes does it seem easiest to balance?
4. Now try to make a sequence of several different balances. Work on making the sequence smooth. Repeat your sequence once you have decided how it will all fit together.
5. When you feel ready, teach your sequence to someone else and let him or her show you his or her sequence.
6. Could you make a different sequence of balances by using other body parts? Make this new sequence longer than your last one.

Phase 2.

7. Now find some ways to balance on:
   (a) Any two supports.
   (b) Any three supports.
8. Support your weight on any three body parts but place them in such a way that it is hard for someone to push you over or upset your position. If the person can push you over easily, move your supports and try again. (If it is hard to push you over, you are in a very stable position.)
9. Now move the three supports and place them in such a way that it is easy for someone to push you over (over-balance). What do you notice about the way you placed the supports this time as compared with item 8?
10. Try to do a headstand (balance upside down while supported by your hands and head). Where should you place the three supports to be most stable? What is the best way to get the rest of your body into balance? Find an easy way to come down from a headstand.
11. What does a photographer use to hold his camera steady? How many supports does it have and why?

Phase 3.

12. Explain to the teacher what you have learned about balance and stability so far.
13. While standing on both feet, how far can you lean in any direction before you fall over (over-balance)? Can you lean far-

ther with your feet close together or far apart?

14. While balancing on your seat, how far can you roll or move in any direction before you fall over? Try the same thing balancing on your back.
15. Take the cardboard triangle and, holding it perpendicular to the floor, place it in a stable position. Now place it in an unstable position. (Resting the triangle on its side is a stable position, supporting it only by the tip is an unstable position.) With the triangle resting on its side or base, how far can it be tilted before it falls over?
16. Take the cardboard pyramid and rest it on its base. How far can you tip it to one side before it falls over? Try doing this with some other things (a chair, a trash can, a book, cardboard boxes of different shapes and sizes).
17. A person's base of support is the space between the supporting parts, including the surfaces of the supports that touch the ground. The farther apart the supports, the bigger the base area. As long as most of our body weight is above the base area we can stay in balance.
18. To conclude this series of tasks, find different ways to balance on two hands. Show some of these ways to me. Why is it so easy to balance on two feet, and yet quite difficult to balance on two hands? Discuss the concepts you have learned in this learning center.

II. Ball skills—Moving a ball with your feet. Skill Level 2. No. 5.

Objective: At this center you will learn how to move and control a ball with your feet.

Equipment: One ball at least six inches in diameter.

Phase 1.

1. Put the ball on the floor and try to move it around with your feet. Keep the ball close to you.
2. Start to walk around and take the ball with you. Change direction occasionally and use both feet in turn. Find different ways to stop the ball by using your feet.
3. Which parts of the surfaces of your feet can you use to move the ball? Which surfaces give the best control? Does using the toe end provide good control?
4. Try to change your speed as well as your direction. Remember to keep the ball close to you. Watch out for other people and try to keep as far away from others as possible. Where should you be looking most of the time?
5. Get a partner and stand facing him or her about five or six steps away. Pass the ball to your partner by using your feet. Which part of the foot helps you to pass accurately? In which direction should your foot be moving as you kick the ball? Does the ball go straight to your partner? After the ball has left your foot, let your

foot continue to move toward your partner. We call this follow through. Are you looking at the ball at the moment of contact?

6. After the ball comes to you from your partner, can you find ways to control it? Stop the ball and control it before you send it back. If you stop the ball by stepping on it, do it very softly, and don't put all your weight on the ball! Why not? How do you stop the ball so that it doesn't bounce away from you?

Phase 2.

7. Find a clear space on a wall so that you can kick (pass) the ball against the wall. Pass the ball so that it comes straight back to you. Are you using the side of your foot to contact the ball? How many sides can we use?
8. Mark some targets on the wall at floor level by using colored tape or chalk. See if you can make the ball hit the targets.
9. Now mark some targets higher up on the wall (at knee height or waist height). Can you kick the ball to hit these higher targets? Where should you contact the ball to make it go higher? Does it matter where your other foot is placed?
10. Discuss with me what you have found out about controlling a ball with your feet. You may have some questions too.

    Note: It may be possible to include some diagrams or wall charts, or illustrations of soccer players kicking a ball. These could be used in the task sequence. A videotape of the children kicking a ball then could be made and analyzed.

Phase 3.

11. With a partner, see if you can pass the ball to your partner while he or she is moving around. Where should you aim the ball?
12. Try to pass to each other while standing still and then while moving. Control the ball before passing it back. Try to look at the ball as you contact it. If you miss the ball it's probably because you did what?
13. On your own, set up a milk carton against a wall. Try to move around with the ball. From four or five yards away try to kick the ball so that you hit the carton. Try doing this as you are moving toward the wall or as you are traveling sideways (parallel) to the wall. Can you do this with either foot?
14. Ask your teacher to watch you kick against the wall and as you move around and pass to a partner. Show that you can control the ball as you move in different directions, change your speed, and use different amounts of force. Keep practicing.

Preparing materials for learning centers does take time and effort. It is suggested that the teacher start with one or two centers and gradually prepare others. Modifications usually must be made as children work through the activities. To make a center "childproof" is difficult, and there should be a way for children to get the teacher's attention if difficulties arise at a center. If the teacher monitors the work of children at the centers, a note can be made of the time it takes to completely work through one set of activities.

If the teacher needs specific activities for certain children to do on their own, individual contracts may be developed.

CONTRACTS

A contract is a kind of individual learning center which can be tailored to meet the specific needs of children who may need remedial help, special drills, or opportunities to apply the skills they have acquired. Children enjoy the sense of responsibility that a contract can provide. Formulating a contract involves a conference between the teacher and the student to discuss what the student will actually do within a certain framework of time. The contract can be formally drawn up and signed by both parties as evidence of an agreement as to what will be done and the time in which it will be completed.

Both a contract and a learning center require a title, objectives, a pre-test or other diagnostic activity (if necessary), a definition of what the student will actually do, and a way to evaluate what has been accomplished. A space should be provided on the contract for signatures.

Example of a contract

VOLLEYBALL THE SERVE 6TH GRADE LEVEL

Objectives:

After completing the activities in this contract you will be able to demonstrate correctly an underarm or overarm volleyball serve which goes over the net in 7 out of 10 attempts.

____

I have read and understand the objectives and I agree to complete them by ______________________.

Signed ______________________
Student

____
Teacher

This contract assumes that the student has no previous experience in serving a volleyball.

Learning activities

1. Look at the pictures on the chart (in the book, on the film loop, on the videotape). The server is trying to hit the ball over the net while standing behind the baseline of the court. (Find out how far the baseline is from the net.)

   How does the server place the feet?

   Let's look at the underarm serve first. Where is the ball held in relation to the body (close to the body or far away)? Which part of the hand is used to hit the ball? Where should you try to hit the ball to make it go high enough to clear the net? (If no net is available a line can be chalked on the wall at about stretch height.)
2. Now let's give it a try! Get a volleyball (or light vinyl ball) and hold it in front of you with your arm fairly straight. Step forward while making a forward swing with your other arm and try to hit the ball away from you. Can you hit the ball out of your hand? Try to toss the ball up a little way just before you hit it. In which direction did it travel? Would the ball have cleared the net? Did you hit the ball with your fist or in some other way? Where were you looking as you hit the ball? Did your hitting arm follow through in the direction you wanted the ball to go?
3. Mark a line on a wall as high as you can stretch. Step away from the wall about four to five paces and serve the ball so that it hits the wall above the line. Each time you are successful, move away from the wall another step and repeat the serve. Review the film loop and compare your performance. Keep moving back until you are at the correct serving distance. What do you need to do to correct your serve if the ball keeps going too low? Can you hit the ball harder sometimes?

   Try to make the serve go in different directions. If you can use a net, try to serve over it.
4. Let's look at another kind of serve now. If you could toss the ball up in the air and hit (serve) it over the net, how might you try to do this? Look at the pictures and then try this kind of overhead serve. You can try hitting the ball with a fist or with the front of your hand. Keep your fingers curled up loosely. Experiment with the upward toss of the ball. How close to or how far away from you should it be tossed? If the ball is too far away on the toss, where does it go when you hit it? After you have hit the ball try to follow through with your arm and body.

   You can try the overhead serve against the wall. As for the underarm serve, you can try to hit it hard or softly. Practice this serve until you can get 7 serves out of 10 over the net when you stand behind the baseline. After you can do this, ask me to watch you. See if you can teach the two ways to serve to someone else.

SOCCER "SHOOTING" 5TH GRADE LEVEL

Objectives:

After completing the activities in this contract you will be able to demonstrate how to kick a soccer ball hard at a goal or target about 20 feet away, hitting the target area 6 times out of 10 attempts.

I have read and understand the objectives and I agree to complete them by ______________________________ .

Signed ______________
Student

____
Teacher

This contract assumes that the student has had some experience in manipulating a ball with the feet and has played some simple passing games by using the feet only to move the ball.

Learning activities

1. In playing soccer the object of the game is to score goals by kicking the ball into a goal. We shall use a target about five feet wide and three feet high as a goal.
2. Let's start by getting a rubber or vinyl ball and finding a clear wall space at which to work
3. Try to kick the ball against the wall fairly hard and yet keep the ball low
4. Did you find a good way to do this? Which part of your foot did you use to contact the ball? The side may be alright, but did you feel that you could kick hard?
5. Let's look at the pictures of a soccer player shooting at the goal. Which part of the foot is being used? (Soccer players usually use the top or instep of the foot where the shoelaces are.) If the ball is stationary, how can you contact the ball with this part of the foot?
6. Try a slow run up to the ball and kick it against the wall with your instep. Where do you have to contact the ball to keep it low? Where should the other foot be placed as you kick? (Try to place the other foot beside the ball or behind the ball in some way.) Where should you be looking at the moment of contact—at the ball or at the target? What helps to give direction to your kick?

7. Make sure that you are pointing your toe under the ball at contact so that you hit the ball with the top of your shoe. Try to kick the ball really hard toward the goal taped on the wall. To keep the ball low you should place the non-kicking foot beside the ball and have the weight well over the ball.
8. Move a little farther from the wall, roll the ball away from you toward the wall, chase after it, and shoot at the target. Practice this until you can do it fairly easily. Can you shoot the rebound back again as the ball comes back toward you from the wall?
9. Chalk some circles about 18 inches in diameter on the wall at different heights. Put one at ground level, one about a foot off the floor, and another about three feet from the floor. Try to shoot at the targets from 15 to 20 feet away. Try this with a stationary ball as well as with one that is rolling away from you.
10. When you feel that you have learned how to shoot, ask me to come and watch you. (You should be able to hit the target at least 6 times out of 10 tries.)

These two examples could be adapted to the local environment, depending on the resource materials available. It helps to have some pictures, charts, or film loops available for children to use. The teacher should be ready to assist when it is necessary. Some children can work on contracts, others at learning centers, and another group can work with the teacher.

Learning centers and contracts can be devised for specific situations or needs. They can also be part of an instructional sequence. If children are expected to develop skills, the centers or contracts can be separate learning modules or form part of "learning packages."

Developing still further the concept of allowing children to learn on their own, perhaps with the opportunity to make choices within a certain framework, they can be introduced to the idea of "open gym."

OPEN GYM

If the teacher has been developing a teaching strategy based on the ideas proposed in this text, that is, encouraging children to explore movement tasks and discover different ways to move, some degree of self-discipline and self-direction should be instilled in children since they are permitted to make choices and work on their own or in small groups. The concept of openness in education implies a certain kind of learning environment, although the term can have various interpretations.

If the school is itself operating on open lines, the teacher of physical education or movement will have other people to talk to about implementation of the open concept in the gymnasium.

The concept of openness is built around the fact that children learn best when they are vitally interested in what they are doing. Children also learn at different rates and do not necessarily all have to learn exactly the same things. A child is curious and enjoys being challenged. The open approach is informal rather than authoritarian, with children being allowed a certain freedom to choose what and how they learn. This freedom also carries with it the feeling that children can be trusted to work more independently and responsibly.

In an open classroom children usually can work on activities for differing amounts of time and bells do not ring every 20 minutes to indicate that it is time to change activities, thus children do not learn in a fragmented way. If, however, there is only one space available for movement, the movement program usually must be scheduled so that all the children in the school have a chance to participate in it. In the open classroom, intact classes are not often taught as a group, rather individual children or small groups often work on all kinds of different subjects. Some children may be involved in mathematics, others in writing or reading, and still others may be involved in a variety of projects. Generally, the teacher receives help from aides or possibly parents. Two or more teachers usually work together with a certain group of children throughout the day. The children may start the school day with one teacher and receive their daily assignments. Children may work at learning centers and use programmed learning, or they may be involved in activities on a contract basis. Physical education teachers have not always seen the possibilities of operating in a different way and have continued to teach mass exercises, relays, and large group games.

In describing what might be done to change to or move toward the concept of a more open situation in physical education, the following points need to be emphasized:

1. If what children learn can be based, in part, upon their needs and interests, they may be more motivated to learn.
2. Children can be guided or directed toward making certain choices in an environment that is structured in a specific way. The children must know which choices are available.
3. Children should be actively involved in their own learning.
4. It helps to have flexible periods of time for movement, although the system can function within a fairly rigid timetable or schedule.
5. The teacher must know what the program goals and objectives are, and when and how to facilitate learning.

6. Maintaining records of childrens' progress will be very important for the teacher in order that he or she may plan effectively for all children and evaluate the program. Teacher aides and even a computer can help here.
7. The environment should be structured in such a way that children can work at learning centers, use contracts or simple task cards, or perhaps work in a small group under the guidance of the teacher.
8. The teacher must develop ways to learn as much as possible about the needs, interests, and abilities of individual children.
9. The program can be developed systematically on a scope and sequence basis. All children may not follow the same plan.

The gymnasium or other space can be set up in different ways. It is helpful if equipment can be left in position for long periods, the entire day, or even part of the day. For work such as gymnastics, part of the space can be set aside for apparatus such as mats, balance beams, and climbing ropes, depending on what the teacher has planned. The remainder of the space can be left clear for floor work, locomotor skills, and other activities. In the area of dance and rhythms, the floor space can be kept very clear so that children can work in small groups with task cards or learning centers, or possibly with the teacher.

Scheduling children into a movement program can be accomplished in various ways, depending on the way the rest of the school functions. In some schools children sign up in advance for movement periods, and they may be told that they must attend a specific number of times during a week or month. This system applies to other curriculum areas as well, and the teacher should keep a record of what each individual is doing. In this system it is possible for children of different ages or grades to be in the same class at the same time, in fact, in some schools children are not assigned to a grade on the basis of age. The teacher must make many adjustments in order to function in such a way, since open gym also may mean that intact classes do not appear every 25 or 30 minutes throughout the day.

Organization and planning take a considerable amount of time both before and after school. The teacher will certainly need help with planning and especially with record keeping. Children also must know what they are going to do, how to record progress, and how to proceed with self-evaluation.

If a school offers computer-assisted instruction, computer cards can be developed for recording levels of skill. Computer cards bear the student's name and the skill level is noted through terminology such as "Has mastered the skill of . . ." or "Is working on the skill of . . ." thus assisting with record keeping. Printouts are produced that list the skills each child has mastered or is working on. The system can be expanded and made more sophisticated if so desired. Handwritten records also can serve the same purpose, but to ask the physical education specialist to maintain individual records on 800 or 900 children is somewhat unrealistic, although this may be possible with smaller numbers.

Through discussion with the teacher, children gradually can assume responsibility for selecting their own activities and objectives and deciding how they will approach learning. They can decide whether they prefer to work alone, with a partner, or as part of a small group. They can determine their own pace and may even design their own experiences.

The teacher may want to try out the entire concept gradually, starting with one group of children to see how the concept works. Time will be needed for the program to develop. Changes to a program should be introduced gradually, with a great deal of planning done beforehand.

FINDING OUT ABOUT CHILDREN

The most obvious way to find out about childrens' needs and interests is to talk to them; however, talking to large numbers of children and recording the data might be very time consuming and may not provide a reliable method for obtaining information. As an alternative, the teacher can develop a simple questionnaire which asks children about their likes and dislikes, feelings, interests, attitudes, and values. Questions and/or statements for the child to complete can be devised. Young children can simply be asked to check a "face" in response to a verbal statement, question, or pictorial representation of a situation. The classroom teacher may be the best person to administer such surveys.

Statements can begin in different ways, such as:

- I like learning best on my own/with a partner/in a group.
- I like being told what to do.
- I am interested in . . . (open ended or list provided).
- I would like to learn more about . . .
- I would like to become better at . . .
- I enjoy . . .
- In my spare time I like to . . .
- I like to be given a chance to find things out for myself.
- I like to have P.E. in the morning/afternoon.
- The things I like doing best are . . .
- I don't enjoy . . .
- Would you like to miss a gym class?
- Are you ever afraid of losing in a competition or race?
- Do you like learning new games?

There are various attitude inventories that a teacher may wish to give to children. (See the study guide at the end of this chapter.) If the above questions and statements are used simply to gather facts about individual children, the results can help the teacher to group children on the basis of similar interests or needs. These facts, combined with the child's level of skill in certain activities, can be a useful aid in classifying and grouping children. The teacher also can utilize the information for planning different instructional strategies. A lack of interest, motivation, and success on the part of children can provide fairly obvious clues at which the teacher needs to look. Pencil and paper inventories are helpful, but through direct observation of children the teacher can collect information about their behavior. (See the suggestion regarding anecdotal records in Chapter 5.)

DOING YOUR OWN THING AS A TEACHER

It is very easy to get into a "rut" when teaching. The pressures of teaching can become very intense, particularly when the teacher is expected to fill so many different roles, such as counselor, clerk, manager, friend, instructor, facilitator, learner, and role model. Trying to fill all of these roles can be a very demanding task; however, teaching can and should be a very rewarding and enjoyable experience. Teaching movement is also an exciting business. As the children work on tasks and make discoveries for themselves the teacher has to be able to develop each child's responses.

The change in behavior which occurs when a completely or partially teacher-dominated situation in the gymnasium becomes one in which decision making is shared between the teacher and the children can be a very rewarding and yet sometimes frustrating experience. To modify teaching behavior from an authoritarian style to one which is more informal and open may take several years. Trying to change can elicit feelings of insecurity and frustration, especially if things do not go right the first time. The rewards come from seeing the children develop their own ideas and create solutions to movement tasks. The whole approach seems to open many doors that had been closed previously because of a slavish adherence to the traditional model, including the use of lesson plans with their list of activities that were implemented without any real understanding of the nature of children or the subject.

Of course, the teacher must believe that what is happening is worthwhile and based on fairly sound principles. Intellectual courage and a lot of support are needed. The teacher's plans to change the program should be discussed with other teachers and possibly with the school principal. The opportunity to meet with and observe other teachers in action does not happen enough in education; pioneering developments usually are made by individual teachers who are moving things along in a gradual way on their own. These teachers must be invited to share their ideas (provided they are willing) through in-service programs or by visitation. It is essential to have some kind of a resource guide. The Saturday morning workshop may get people excited about change, but it may not provide enough material or theory for any serious long-term adoption or trial. The motto of teaching might be "Try all things," and then hold on to what seems to work best for you in your situation.

Study Guide

Tyler, Ralph W. *Basic Principles of Curriculum and Instruction.* Chicago: The University of Chicago Press, 1949.

This text can provide the teacher with a framework on which to develop a curriculum.

Eraut, M., *et al. The Analysis of Curriculum Materials.* University of Sussex. Education Area, Occasional Paper No. 2., 1975.

This is another interesting model on which a curriculum can be based.

Goals and objectives have been discussed in an earlier chapter (Chapter 2). The reader also should examine local school district, state, and national curriculum guidelines.

The sources provide information on different instructional methodologies.

Siedentop. *Developing Teaching Skills in Physical Education.* Boston: Houghton Mifflin, 1976.

The author has included a chapter on planning for instruction.

Hellison, D., ed. *Personalized Learning in Physical Education.* Washington, D.C.: American Alliance for Health, Physical Education, and Recreation, 1976.

Heitmann, H. M., and Kneer, M. E. *Physical Education Instructional Techniques.* Englewood Cliffs, New Jersey: Prentice-Hall, Inc., 1976.

Singer, R.N., and Dick, W. *Teaching Physical Education: A Systems Approach.* Boston: Houghton Mifflin, 1976.

Ohio State Department of Education. *Elementary School Physical Education: Beliefs, Goals, Objectives, Activities.* Columbus, Ohio: 1978.

Florida Educational Research and Development Council. *The Learning Centers Approach to Instruction.* Research Bulletin. Gainesville, Florida: FERDC., Vol. 8, No. 4. Fall 1973.

Barth. "So You Want to Change to an Open Classroom." In, the Phi Delta Kappan for October 1971.

This last article may help teachers clarify their ideas about open education.

Seminar Questions and Activities

1. Discuss the advantages and disadvantages of writing behavioral objectives for an elementary school physical education curriculum.
2. What effect might the way in which a school is organized or operated have on the development of a physical education program?

3. Examine the most recent copy of a local or state curriculum in physical education. Compare the stated goals and beliefs with AAHPERD's position paper, "Essentials of a Quality Elementary School Physical Education Program." What, if any, are the main differences?
4. Develop a set of activities for a learning center designed to develop basic skills. Choose a specific area such as a locomotor or manipulative skill. Try the center out with your class or a group of children. Include some way for students to do some self-evaluation.
5. Make a list of movement themes that you could use to develop manipulative skills in Grades 5 and 6. Indicate the sub-themes that could be used with each main theme.
6. Write a description of your idea of an open gym program. How could this plan be adapted to a school that was organized traditionally?
7. How can the teacher utilize the information gathered about individual children's needs, interests, and learning preferences to plan different instructional strategies for them?

Bibliography

AAHPER. *Essentials of a Quality Elementary School Physical Education Program.* Washington, D.C.: American Association for Health, Physical Education, and Recreation, 1970.

Bloom, Benjamin S. *Human Characteristics and School Learning.* New York: McGrawHill Book Co. 1976.

Foster, Ruth. *Knowing in My Bones.* London: A and C Black, 1977.

Mager, Robert F. *Preparing Instructional Objectives.* Belmont, California: Fearon Publishers, 1962.

11 evaluation: discussion and guidelines

Introduction

As students work toward achieving the objectives of the movement program under the guidance of the teacher, they will need to know how well they are progressing. Children will gain some notion about their progress or success from their interpretation of the comments or other feedback offered by the teacher. Children generally have a keen sense of their relative place in the order of things. They realize that some of their peers are better than they are at certain activities, and that some are probably worse. There may or may not be agreement between these two sources of information about progress or success as understood by the child. Therefore, there is a need to examine ways in which the knowledge, skill, and attitudes acquired by the learner can be assessed or evaluated, and to decide how the results of such evaluation can be communicated to the child, the parent, and the administrator.

There may be several reasons why children do not achieve the stated goals of a program. In the first instance, the expectations incorporated in the objectives and goals might be unrealistic for the developmental level of the children. Next, the teacher may not be doing a very good job of facilitating learning. It may be that not enough time is allocated to physical education, or that the facilities and equipment are inadequate for children to develop and master certain skills. In some school districts teachers may be held accountable for the failure of children to learn. The teacher's accountability for the learning of his or her students is necessary at all times, not just when it is mandated by the school board or by state legislation.

Thus, in terms of the total effectiveness of an instructional system, evaluation must be made of the student, the program, and the skills of the teacher.

TWO ASPECTS OF EVALUATION

Teaching behavior in movement education largely is shaped by the performance or responses of students to the tasks or problems presented by the teacher. These responses should be continuously monitored by the teacher since they can provide indications as to the most appropriate developmental course for each student. This monitoring and observation or assessment is a form of evaluation known as *formative* evaluation since, as the name implies, teaching behavior and student learning can be formed or shaped as a result. In this process the teacher is trying to determine what is the next best thing for the student to do, such as repeat a particular skill, proceed to the next step in the learning sequence, or review an earlier step, depending on the performance of the student.

Good teachers are continously monitoring and observing their students and thus making decisions about their teaching. This may not be considered a form of evaluation in the usual sense of the word, which more often means a process implemented at the end of a unit or learning sequence. Skill levels, knowledge, and attitudes are thus assessed as teachers try to measure the total sum of learning. This kind of evaluation is known as *summative*. The teacher can perform summative evaluations at any time in an attempt to assess the student's learning level. Such devices as quizzes or tests are utilized usually without any effect on the pattern of instruction, and the results combined to produce a final grade. Part of the art and science of teaching is the use of formative evaluation for informal judgments about the suitable cues or tasks for students. In utilizing such evaluation a teaching cycle is developed which consists of presenting an initial task, monitoring the children's responses, deciding on additional tasks or cues (for individual children, small groups, or the entire class), monitoring these new tasks, and so on.

Current evaluative and grading practices

There is no single, easy answer or solution to the question of how students should be evaluated. A brief look at existing practices can give some idea of the wide variations in the methods teachers use to evaluate students and communicate the results of such evaluations to others.

In most schools, teachers are expected to complete a report card of some kind for each student they teach. This usually is done every quarter or at the end of a similar grading period. Some schools or school districts have separate report cards for physical education; however space usually is provided on the regular report card to record the physical education grade.

If a sample of report cards is examined, many different ways can be found of reporting the results of some kind of evaluation. In evaluating skills, a letter grade is sometimes given, with or without a written comment. Checklists sometimes are used that list the various components of the skill and then categorize them under such headings as "highly proficient," "average proficiency," or "has difficulty," in terms of the student's level of achievement or progress. Instead of letter grades there may be descriptive categories such as "above," "below," or "at" grade level, which is itself rather meaningless. Some report cards simply use pass or fail designations rather than three or more categories or levels. Other descriptive categories can be found as well, such as the ubiquitous "satisfactory" "needs improvement," "is improving," or "doing well."

The skills may be broadly classified as basic skills or cited individually along with activities such as running, jumping, balancing, and throwing. Gymnastics, rhythms and dance, games, and physical fitness often are included.

In schools which utilize computer-assisted grading or record keeping, a simple system can be developed to record progress. Students can be described as having "mastered the skill of . . ." or "is working on the skill of. . . ." The skill objectives are described in behavioral terms so that it is clearly understood exactly what the student is doing. Computer cards are available that bear the student's name and also cards having skill descriptions. A printout is obtained for each child that lists the skills mastered and those which are still being learned. Different levels of competence can be devised to show mastery in the areas of motor skill and knowledge. In schools where the curriculum is developed around the concept of continuous progress, the teacher may be able to work with all the children who have not yet mastered certain skills. A computer can print lists of children who take physical education at special times.

Even without a computer, the teacher can devise ways to record the progress of special groups of children. Cards can be made that list the required skills, with one card developed for each student. A hole can be punched in the edge of the card opposite to the description of a skill if the student has mastered that skill, and an open slot is made if the student is still working on the skill. The teacher may then insert a knitting needle through a stack of cards at a particular skill, and upon lifting the needle the cards of those students who have mastered the skill will appear. Those cards remaining in the stack will be the cards of those students who are still working on that skill. The idea here is that there are various ways to work with special groups of children rather than always using intact classes. Evaluative procedures can be based on the concept of mastery and can be as simple or as elaborate as the teacher feels necessary.

Knowledge and understanding of physical activity and exercise is not often found as a separate category on report cards. Knowledge of the rules of a game usually is combined with the skill grade given for that game.

Affective outcomes, as described by such attributes as attitude, effort, citizenship, sportsmanship, ability to get along with others, and participation, sometimes are assigned a letter grade or may be given a value on a descriptive scale of attainment.

ASSIGNING GRADES

How teachers arrive at or make judgments about their students is an interesting topic. Quite often grades are arrived at in a very subjective manner, that is, without the support of any kind of objective measurement or testing. In observing children's performance and behavior in a movement education setting, it is relatively easy to pick out the highly skilled and talented children as well as those with behavior problems. Poorly skilled children also will be fairly obvious. However, there will be a large group of children among whom it is difficult to differentiate on either a skill or attitude basis. This "average" group of children could comprise up to two thirds of a class, and without any objective data the teacher would be hard pressed to assign a meaningful grade.

The movement teacher may see a large number of children in different classes, thus compounding the problem of assigning grades. The teacher's own personal biases and other impressions of children may tend to color the judgments made about children. The grade could reflect the values of the teacher rather than the competencies of the student. In making an adequate and meaningful evaluation, the teacher confronts a challenging task in terms of even getting to know the children's names, let alone making intelligent comments to parents about their child's progress. In addition such evaluations may be required every nine weeks. This fact alone probably has forced many teachers to take the easiest route possible, that is, subjective evaluation with little objective support. Many teachers would prefer not to assign grades, at least in the primary classes. This does not mean that they would not evaluate the children, but merely that they would escape what is often a mockery of true evaluation imposed on teachers by a school administration that does not really understand or want to acknowledge the nature of the problem.

Another area of concern is with the nature of the skill tests that often are administered to children. Many scores as recorded may not be reliable. That is, if the children repeated the test within a few days, would they get close to the previous score (other things being equal)? This may be an even more critical question if children are permitted only one or two trials of a particular test. There may also be a concern about whether the test measures what it is supposed to measure.

What does a letter grade represent?

An assigned letter grade can imply different things and, unless the basis of the grade is known and fully understood, may not be too meaningful. Some teachers may grade on a curve, that is, with a certain percentage of A's, B's, C's, D's, and F's. Other teachers may grade on improvement of skill, while still others may assign grades that are a composite of several different factors. A single letter grade therefore can only be understood if its derivation is clearly stated.

Quite often a teacher will assign scores or points for skill tests that are tallied at the end of the grading period to give a cumulative total that usually is converted to a letter grade. A problem that arises here is in deciding the cutoff points that separate an A from a B or a C from a D.

If a teacher bases a grade on the degree of improvement a student makes, it implies that the teacher knows the entry skill levels of the students and has some way of estimating or measuring progress. Assigning letter grades in this instance could be very misleading, since the students who made the greatest amount of progress or improvement may not be as highly skilled as someone who made a lesser amount of progress. Letter grades and written comments together can provide a better understanding of a child's progress.

GRADING AND ITS EFFECT ON THE STUDENT

One of the key aspects of teaching movement education is the development in the child of the feeling that his or her solutions and ideas elicited in response to tasks presented by the teacher will be accepted and encouraged. (The classroom climate necessary for this feeling to emerge was discussed in Chapter 5.) The method allows children to make choices, exercise judgment, reach conclusions, solve problems, discover concepts, and so on. The teacher must make fairly continuous judgments and assessments as to how well each student is succeeding at the task. These judgments generally will express approval rather than disapproval, unless the child does not respond to the task, perhaps deciding to do something else, such as interfere with someone else or behave in a way that disturbs others. Bloom (1976) discusses the effects on children of approval or disapproval and indicates that teachers usually must make such judgments in fairly competitive situations. The students also come to see themselves in relation to their peers with respect to their own accomplishments, and their feelings of success can influence how new or succeeding tasks will be approached.

As children produce a variety of responses to movement tasks, the teacher should try to observe them and provide appropriate feedback. Competition among children, in terms of striving to be first or best, should be de-emphasized, with the teacher making judgments based on other factors. In movement education the teacher must be sure that all children are made to feel that their responses count, not just those of the more creative children. If children have the opportunity to be successful in terms of their own abilities, their self-esteem and self-concept will be enhanced. Children should be encouraged to think about the quality of their movements rather than about who is the "best." Understanding and appreciating quality in movement can be developed through directed observation and discussion.

This does not mean that self-testing or competition with one's peers will not occur, since self-testing does occur constantly in movement education as children confront the challenges presented by tasks and problems. Children often challenge each other to run a race, jump, or throw. This may happen on the playground, in the park, or in the gymnasium, and it is a perfectly natural thing for children to want to do.

During the remainder of the school day, many children may feel that they are being judged continuously on their skills in reading, mathematics, and in other curriculum areas. Bloom (1976) has stated that test results are being used as a "primary motivational technique." One of the problems with this concept is that generally the same children are the "winners," holding this position throughout all the years spent in school. Successful experiences provide their own reinforcement and motivation, whereas experiences in failure can be very discouraging. We can have "dropouts" from physical education as early as kindergarten, and as teachers we must make sure that this does not happen.

The preceding discussion gives some indication of the state of the art in evaluation and grading. The picture is quite confusing, and could leave a new teacher wondering exactly how to proceed in evaluating students. Within the framework of the suggestions made in this text for teachers to facilitate the movement education of children, judgments must be made as to whether children are progressing toward the objectives that have been proposed. The steps a teacher should take to develop a system of evaluation are as follows:

1. Establish broad goals and objectives for the total program. Decide whether these will pertain to a single grade level or class or to the total movement program in a school.
2. Decide how children's progress and skill attainment will be evaluated.
3. Decide how this progress and attainment will be reported.
4. Establish a way to evaluate the program. This may include a review of goals and objectives, the curriculum content, facilities and equipment, organizational procedures, and so on.
5. Decide how teaching effectiveness will be evaluated.

GOALS AND OBJECTIVES

As the teacher begins to formulate goals and objectives, he or she may use this text as a source. The teacher also can examine other sources, such as local and state curriculum guides and position papers. (See the bibliography at the end of the chapter.) Goals and objectives should be discussed with, and possibly approved by, the school principal and other district curriculum consultants. Basically, the goals and objectives should be well grounded in acceptable current practices and yet be compatible with the teacher's own values and beliefs about education, children, and learning. In a sense, a curriculum should be school based insofar as it reflects the educational philosophy of the school district, the school, and the teachers.

The broad, interrelated goals of a movement program as suggested in this text were developed under the three headings of physical, socioemotional and intellectual aspects of movement. (The reader should refer back to Chapter 2 for a discussion of these goals and objectives.) After identifying the broad goals, the teacher should develop the program content. The teacher should determine whether to use behavioral objectives or performance objectives for the three areas of knowledge, skill, and attitude. Evaluation will be based on the degree to which individual children achieve the stated objectives.

Evaluating children's progress

If the teacher uses the approaches to teaching suggested in this book, formative evaluation will take place continuously as he or she monitors and observes student responses to tasks and challenges. Even in a direct teaching situation the teacher observes what the children are doing. This observation provides the basis for the next task or question for each child or for a group of children. At the end of a lesson the teacher should record what the children tried or achieved. A teacher often is faced with a continuous sequence of classes which arrive at and depart from the gym with monotonous regularity, prohibiting the teacher from taking a break of even five minutes in which to think about, organize, or record information pertaining to the previous class. On-the-spot recording is difficult, and yet if left until the end of the day, recording may be even more difficult. It is very easy to forget details concerning individual children, whereas it is relatively easy to record whether lesson plans were covered and objectives achieved.

As children are encouraged to work at their own rate and demonstrate their different interests and abilities, it will become incumbent on the teacher to make some attempt at maintaining records of children's progress. Checklists can be developed that correspond to the particular skill or theme being worked on. There is no need to check off individual components of a skill, but it is important to record the degree to which children are mastering the main aspects of a task.

Another helpful way in which teachers may record progress is by means of an anecdotal record. (See the examples in Chapter 5, page 86.) In this system, a list of children in each class is kept, and the teacher records relevant information as it occurs. Information that can be recorded could include notes on behavior, skill level, attitude, participation, relationships, interests, degree of persistence, self-direction, and self-discipline, in fact, anything the teacher feels it is important to note about the child. A coding system could be used to save time. Observations should be dated and described in such a way that they will be meaningful at a later date.

Simple skill tests can be devised to measure a child's status in different areas. Locomotor skills can be evaluated in this way as well as such concepts as balance and manipulative skills. If the teacher is working with themes, simple assessments can be made as children show mastery of tasks or sequences. In the area of games and dance, performance can be assessed in terms of skill level, enjoyment, participation, respect for rules, relationships with and toward others, creative work, and quality of movement.

Knowledge tests also can be given to measure accomplishment in such areas as movement concepts and vocabulary, understanding essential facts and concepts in health, exercise, body mechanics, technique and physiology, and rules of games. The AAHPER Cooperative Physical Education Test has a form suitable for use with children in Grades 4 through 6; the test provides a measure of children's grasp of concepts and knowledge about movement.

Physical fitness and testing was discussed in Chapter 2. Measures of self-concept and attitude toward school and physical education can be used. Surveys can be developed that will provide the teacher with information about whether the program is achieving its goals with children.

A CAUTIONARY WORD

The progress of children in the areas of learning skills, acquiring attitudes, and gaining knowledge usually is a gradual process. The teacher who is with the children on a regular basis may not always be aware of the amount of progress children are making. An example of this can sometimes be found at the beginning of the school year in the teacher's lounge, where a teacher may be heard grumbling about the worst third grade class he or she has ever had! What the teacher is doing is comparing the new class with that he or she had just taught for a year. In other words, a comparison is being made between children who have just finished third grade and those who are just beginning it. Skill improvement, growth, maturation, and other changes in children are taking place continuously, so the teacher may not always notice them on a day-to-day basis. Measurement and checklists will provide more concrete evidence of progress.

REPORTING CHILDREN'S PROGRESS

The teacher will have to decide on the best way to report progress to the children themselves and to others. In some respects this will depend on the current practices of the rest of the school with regard to the reporting of grades or evaluations. Separate report cards are useful for movement education, providing that completing them does not become too time consuming. If the program is based on sound written objectives, parents and other individuals who may be concerned with the children's progress will better understand the goals of the program and will welcome and accept a progress report.

A few of the alternative ways of reporting the results of evaluation were presented earlier in this chapter. To communicate the results of evaluation the teacher can choose between checklists, letter grades (with or without written comments), statements concerning the skills that have been mastered and the skills that are still being learned, and possibly even computer printouts. Generally, the teacher should comment on the child's motor skills, knowledge, and attitude. Other comments may be added as necessary, depending upon the aspects of the program which the teacher feels are important or concern the development of the children. On some report cards there is a place for the parent to sign, ask questions, or make comments.

Many schools have parent-teacher conferences in which the parents come to the school to discuss their child's progress with different teachers. The physical education teacher is not always a high priority on a parent's list of people with whom he or she wants to talk. The parent is often more concerned with other subjects, such as reading or mathematics. If a good movement program is provided, the children themselves will be the best advertisement for it. Fliers can be sent home to explain the program, parents can be invited to observe the program, and special events can be developed to show the scope and variety of skills that children can acquire.

If a teacher is faced with a parent-teacher conference, the teacher obviously will need to be able to make intelligent comments about the particular child involved, again pointing out the desirability of having available reliable data on which to base any comments.

EVALUATING THE PROGRAM

The teacher should take stock of the total program each year. Goals and objectives should be reviewed to see if they remain realistic, in line with current practices, and compatible with the educational policies of the school. The degree to which students achieve the established goals also should influence any examination of the goals. The program also should be considered from the point of view as to what was accomplished at each grade level in the different areas of the curriculum. The allocation of time can then be changed if the teacher feels it is necessary. The students should be polled to ascertain their feelings about the program. A review of the children's needs and interests also can be made, and input about the program solicited from parents.

Facilities and equipment should be examined to see if any improvements are needed and listed in the budget. Movement education should get a fair share of the budget, and long-range plans can be made to cover several years.

The program should be coeducational as there is no real reason to separate boys and girls in movement education. Handicapped students should be accommodated in the regular program as much as possible. The movement education teacher can provide a great deal of input in developing individual education plans for children with special needs.

Opportunities for after-school intramural programs should be available for all children; however, intramurals should not take the place of instructional activity.

Contact should be made with the junior high school physical education teachers to discuss the need for program continuity and the possible alignment of curricula.

Finally, the evaluation procedures should be examined to ascertain that the most efficient and yet effective procedures are being used.

EVALUATING THE TEACHER

It is not an easy task for teachers to evaluate themselves. The teacher may possibly enlist a colleague to observe him or her as he or she teaches. Some schools utilize a form of group evaluation which is essentially a peer group system. This kind of evaluation of teaching effectiveness has to be seen in a positive, nonthreatening way in order for it to improve teaching.

The following questions need to be asked in an evaluation of teaching:

- Is the best use being made of the available time, space, and equipment?
- Is the instruction geared to the individual needs, interests, and abilities of students?
- Does the teacher encourage participation by students, not only in the program content, but also as to what, when, and how they learn?

Other questions may be asked about the kind of interaction occurring between teacher and student, such as "Does the teacher use a conversational manner, plan daily, and stay up-to-date?" (There are a number of ways of doing this; see the study guide at the end of the chapter.) The teacher's relationships with the rest of the faculty and staff also need to be examined as well as the status of the program in the school, that is, is the movement education program a part of the total school curriculum and not separate from it? The movement education teacher should occasionally try to visit children in their regular classroom; similarly, the classroom teacher should observe children in movement education.

Lessons can be videotaped or an audio tape made and played back to provide the teacher with a feeling for how much of the lesson was spent in giving instructions, managing or organizing the program, and developing student-teacher interaction. The quality and amount of feedback offered to students also can be investigated. Two other important questions that also need to be examined are "Does the instruction appear to be geared to cater to different rates of learning?" and "Is quality of movement being developed?" The opinions of the children may be solicited by using a specially developed inventory to find out how they feel about the teacher.

Teaching is not a popularity contest, and the teacher should set and demand high standards from the children at all times. How the children behave in the gymnasium is important. The movement education teacher has a responsibility and an opportunity to develop appropriate behavior and respect for equipment and other people as children participate in the program.

The last word

Teachers must know what they are evaluating and why. Testing for the sake of testing does happen, but it wastes a great deal of time that could be put to better use. Testing and measuring merely because "We always do it," and doing nothing with the results, is really intellectual incompetence and there is no excuse for it. Evaluation can become a way of life, and we must be careful that we do not evaluate instead of teach. The question of whether children should ever fail in movement education has not been discussed in this text since no child should fail or receive an "F" on a report card if he or she has done his or her best. Nor should the results of physical fitness tests form a large part of a grade. Evaluation should be a positive process designed to facilitate learning and encourage the development of an awareness of one's own limitations and capabilities.

Summative evaluation tends to measure skill levels at a certain point in time, and this fact should be remembered. If children learn at different rates, then formative evaluation, as an ongoing, continuous process, provides a better tool to monitor and assess children's progress as they grow, develop, mature, and learn.

Bibliography

Study Guide

Various sources can be examined for further study of evaluative procedures.

Gilliom, B. C. *Basic Movement Education: Rationale and Teaching Units.* Reading, Mass.: Addison Wesley, 1970.

This book indicates how teachers can use checklists of quality factors after the children have explored a problem and its sub-problems. (See especially pp. 42–43.)

AAHPER. *Essentials of a Quality Elementary School Physical Education Program.* Washington, D.C. American Association for Health, Physical Education, and Recreation, 1970. (Revised edition due 1979–80.)

McGee, R. "Evaluation of Processes and Products." *In Physical Education for Children: A Focus on the Teaching Process.* Logsdon, B. J., *et al.* Philadelphia: Lea and Febiger, 1977.

Mauldon, E., and Layson, J. *Teaching Gymnastics.* London: Macdonald and Evans, 1965. (See Chapter 2, Movement Observation, pp. 21–31.)

Kruger, H., and Kruger, J. M. *Movement Education in Physical Education.* Dubuque, Iowa: Wm. C. Brown, 1977. (See pp. 486–487.)

This source offers a sample report card.

Barrett, Kate R. "Studying Teaching—A Means for Becoming a More Effective Teacher." *In Physical Education for Children: A Focus on the Teaching Process.* Logsdon, B. J., *et al.* Philadelphia: Lea and Febiger, 1977.

Locke, Lawrence F. "Research on Teaching Physical Education: New Hope for a Dismal Science." *Quest.* Monograph 28. Summer 1977, pp. 2–16.

Cheffers, John. "Observing Teaching Systematically." *Quest.* Monograph 28. Summer 1977, pp. 17–28.

Siedentop, Daryl. "Systematic Improvement of Teaching Skills." *In Developing Teaching Skills in Physical Education.* Boston: Houghton Mifflin, 1976.

Skills tests can be examined in:

Johnson, B. L., and Nelson, J. K. *Practical Measurements for Evaluation in Physical Education.* Minneapolis: Burgess, 1974.

A discussion of teaching and teaching skills is provided in these sources.

AAHPER. *Youth Fitness Test.* Washington, D.C.: The American Alliance of Health, Physical Education, and Recreation, 1976.

The teacher will find this source valuable in assessing physical fitness.

Cheffers, John T., *et al.* "The Development of an Elementary Physical Education Attitude Scale." *In Physical Educator.* Vol. 33, No. 1, March 1976.

A description of an attitude test and additional references applicable to attitude measurement are discussed here.

Ohio State Department of Education. *Self Appraisal Checklist for Elementary School Physical Education.* Columbus, Ohio: Ohio State Department of Education, 1978.

This provides a useful program evaluation.

Educational Testing Service. *AAHPER Cooperative Physical Education Tests.* Princeton, New Jersey: Cooperative Tests and Services, Educational Testing Service.

Bloom, Benjamin S. *Human Characteristics and School Learning.* New York: McGraw Hill, 1976.

Seminar Questions and Activities

1. Try to obtain some physical education report cards from local schools. Examine the factors to which teachers must assign a grade. Describe the information which the report card communicates about a child's status or progress in physical education.
2. Design a report card for movement education that does not utilize letter grades and is based upon a clear statement of objectives. How could such a report card indicate the degree of an individual's improvement as well as his or her status within a group?
3. How can the teacher help children to develop skills in self-evaluation?
4. Outline the broad areas that need to be covered in an evaluation of a total movement program. Describe how a teacher could develop a method for evaluating the total program.
5. Observing children is a necessary part of the teaching process. Draw up a list of guidelines which a teacher could follow in observing children's responses to movement tasks.
6. Distinguish between the terms "evaluation" and "grading." Can we have one without the other?

appendix ACTIVITY SPACES AND EQUIPMENT

A vital factor in a movement program is the development of an exciting and challenging environment for activity. Many elementary schools do not have a gymnasium built expressly for the purpose of physical education (purpose-built), although there are signs that in some areas more schools are adding gymnasiums. More often there is a multi-purpose room, which is often jokingly referred to as the "multi-useless" room! This is because the room probably is used as a cafeteria, for movies, concerts, meetings, and music classes, and for physical education in whatever time is left. In certain parts of the country physical education takes place outside or else in the regular classroom, and some teachers have had to teach physical education in the hallways and foyers of the school.

The Purpose-Built Gymnasium

Architects who design gymnasia do not always seem to realize that these are places in which teachers are going to teach, and that in doing so they must be able to communicate effectively with children without the need to shout. Usually gymnasia are simply vast

Fig. A-1 *A typical elementary school gynmasium.*

echo chambers in which a bouncing ball sounds like a bass drum and a teacher's voice is lost in a blur of sound or cannnot be heard by anyone standing more than 10 feet away! Good acoustic design is of prime importance in the construction of a gymnasium. Acoustic tiles can be used in ceilings and walls can be sprayed with foam above 10 feet to deaden sound reflections. Floors can be of a rubber composition or covered with indoor-outdoor carpet. There must be adequate ventilation and heating systems. Lighting should be fluorescent and recessed in a flat ceiling.

Generally, 60 feet by 40 feet will be an adequate size for a gymnasium, although if the gym is to be used for community education or recreation programs, 70 feet by 40 feet or even larger would be better. The ceiling should be at least 20 feet high, with roof beams that are strong enough to support climbing ropes and cargo nets.

A storage room of adequate size with large double hanging or sliding doors should open into the gymnasium. Storage space must be adequate for small items such as balls, beanbags, hoops, individual mats, and jump ropes. In addition, there should be suitable storage space for such small items as milk cartons, traffic cones, hockey sticks, and so on. Larger items such as car tires, balance beams, tumbling mats, nets, and any other large items of equipment also must be accommodated. It is important that all

Fig. A-2 *Indoor equipment.*

items of equipment be accessible and easy to move without the need to take everything else out first.

It is useful to keep one wall of the gymnasium clear so that balls can be rebounded from it. Hooks will be needed for nets. Power outlets and recessed drinking fountains should be suitably placed.

An office that includes a desk and telephone as well as a locker and shower should be provided for the teacher.

In a large elementary school it is highly desirable to have another teaching station in addition to the gymnasium so that two classes can be scheduled at the same time without a need to share the same space. (Of course, this assumes that there are two teachers available in the school.) Often this other space will be a cafeteria which can only be used for part of the day. Music classes should not be scheduled for the stage of a gym or multi-purpose room, since this is not fair to either program as one would disturb the other.

EQUIPMENT AND APPARATUS

Equipment and apparatus generally will be either fixed or portable. In the list below items are classified as large, small, and improvised.

Large Apparatus

APPARATUS FOR CLIMBING, HANGING, SWINGING

Cargo Net. Cargo nets are suspended from the ceiling or roof beams and pulled out of the way when not in use.

Chinning Bars. These should be placed at different heights and folded against the wall when not in use. The heights should be such that children in kindergarten as well as in sixth grade can hang by their arms with their feet clearing the floor.

Climbing Apparatus. These usually are portable for indoor use or fixed in position on the playground. There are many different kinds of commercial equipment available that combine trestles, ladders, planks, and balance beams. (See catalog listings at the end of this chapter.)

Climbing Peg Board. These are boards of different shapes and sizes with peg holes that start at about shoulder height. They are fixed to the wall. Children hold short pegs and climb by moving the pegs into different holes.

Horizontal/Turning Bars. A portable bar that can be adjusted to different heights is desirable.

Parallel Bars. This equipment provides an interesting challenge to children, especially if the bars can be converted to uneven bars.

BALANCING EQUIPMENT

Balance Beams. These can range from very simple lengths of two-by-four lumber to adjustable beams which can be placed at different heights.

Balance Beam Benches. These are benches which become balance beams when turned over. They can be used in combination to provide different challenges and uses.

JUMPING EQUIPMENT

Agility Ramps. These are sloping wooden ramps about 5 to 6 feet long and about 12 to 15 inches wide. The raised end can be up to 18 inches off the ground. Agility ramps are fairly easy to construct (see the illustration, page 117, page 197).

Tumbling Mats/Crash Pad. Tumbling mats should be lightweight and have a washable surface. Children should be able to carry them fairly easily. Some mats fold easily into small sections. Enough surface area is needed to allow an entire class to work on the mats at the same time.

Crash Pads. These mats are thick (six to nine inches) and are useful for landing when children jump down from a height or perform the running long jump or high jump.

Vaulting Horse. A junior size horse is needed.

Small Apparatus

Balls. A variety of different kinds of balls should be collected.

Fleece or yarn balls. These come in different sizes.

Foam Nerf or All balls.

Tennis balls. Try local tennis or sports clubs to obtain old balls.

Playground balls. These balls come in different sizes ranging from 6 to 15 inches.

Cage ball. A cage ball has a 24- or 36-inch diameter.

Whiffle balls. These are plastic balls with holes and are of softball size.

BALLS FOR SPECIFIC SPORTS

Footballs, basketballs, volleyballs, soccer balls, and softballs. Probably half a dozen of each type is needed. Junior sizes should be used when appropriate. In the early stages of skill learning children can use playground or vinyl balls.

Beanbags. Enough beanbags are needed to provide one for each child.

Jump Ropes. Ropes can be cut from sash cord. The ends can be covered with plastic tape of different colors to indicate the rope size.

Hoops. Hoops can be purchased commercially. They usually are plastic (see improvised equipment list) and different sizes are useful.

Striking Implements

Paddle bats, plastic hockey sticks, badminton racquets, softball bats.

Improvised or Inexpensively Obtained (or Constructed) Equipment

Balls. Balls can be made from wadded newspaper wrapped with masking tape or covered with old pantyhose and sewn up. Yarn balls (pom-poms) also can be made.

Balloons. Packets usually can be purchased cheaply in a supermarket.

Bowling pins. Try the nearest bowling alley for old pins.

Cones. These can be purchased commercially or made from plastic bottles or milk cartons.

Cardboard cartons and boxes. These are useful for storing equipment and also can be used for jumping activities, etc.

Deck tennis rings (quoits). These can be obtained from sporting goods stores.

Fig. A-3 *Tire tree.*

Elastic rope or shock cord. Automotive supply stores carry this item.

Frisbees.

Goals. Useful for indoor soccer or hockey, goals should be about five feet wide and three feet high.

Hoops. Old bicycle tires or car tires can serve as hoops, or they can be made from plastic water pipe joined with connectors or a dowel.

Individual Mats. Carpet squares make adequate mats.

Milk cartons. Cartons should be washed out first. They are useful as markers, targets, or supports for cones for jumping activities.

Parachute. Try surplus stores for parachutes. Figure out the size that will comfortably fit the indoor space.

Paddle bats. These can be made from coat hangers which are bent into shape and covered with pantyhose.

Rhythm or Lummi sticks. Make sticks from a dowel three-quarters of an inch in diameter. Cut the pieces about 12 inches long. They can be painted in different colors.

Scooters. Scooters can be made by screwing castors to a piece of three-quarter-inch plywood. Round the corners and cover the edge with rubber strips or carpet.

Skateboards.

Wooden boxes. Boxes should be big enough and strong enough for children to stand on and jump off. The height should range from 6 and 9 to 12 inches high.

Miscellaneous Items

It will be useful to have:

- A drum and other percussion instruments.
- Record player and records.
- A whistle (for officiating games).
- Adjustable basketball hoops and backboards.
- A stop watch and measuring tape.
- Badminton shuttles.
- Plastic hockey pucks.
- Batting tees.
- Softball bases and mitts.

If a teacher can assemble most of the items listed, a good start will have been made toward creating an exciting learning environment. A child should be able to have a ball, jump rope, or hoop for class activities. No one should need to wait for a turn because there is not enough equipment. Many pieces of equipment can be improvised; this Appendix has only indicated some of the more desirable items which the author believes to be necessary to a movement program.

OUTSIDE APPARATUS

Some kind of hard-surfaced play area is necessary for games and other activities to be performed outside. The area should be well drained and free of broken glass and rocks. It is a good idea to have separate areas for the primary and intermediate grades so that they can be separated at recess if necessary and also so that equipment is more suitable to the different age levels.

The teacher can mark those lines which he or she feels necessary both indoors and outdoors. A court boundary, a halfway line, and some different sized circles would be basic essentials. Basketball courts also may be marked out.

The rest of the playground area should be grass. Distances of 50 yards or longer should be marked and the children informed where the measured distances are located. Climbing apparatus, swings, slides, balance beams, turning bars, parallel bars, and other pieces of equipment should be situated so that a teacher can keep a close watch on both the hard-surfaced play area and on the

Fig. A-4 *Hanging rings.*

other equipment as well. There are many innovative ways to design playgrounds using logs, utility poles, tires, creative climbing equipment such as geodomes, and other imaginative items which are usually made of wood or tubular metal.

A smooth outside wall is useful for throwing and catching balls, as are sandpits and a softball area with backstop netting.

Safety is a prime consideration for both indoor and outdoor areas. The teacher should check daily to make sure that equipment is safe and does not present any hazards to children. The children can be encouraged to report any damaged or unsafe apparatus.

Children need to be taught how to handle apparatus. In general, they should be encouraged to lift things rather than drag them over the floor.

The cleanliness of the gymnasium is very important and the teacher should maintain a working relationship with the school custodian. Floors especially need to be cleaned daily and children should leave their street shoes outside the gym area. If a cafeteria is used for physical education it is important that the floor be cleaned after the lunch period and before movement education resumes in the afternoon.

Fig. A-5 *Outdoor playground.*

Fig. A-6 *A geodome.*

Fig. A-7
Log work.

Finally, the current resources of a school, including facilities and equipment, should not define the program, rather the program should be planned and then a determined effort made to obtain the necessary resources.

Study Guide

To obtain some ideas on outdoor playgrounds, the following sources may be helpful

Rasmus, Caroline J. "A Formula for Play: Child + Space + Imagination." *In Physical Education for Children's Healthful Living.* Association for Childhood Education International. Washington, D.C., 1968.

This article discusses playground innovations and junk and adventure playgrounds.

Hurtwood, Lady Allen of. *New Playgrounds.* London: E. T. Heron and Co., Ltd., 1966.

AAHPER. *Echoes of Influence.* Washington, D.C.: American Alliance for Health, Physical Education, and Recreation, 1977.

This collection of articles has a section on play and playgrounds (pp. 112–119).

Sinclair, Caroline B. *Movement of the Young Child: Ages Two to Six.* Columbus, Ohio: Charles E. Merrill, 1973. This text has a chapter that deals with equipment (pp. 79–95).

Werner, Peter H., and Simmons, Richard A. *Inexpensive Physical Education Equipment for Children.* Minneapolis: Burgess Publishing Company, 1976.

Many different ideas about obtaining equipment at little or no cost for the gymnasium as well as the playground are provided in this book.

Flinchum, Betty M. *Motor Development in Early Childhood.* Saint Louis: The C.V. Mosby Co., 1975.

A chapter in this book is devoted to simple ideas on equipment and instructions for making different items of equipment.

Ohio State Department of Education. *Elementary School Physical Education: Beliefs, Goals, Objectives and Activities.* Columbus, Ohio 1978. See pages 91–94 for ideas about equipment to buy and make.

Seminar Questions and Activities

1. Draw up a design or blueprint for a gymnasium and indicate the main dimensions and the siting of fixed equipment, storage space, lighting, heating, and ventilation. Describe the materials to be used for the floor, walls, and ceiling. Show any floor markings you would use.
2. Design an outside playground for a school that has separate areas for primary and intermediate grades. Indicate the main dimensions and show the siting of hard-surfaced areas and any equipment in relation to the school building.
3. Design an adventure playground for elementary school children.
4. Survey several local elementary school playgrounds and compare their design, layout, and equipment with an acceptable model.

Resources

Equipment catalogs can be collected and examined for ideas and possible equipment purchase. The following companies carry equipment that is suitable for use in an elementary school:

Cosom, P.O. Box 701, Lakeville, MN, 55044.
Cran Barry, Inc. 2 Lincoln Ave., P.O. Box 448, Marblehead, MA, 01945.
Ed-Nu Inc., 5115 Route 38, Pennsauken, NJ, 08108 (especially good for hoops).
Elementary Gym Closet, Inc. 2511 Leach Road, Pontiac, MI 48057.
Game Time, Inc. 900 Anderson Road, Litchfield, MI, 49252.
J.E. Gregory, 922 W. 1st Avenue, Suite 221, Spokane, WA, 99204.
Gym Master, 3200 S. Zuni St., Englewood, CO, 80110.
The Gym Thing, 19 W. Pennsylvania Avenue, Towson, MD, 21204.
Jayfro Corp., P.O. Box 400, Waterford, CT, 06385.
The Lind Climber Co., 807 Reba Place, Evanston, IL, 60202.
Nissen, 930 27th Avenue S.W., Cedar Rapids, IA, 52406.
Program Aids, Dept. 106, 161 MacQuesten Parkway, Mount Vernon, NY, 10550.
Snitz Manufacturing Co., 2096 Church Street, East Troy, WI, 53120.
Things from Bell, 12 S. Main St., Homer, NY, 13077.
United Canvas and Sling, Inc., 248 River St., Hackensack, NJ, 07601.
Wolverine Sports, 245 State Circle, Ann Arbor, MI, 48104.

For records, catalogs can be obtained from:

Kimbo Educational, P.O. Box 477, Long Branch, NJ, 07740.
Hoctor Educational Records, Waldwick, NJ, 07463.

INDEX

N

O

P

Q

R

S

T

V